Masculinity Besieged?

Issues of Modernity

and Male Subjectivity

in Chinese Literature of the

Late Twentieth Century

Masculinity Besieged?

Xueping Zhong

Duke University Press   Durham and London   2000

© 2000 Duke University Press

All rights reserved

Printed in the United States of America on acid-free paper ∞

Typeset in Stone Serif and Sans by Keystone Typesetting, Inc.

Library of Congress Cataloging-in-Publication Data appear on

the last printed page of this book.

For my parents

Contents

Acknowledgments

I would like to begin by thanking my former advisors and mentors at the University of Iowa, Rudolf Kuenzli, Thomas Lewis, Tonglin Lu, Maureen Robertson, David Arkush, and David Hamilton. I am grateful for their help and support, and for their encouragement and trust as I explored difficult issues. My gratitude also goes to Marilyn Young and Gail Hershatter for supporting my work in general, for reading portions of this book, and for providing constructive suggestions; to my friends Zhang Zhen, Lin Chun, and Magnus Fiskesjö for reading various portions of this book and for providing thoughtful and extensive comments and suggestions; to Lili Chen, Rey Chow, Sharon Hom, Norma Field, Helen Koh, Heh-Rahn Park, Ellen Widmer, Ming-bao Yue, and Judith Zeitlin for offering support or reading portions of the manuscript at different stages of its development. Finally, I would also like to thank my colleagues at Tufts University, Charles Nelson, Lynda Shaffer, Liz Ammons, Greg Carleton, and Peter McIsaac for offering suggestions, encouragement, and comments that helped sustain me throughout the process of finishing the manuscript.

Let me also thank the Modern China Seminar of Columbia University for inviting me to present an earlier version of one of the chapters. I am grateful to the Gender Studies Workshop of the University of Chicago, where I received constructive comments and suggestions. Thanks also to the Tufts Faculty Research Award Committee for granting me the Mellon Fellowship, which made it possible for me to finish the manuscript. And I would also like to thank my colleagues in the Department of German, Russian, and Asian Languages and Literature of Tufts University for offering opportunities to present portions of my book and for sharing their thoughts with me.

There are a few people to whom I am especially indebted: my editor at Duke University Press, Ken Wissoker, for his support and his faith in the subject matter of the book, and his two anonymous readers for their constructive comments and suggestions. My special thanks also go to Susan Greenberg for her wholehearted support throughout the years of my writing and for her admirable editorial skills. I am equally indebted to David Greenberg for his careful reading of all the chapters and for his great sense of humor that brought laughter to my protracted hours of writing. Finally, my most special gratitude and appreciation are reserved for Malcolm Griffith, whose help throughout the years of my graduate study and of writing the book and whose sharp eye and constant demands for clarity have been invaluable to my growth both as a scholar and as someone who writes in English as a second language.

Masculinity Besieged?

Introduction

Raising the Issue

Nearly three decades ago, Benjamin Schwartz questioned the categorizing of Chinese intellectuals as either traditional or modern: "If tradition cannot be reduced to a simple integrated system, what can we say of modernity? Since our focus here is on intellectuals, we must be interested in modernity not merely as descriptive of certain processes of action but also as embodied in certain modes of thought and sensibility."[1]

If we take Schwartz's statement that (Chinese) modernity is to be understood "also as *embodied* in certain modes of thought and sensibility" and if we recognize that his focus is on Chinese intellectuals, the next question we can ask is this: In what ways can we also see that Chinese intellectuals em*body* Chinese modernity?[2] That is, besides understanding Chinese modernity as "certain modes of thought and sensibility," in what ways can we also understand it as simultaneously expressed through the *bodies* of the intellectuals that mediate those "modes of thought and sensibility"? And in what ways does the gender of these *bodies* figure in all of this?[3]

By way of the word "body," I hope to draw attention to what Schwartz's passage assumes and what remains invisible within it: the role played by Chinese (male) intellectuals' gendered position in the formation of and quest for

Chinese modernity and, conversely, the ways in which the quest for modernity inform the gendered position of Chinese intellectuals. And, by extension, to draw attention to an issue that the study of Chinese modernity has yet to explore: the relationships among modernity, men, and issues of masculinity. If it is important to recognize that Chinese modernity, like tradition, cannot be reduced to one integrated system, in what ways have intellectuals also *embodied* this nonreducibility and for what reasons?

One point of entry for exploring these issues is this question: What happened to the relationship between men and modernity in China when the rise of the latter challenged the dominance of traditional Chinese discourse? Indeed, if the processes of modernization in the realms of economy, politics, and social structures entailed ruptures and displacements of various social groupings and individuals, and if the onslaught of (Chinese) modernity entailed inevitable paradigm shifts, what happened to the male subject position within these changes? In what ways was the male subject displaced, and where can we locate the displacements that took place? Finally, in what ways was he reconfigured in the scheme of modernity, and what are the implications of such reconfigurations?

Given the specific implications of these questions, I must make clear at the outset that, by "Chinese men," I do not mean all men in China. Rather, I refer both in general and specific terms to (modern and contemporary) Chinese male intellectuals, especially writers and critics who constitute the most vocal component of modern Chinese intellectual forces. As such, they have also constituted the most active force in China's response to the Enlightenment-informed modes of modern thought and system and to other modes of modernity (such as that of the Soviet Union and of Mao-era China), struggling, for over a century, to make sense of where China might fit in the schemes of the modern world.

In recent years, studies have examined modern Chinese intellectuals' relationship with women, and these studies have generated critical attention to the gendered identity of Chinese male intellectuals.[4] Focusing on the May Fourth intellectuals' attention to women's issues, and especially their sympathy for women, critics have started questioning the patriarchal implications embedded in this male sympathy. They have argued that, on the one hand, part of the formation of Chinese modernity discourse was closely related to intellectuals' sympathy for the plight of Chinese women and their strong interest in liberating them from oppression. On the other hand, critics have also questioned the paternalistic nature of the relationship between male intellectuals and the object of their sympathy. As such, critics have charged that male sympathy for women must also be understood as symptomatic of the patriarchal nature of the gendered subject position of Chinese male intellectuals.

For the most part, however, these discussions have not considered issues of masculinity, especially the question of how the pursuit of modernity has informed the (changes in) male subjectivity, the male's sense of himself, and how such changes have, in turn, informed the relationships among men, masculinity, and modernity.[5] And yet, the gendered position of Chinese male intellectuals involves more than their paternalistic relationship with women and women's issues.[6] In fact, as the twentieth century is drawing to an end and we look back to (re)examine the role of Chinese male intellectuals' gendered position in China's quest for modernity, we must ask the following questions: What has become of the male intellectuals' relationship with women now, especially when Chinese women's positions have undergone tremendous changes and when women have come to see themselves as men's equals? How do we understand the changes in this relationship? What do they tell us about being men in modern China, and in what ways do they compel us to explore the gendered position of Chinese male intellectuals? Implied in these questions, I believe, is a contention that issues involving Chinese male subjectivity are such that they cannot be reduced, to echo Schwartz, to "a simple integrated system"—in this case, men's sympathy (or lack thereof) for women.

To expand on the existing discussions, therefore, I focus on the following question: In what ways is Chinese modernity, especially Chinese male intellectuals' quest for it, closely related to the changing male positions in modern China, and how have such changes affected the formation of Chinese modernity and the trajectory of China's quest for it and, by extension, the subject positions of male intellectuals?

In this book, I explore these questions by examining male representations of men in the literature of the 1980s, a decade in which the intricate dynamics among men, masculinity, and modernity (re)surfaced and when China found itself at yet another important historical turning point. Through discussing the issues that strongly concern the male writers and doing so against the backdrop of the questions raised above, I explore the extent to which these male-oriented issues indicate both a continuation of and conflicts and contradictions within the modern Chinese intellectual legacy. More specifically, I examine the ways that legacy has been affecting and affected by the central concerns of Chinese intellectuals as gendered beings. As such, I argue that examining the relationship between Chinese male intellectuals' sense of themselves and modernity is crucial to our understanding of China's quest for modernity.

Defining "Chinese Men" in the Literature of the 1980s

During the decade of the 1980s, for reasons I explore further in the next chapter, there was a rather unprecedented and uniquely shared concern, especially among male writers, about the (gender and sexual) identity of men. For many contemporary Chinese male writers, the question of men was not at all a peripheral one. Indeed, part of my interest in the issue derives initially from what I saw as an acute male interest in the question of men found in post–Cultural Revolution literature. It is the prominence of such a male interest and, for that matter, its larger historical, political, and cultural implications that generated a need in my mind for a substantive study of the issues either explicitly or implicitly presented to us in that literature.

One can safely suggest that literary attention to men as gendered beings in post–Cultural Revolution literature started with a number of women writers' critical representations of men. In the early 1980s, for example, Zhang Jie and Zhang Xinxin wrote stories concerning relationships between the sexes that in many ways were critical of men. Zhang Jie's "Fang zhou" (The ark) portrays three middle-aged women and their struggles with men who are either their (former or estranged) husbands or colleagues or bosses.[7] Her portrayals are less than favorable and caused discomfort among critics, who expressed concerns about her being harsh and "unfair."[8] Similarly, in some of her early stories, such as "Zai tongyi dipingxian shang" (On the same horizon), "Wo zai naer cuoguo le ni?" (How did I miss you?), and "Zuihou de tingbodi" (The last anchor point), Zhang Xinxin tackles gender relationships by questioning the inability of men to treat a "strong" woman on an equal footing.[9] In "Women zhege nianji de meng" (Dreams of our generation), she associates the broken dreams of the female narrator not only with the broken dreams of the Chinese Communist Party's (CCP) ideology but also with the banal quality of the men in her life. In these stories, we can clearly see women adopting a critical view of men. Regardless of whether such views are often themselves mixed with an idealism derived from patriarchal ideals of men, the stories constituted the strongest criticism of (Chinese) men to date.

Meanwhile, toward the mid-1980s, China began to witness an explosion of literary stylistic experimentation. Accompanying this stylistic renaissance was a change in literary representations of men; many male writers began to experiment with new forms and styles and often turned inward to represent "themselves."[10] Men's issues began to appear in a different light: on the one hand, "maleness" came to symbolize an oppositional gesture against the dominant discourse; on the other hand, men appeared as embodiments of dilemmas—political, historical, and cultural—and their "problems" dominated a discourse centering on a weak/strong dichotomy concerning the uncertainty of male identity. In short, there is an ambivalence in the representations of men: they are considered "weak," but they want to be (and it is thought that they should be) strong.

Of course, these complex and contradictory male concerns in post–Cultural Revolution literature are manifestations of the changes taking place at large in China. Starting in the early 1980s with the controversies over Zhang Jie's and Zhang Xinxin's not-so-sympathetic representations of men, the term *yinsheng yangshuai* or "the rise of the feminine and the decline of the masculine" emerged and quickly became a popularly accepted perception of the status of Chinese men (and women). Its political implications notwithstanding—as an indirect critique of the CCP's political oppression as well as its gender equality policies[11]—the notion that women were too strong and men too weak was taken as an abnormal phenomenon that had to be corrected.[12] Among the first in voicing this sentiment was what was later known as the "looking-for-real-men literature" or *xunzhao nanzihan wenxue*.[13] Other cultural media—magazines, film, and TV—followed suit in their response to the "need" for "real men." Images of strong or real men, borrowed from America and Japan and symbolized by Sylvester Stallone and Takakura Ken, emphasized a "manly" physical appearance,[14] and these images soon took on a Chinese identity in the figure of a Chinese man from the plateau of China's northwest (*xibeifeng* or "northwesterly wind"), untainted by the (supposed) decline of the masculine.[15] Now, this obsession with weakness is nothing new to the post-Mao era (an issue to which I return in later chapters), but its

erotic and sexual implications not only mark the specificity of the time period but also reveal more fully the gendered nature of the obsession possessed
by (and possessing) many contemporary Chinese male writers.

Furthermore, the literary and media interest in searching for a strong male
identity is part of the ethos of the decade of the 1980s. With the lessening of
the intrusive control of the official propaganda apparatuses, the cultural and
discursive power of the 1980s essentially shifted and belonged to male writers
and intellectuals who occupied center stage of the cultural scene (before, of
course, the onslaught of mass culture and consequently the decentering of
the role of literature and of the writers and critics in the 1990s). Indeed, with
the Cultural Revolution officially ended in the late 1970s, the 1980s witnessed
male intellectuals' rapid arrival at the cultural forefront. Looking back on it
now, we can see that the decade is not only permanently associated with a
number of major political events (such as the debate over *yihua* or alienation,
political campaigns against "bourgeois spiritual pollution," and most of all
the 1989 students' demonstration and the June Fourth incident) but also
with the writer and critic-led cultural movement, which was marked by a new
culture fever (*wenhua re*), by a literary renaissance in which writers enthusiastically experimented with new styles and new ways of telling (or not telling)
stories, and by the so-called return of the May Fourth spirit (*wusi jingsheng de
huigui*), when writers and critics looked to that spirit for their intellectual
heritage. In fact, the prominence of the intellectuals was such that they were
proudly identified as *wenhua jingying* or cultural elites, who, with few ex-
ceptions, were men. As a term that glorified the status of the intellectuals,
wenhua jingying manifested the spirit of the time, which featured the male
intellectuals as they commanded public attention and exerted strong influence on social, cultural, and political issues of the time.

By now, it should be clear that by "Chinese men" I do not mean all men in
China. Rather, to expand on my earlier point, I refer first of all to the male
voices, or the male subject position, manifested through a body of literature
expressing various concerns about male gender, sexual, and cultural identity.
As such, male representations of men in post–Cultural Revolution literature—specifically in the 1980s—provide us with important insights into those
who have access to means of representation, namely, writers and critics,
whose desires and anxieties are also manifestations of the historical complexity in which they exist. What interests me the most in conducting this study,

therefore, is not merely collecting and commenting on a number of male issues, but exploring the sexual/textual politics in the male search for identity manifested in the telling of many of the stories. I am interested in examining the implications of such politics and how the literary concern is related to this distinctively male-centered cultural scene at large in the 1980s.

Second, because I believe that most of the post-Mao Chinese literature has been a significant part of the intellectual endeavor of modern Chinese intellectuals, a fundamental question I also address in this book is precisely the relationship between male representations of men and the position and role of Chinese intellectuals in China's quest for and ambivalence toward modernity.[16] And by extension, I address the ways in which we understand this male interest in conjunction with the extent to which men as gendered beings have figured and how masculinity has been contested in Chinese modernity.[17]

The Question of Chinese Male Subjectivity

"The question of men," in this sense, can also be identified in terms of the gendered subject positions—gendered subjectivity—of the intellectuals in question. Employing the notion of male subjectivity here, however, is not a blind purchase within the current academic jargon economy. Although the existing theoretical debate over the notion of subjectivity has put anyone using the concept on the alert and an indulgence in the concept can lead to pessimism and a lack of a sense of agency, nevertheless, its complex implications and the open-endedness of that complexity can continue to provide useful insights. My use of the concept here hinges on the emphasis on the *relationship between history and the individual* that the concept embodies. I apply it in the sense Adorno discussed in his treatment of the concept of the individual, which is part of his critique of the Enlightenment: "that individuals are constituted out of overlapping and often conflicting relational contexts."[18] It is important, that is, to realize that history is not constituted by binary relations that keep individuals in either/or positions: strong or weak, the master or the slave. Additional lessons can be learned, according to Martin Jay's interpretation of Adorno, "from an investigation of two other aspects of the whole, namely, culture and the individual psyche which traditional Marxism had tended to neglect" (85). These lessons include, as Adorno started to insist decades ago, seeing "the power of those heterogeneous fragments that slip through the conceptual net" (21). These "fragments" may well pertain to such issues as "the contradictory meanings of subject as active agent, the source of one's own destiny, and as passive object of domination, the plaything of an other to whose will one is 'subjected'" (60). Even though the Frankfurt School's insistence on cultural aspects of history has been periodically questioned and criticized for its lack of attention to the role of the economy, the issues it raised half a century ago are not only still highly relevant to our understanding of the West but are increasingly so to the study of non-Western cultures. Indeed, the school's insistence on seeing the constructedness and conflicts within the individual in relation to history can be highly instrumental in our understanding of, among other things, the relationships between Chinese men and the contexts in which they exist.

As for history, Jean Laplanche has carefully discussed it in his reconceptualization of the notion of ego and in his efforts to clarify the difference between the notion of individual and that of ego. Echoing Adorno's insistence on the importance of understanding individuals as constructed out of "overlapping and often conflicting relational contexts," Laplanche argues that the individual should not be seen as the "totality itself" but as "a part of the totality" and as "an 'agency.'" And, for that reason, "as one of the protagonists in the conflict splitting the individual."[19] With a firm grounding in history and the specific human interactions conditioned by and conditioning the former, the notion of "the contradictory meanings of subject" and Laplanche's reinterpreted meaning of the ego are particularly illuminating in our efforts to understand the subject positions of Chinese men in question. More specifically, they help shed light on our understanding of why the ambivalence concerning Chinese male weakness continues to affect the perception of male weakness and the male search for a masculine identity.

In the context of this book and of the larger issues mentioned above, therefore, the notion of male subjectivity is understood with the following questions in mind: What are the issues that most concern contemporary male Chinese intellectuals, and why? In what ways do their concerns embody the paradoxes, conflicts, and contradictions in modern Chinese history? How do we understand the role of the displaced male subjects, their anxiety, and the extent to which their manifested desires signify both a connection between masculinity and Chinese modernity and the tension within? Above all, in what ways is all of this symptomatic of both a collective intellectual orientation *and* the characteristic of Chinese male subjectivity that is particular to modern and contemporary Chinese male intellectuals?

Approaching Issues of Chinese Masculinity

Against the backdrop of these questions, the Chinese male search for masculinity can be understood as a multifaceted one across a number of paradigms: questions of male sexuality, male desire, male anxiety, and male relationships with women; sexual politics played by the power structure—the Party-state and its ideology—and sexual/textual politics manifested in male representations of men, and the relationship between the two; modern and recent Chinese history and the role and positions of modern and contemporary Chinese intellectuals within that history.[20] Because these issues are not divided evenly into categories or paradigms in a comfortably balanced relationship with each other, this study is also an effort to find a new ground on which my discussion of the subject can be conducted effectively.

To find such a ground, an initial step is to move beyond the persistent stance in reading contemporary Chinese literature, especially representations of men or male-related themes, "allegorically."[21] That is, to move beyond the assumption that "Third World" literature is political by nature. Or conversely, because an allegorical approach to Chinese literature can still be a valid one given the specific historical context, the step to take is to put men as gendered individuals back into the scheme of allegory, thus expanding an allegorical reading of contemporary Chinese literature by including, rather than displacing, such an equally important (and political) approach as a gendered one. Otherwise, a narrow interpretation of the notion of allegory as prioritizing the political (as in politics) can result only in an encapsulation in which only one set of issues gets privileged. This, it seems to me, is where the criticism of the "Third World" allegory lies: it further makes uneven, rather than level, the field between approaches to Western and non-Western literatures and cultures and, by implication, further simplifies the complexity of non-Western historical contexts. When it comes to the Chinese situation, it then becomes problematic when the politicization of male gender anxiety (over "male weakness") is reduced and yet in actuality is not reducible to politics only.

I intend to move the reading of prominent post–Cultural Revolution male writers beyond the existing center/margin dichotomy, which categorically identifies the center as the Party-state or the CCP's regime or the official ideology and the margin as the writers who are perceived as politically oppositional to the center. To do so is to recognize the writers as social, gendered, and sexual beings (which male writers themselves have tried to demonstrate in literature) whose subjectivity should be recognized as not only simply in opposition to or critical of the state. On the one hand, as some critics have argued, echoing this center/margin dichotomy, I fully recognize that in relation to the high-handed control of the CCP's power machine, most Chinese men as individuals have not always enjoyed a more powerful position than Chinese women; as subjects of the Party-state, Chinese men can be as vulnerable as and at times even more vulnerable than women.[22] On the other hand, we also need to realize that, if male vulnerability provides (in this case) Chinese male intellectuals with a moral power to criticize, a similarly important question to ask is how such moral power has been exercised: Who are the "feminized" or "oppressed" men who can and do speak, and what do they bring with them? We need to ask, as some critics have, what it means when humanist and modernist endeavors in contemporary Chinese literature subsequently suggest that misogyny be taken as part of "human nature" (in men).[23]

As a critic (and a woman from the PRC), my discomfort with the center/margin dichotomy and the characterization of the male position as "feminine" (and therefore oppositional) inherent in the allegorical reading of contemporary Chinese literature is twofold. First, it has to do precisely with the gendered dichotomy—masculine versus feminine—that is employed as an analogy to this center/margin dichotomy: the marginal (male) intellectual occupies the position of the "feminine" in relation to the power structure—the Party-state apparatuses—which is identified as "masculine." Such a dichotomy displaces women altogether. Second, in the contemporary Chinese context, it tends to operate in a disturbingly familiar pattern in which women are either excluded from the debate or identified with the power structure, namely, with the oppressors of men.[24] My discomfort comes from this: because I am not a "feminized" Chinese man who can claim his moral authority over his oppressor, paradoxically, therefore, I cannot occupy what is essentially a center-validated (and centrifugal) marginal position either. In this sense, unless a woman critic always shares or identifies with the positionality of the "marginal male," the legitimacy of her critical stance can be curtailed.

Although I recognize that, politically, margins are often shared by both sexes, I believe, as is shown by many studies of men's issues in other contexts, that the sharing does not always take place on the same level. To be sure, arguing against Western hegemony in defining masculine ideals, critics in the West have rightly insisted on the importance of recognizing the existence of different masculinities and the importance of acknowledging such difference. However, keeping in mind the central ambivalence regarding Chinese "male weakness," the question is whether such a recognition of diverse masculinities is enough for us to understand the male gender anxiety found in Chinese literature of the 1980s. There, Chinese men are seen as "weak" and "unmanly." And yet, if that can be argued as masculinity of a different kind (an issue I discuss in chapter 1), it does not seem to be what Chinese male writers are content with. If anything, their gender anxiety persists. So does their persistence in searching for a strong male identity.

In this sense, I argue that the presumed Chinese male weakness (along with a male desire for strong masculine identity) is symptomatic of the displacements or reconfigurations of male subject positions in the modern Chinese context. And the symptom—the presumed male weakness—constitutes the very rupture of Chinese male identity to which intellectuals keep returning.

In this study, identifying Chinese male gender anxiety over masculinity as a preoccupation with the lack of a male power position, I call this preoccupation a male "marginality complex."[25] It pertains both to a sense of crisis of male identity and to the presence of the ideology of masculinism that, according to Arthur Brittan, who argues for a need to understand the difference between masculinity and masculinism, is also the ideology of patriarchy.[26] Given the paradox within, I do not perceive that the marginality of Chinese male subjectivity in question exists in the same way Kaja Silverman discusses in her book *Male Subjectivity at the Margins*. Instead of embracing the marginality (as Silverman attempts to demonstrate), the Chinese male marginality complex is filled with the desire to overcome the marginalized position by moving toward the center, a marginal positionality that ultimately, in Rey Chow's words, "support[s] . . . the center."[27] It is this centrifugal direction, in other words, that marks the specificity of Chinese male marginality anxiety.

And the essence of this anxiety is justified by the embedded masculinism that "naturalizes male domination . . . takes it for granted that there is a fundamental difference between men and women . . . assumes that heterosexuality is normal . . . accepts without question the sexual division of labor, and . . . sanctions the political and dominant role of men in the public and private spheres."[28]

My study of the Chinese male marginality complex, in this sense, has to account for (1) the historical specificities that in various ways have marginalized men in relation to their Western counterparts and to the Party-state and have also effected a strong concern over marginality; (2) how such a concern conditioned the numerous other factors that overdetermine the centrifugal direction that the marginalized male is taking; (3) the fact that issues of masculinity constitute an intrinsic part of our understanding of Chinese modernity; and (4) why a particular version of masculinity is preferred and what perpetuates its desirability and with what consequence.

Throughout this book, I follow and examine the trajectory of the various male reactions, manifested in literature, toward the issue of male weakness, reactions that range from male desires for sexual potency or the anxiety over the lack thereof, to male ambivalence over the body and self, and finally to man's anxiety to transcend the ambivalence by displacing his "ugliness" onto woman's body and by searching for "the sublime" to relocate his new self. I explore how the obsession with male weakness is historically conditioned, how the male reaction toward it is also symptomatic of the complexity of many of the conflicting historical conditions of Chinese modernity, and why because of all this my study is necessary.

Chapter 1 investigates the historical trajectory that led to the contemporary concern about masculinity in literature. Here, I present and interrogate the few existing studies of Chinese men. The common aspect of these studies lies in the fact that, in various ways, they all suggest that the subject positions of Chinese men are different from that of their Western counterparts. My interest, however, is not in presenting these discussions to prove that Chinese men are somehow different. Rather, I am interested in presenting a discursive trajectory that will lead my discussion into the question of how all of this anticipates the ways in which contemporary Chinese male intellectuals react toward their roles as men in contemporary China, perceive their role as intellectuals in modern Chinese history, and demonstrate the tendency to be obsessed with the notion of male weakness. In doing so, I take the questions, contradictions, and assumptions within these studies as points of departure to explore further the contested notions of subjectivity, (Chinese) masculinity, and Chinese intellectuals' articulation of a crisis of male identity. I demonstrate how the complexity of modern Chinese history can be brought to bear in mapping a process that not only effected male gender anxiety but also preserved the ideology of masculinism, both of which were to be manifested in post-Mao Chinese literature.

Chapters 2 through 5 offer textual and historical readings in which I examine how the obsession with male weakness manifests itself in realms of sexuality, in the search for the self, and in the quest for cultural identity. In Chapter 2, I examine stories by Zhang Xianliang and Liu Heng, who in various ways represent male anxiety about (male) sexuality. In post-Mao China, the realm of sexuality has been considered a realm of liberation where (especially) men finally are able to express their desires. I discuss how male sexuality is expressed as a reaction against political oppression and repression, thereby restoring a recognition and celebration of "human nature." I also focus on why, at the same time, there is a constant awkwardness or discomfort on the part of many of those two authors' male protagonists over their own bodies. I am curious about the link between this male discomfort and the writers' representations of (hetero)sexual relationships and the ways this discomfort gets transferred onto women's bodies and female sexuality. I explore the extent to which the transference secures a narcissistic position for the male protagonists from which they manage to aestheticize the discomfort over their own bodies, and I ask what it means when they aestheticize the discomfort rather than their own bodies. All of this leads to the question of how the marginal male deals with his own sexual identity in relation to the state and to women.

In chapter 3, I discuss stories by three prominent writers, Han Shaogong, Yu Hua, and Wang Shuo, whose writings enjoy a wide readership not only among the well educated but also among urban working and middle classes. I examine how, in spite of their stylistic and generational differences, they share one feature in common: writing about marginal male figures. And I discuss how, each in his own way, their use of the marginal male and antiheroes helps create a new version of what I see as a male-centered modern and modernist discourse, and what the implications of such a discourse are when it is established as a new aesthetic order.

In chapter 4, I examine the self-loathing voices found in male writers in general and in Mo Yan in particular. Focusing on the narrative voice in his *Red Sorghum,* I explore why many stories by Mo Yan—a writer highly regarded for his stories of peasants, for his innovative narrative style, and for the intensity effected by that style—are also curiously full of ambivalence and a strong sense of contempt for the male self. This male self-contempt is oriented around a comparison between, to use Mo Yan's own metaphor, the hybrid sorghum and the red sorghum, the latter symbolizing the better—masculine—self. The search for the better self (which often takes the form of a peasant-turned-bandit) constitutes a male search for "real men." The seemingly masochistic obsession with one's own ugliness and where it ultimately leads are some of the fundamental questions I explore in the examination of Mo's novel.

Chapter 5 begins by exploring representations of the Chinese male archetype found in the so-called roots-seeking literature, focusing especially on the anxiety over the fear of "losing identity" and over recreating "strong" men in relation to their desire for Chinese culture to be potent geopolitically. I place this conflation within modern Chinese intellectual history and in relation to the anxiety over China's ability to respond to modernity, and I speculate on the problems inherent in that conflation. I then return to the question of the male marginality complex and argue that the conflation of male desire for a strong and potent self is part and parcel of Chinese cultural nationalism, which often treads a fine line between a cultural/national nihilism and a cultural/national chauvinism. What is more, such a tendency can also pose increasing problems for women's positions and identity in China, and requires us constantly to challenge masculinist-oriented cultural nationalism.

The study ends with an afterword in which I place my overall discussion against the backdrop of the 1990s. As Chinese intellectuals become increasingly diverse in their commitment to the magic of modernization and globalization, I wonder how all of that will affect and reconfigure their gendered positions and, in turn, their relationship with increasingly stratified groups of Chinese men and women.

Chapter 1

Masculinity Besieged?

Toward an Understanding

of Chinese Modernity

and Male Subjectivity

As I briefly mentioned in the introduction, post-Mao Chinese literature and culture in the 1980s witnessed a particularly strong concern over a male lack of "masculine" identity, and the concern suggested a sense of siege and a desire to break out. My goal is to investigate what "masculinity" meant in that context and to examine its various manifestations and larger implications. In this chapter, I turn to history first for a better understanding of the trajectory that led to the contemporary concern over masculinity and the sense of besiegedness. I do so by focusing on a number of key notions and related issues, ranging from concepts such as the self, desire, and lack, to the historical, social, and political implications of these concepts in relation to China's quest for modernity, to the existing perceptions of modern Chinese men, to Chinese male intellectuals' search for their own identity, and finally to the post-Mao popular assumption of *yinsheng yangshai* (women are too strong and men are too weak) and how to understand it in conjunction both with China's early-twentieth-century quest for modernity and with the PRC's post-1949 pursuit of modernization.

An understanding of the historical context does not alone yield a fuller understanding of the issue in question. This is not only because most of the existing (Chinese) historical narratives are yet to be more fully engendered, but also because the historical, as it is conventionally understood in most (historical) narratives, often discredits the psyche as "ahistorical," and thus excludes the possibility or the necessity of examining the "historically precipitated but psychoanalytically specific" aspects of the historical.[1] A better understanding of Chinese male subjectivity calls for an inquiry into the psychosocial, or the "psychoanalytically specific," aspects of the historical of Chinese modernity.

I believe there is a space where the historical and the psyche intersect, where history cannot exist without human or individual or subjective participation. In *Male Subjectivity at the Margins,* Kaja Silverman links the historical and the psyche when she defines the term "historical trauma" as "a historically precipitated but psychologically specific disruption, with ramifications extending far beyond the individual psyche."[2] In this sense, the psyche is more than just about the individual; perceived through Silverman's definition, it is about the social *construction* or *configuration* of the individual psyche, or the *construction of subjectivity.* Historical trauma is the very juncture where the link between the historical and the psyche becomes visible. And the interdependence between history and human participation is the very space within which social, cultural, political, and psychological activities take place. Put differently, this interdependence constitutes the "materiality" of the space, as Judith Butler would suggest, within which the complexity of the historical is to be understood.[3]

Although this poststructuralist view of the historical continues to be subject to debate, its attention to the role that signs and language play in the (re)formation of power, knowledge, hegemony, and the survival of human communities and to the human participation in such (re)formation adds a necessary and important understanding to the cultural and ideological dimensions of the historical. In historicizing modern Chinese male subjectivity, therefore, I find such claims as "Chinese men are weakened by the CCP's power structure" and "Chinese male configurations are different from those in the West" not satisfying. They imply a passive subject formation or construction without indicating precisely *the interdependence between history and human participation* on social, political, cultural, and discursive levels.

In the following discussion, situating my examination of Chinese male subjectivity in modern Chinese history, I venture into uncharted territories—via the notion of desire—to examine how modern Chinese intellectuals are not only the agents of Chinese Enlightenment (in the sense that they were

responsible for introducing Western ideas and smashing the old and traditional cultural heritage),[4] but are also products of their own desire, a desire
conditioned by China's modern encounter with the West and by the rise of
Chinese modernity. I explore these issues within two related and yet different
contexts. First, I place the discussion within the context of modern Chinese
intellectuals' quest for modernity, which is arguably both part of the political, social, and cultural changes taking place throughout twentieth-century
China and a unique component of modern Chinese history with its own
specific trajectory in relation to those changes. Furthermore, because this
specific trajectory has always been conditioned and affected by the ups and
downs of political and historical events, when it comes to the post-Mao era,
additional understanding of recent Chinese history is also necessary. Second,
therefore, I discuss the issues within the context of the *yinsheng yangshuai*
(the rise of the feminine and the decline of the masculine) phenomenon,
specifically in conjunction with what I identify as the CCP's pursuit of modernity. If the CCP has exerted a direct impact on the lives of contemporary
male writer intellectuals and if the latter's desire to search for strong cultural
and masculine identities is to be understood as an oppositional move in reaction to that impact, in what ways is their oppositional stance also conditioned by that part of history and by their own participation in it? My hope,
in short, is to explore the ways these two different and yet overlapping historical contexts constitute the very historical juncture from which the post-Mao
male writers emerged and against which they responded.

The "Self" in the Formation of Modern Chinese Male Subjectivity

In their efforts to revitalize Confucianism, some contemporary believers
have looked to the notion of the self and "self-cultivation" for an entry point.
Tu Wei-ming, a leading scholar of Confucianism and an advocate of the contemporary neo-Confucianist movement, for example, argues that "Confucian learning, in its inception, took the cultivation of the self as its point of
departure," and he adds that learning and self-cultivation have always been
the essence of Confucianism.[5] He contends that the task of the Confucianist
movement today is to envision a new polity based on a revival of this Confucian essence. His criticism of the May Fourth intellectuals ("May Fourth
Westernizers," in his words) is centered on their "iconoclastic attacks" on

traditional Chinese culture represented by Confucianism, acts that, according to Tu, throw the baby out with the bathwater. One can infer the following logic from Tu's criticism of the May Fourth intellectuals: If not for the May Fourth "iconoclastic" rejection of Confucianism, China (or the PRC, to be exact, for he has already made clear that other Chinese communities such as Taiwan, Hong Kong, and Singapore have not been affected by the aftermath of the May Fourth movement and have benefited from their holding onto Confucian values by becoming contemporary little economic giants) might not face so much crisis today (or, for that matter, may not have gone through the Communist Revolution either). Using those other Chinese communities as examples of the success of Confucianism in the modern world, Tu is convinced that modern China's refusal of Confucianism was a bad judgment call on the part of the May Fourth intellectuals, and helped turn China into a place of endless turmoil.[6]

What is at issue here is not whether Confucianism as a social theology can help strengthen a society and make it more humane; what is at issue is the fact that Tu's criticism of the May Fourth intellectuals, which is based on a deep belief in the humanity of Confucianism, turns history on its head. That is, from his contemporary vantage point concerning today's China, the link between the present and history is only thinly connected on the point of the "iconoclastic rebels" of May Fourth. The complex history of modern China is reduced to "wrong" moves made by modern Chinese intellectuals in relation to Confucianism. Though I am not arguing for a historical determinism, I do believe that contemporary Confucianists fail to come to terms with the historical factors that led to the "iconoclastic" attacks in the May Fourth cultural movement.[7] To argue this point, let us come back to the very accusation made against the May Fourth intellectuals for having thrown the baby out with the dirty bathwater, and ask: What is the "baby" that was supposedly thrown out (assuming that the "baby" here pertains, in part, to the values and principles surrounding the cultivation of a Confucian self)?

Generally speaking, the Confucian self, as constructed by various interpretations, denotes a belief that humans are originally good but need to be perfected through learning. A self is always perfectible; perfectibility, in essence, constitutes the self. A perfected self, in turn, is a sage with the qualities suitable for a king. What is assumed and needs to be made visible here is that the self is always a male self. This seemingly forward-looking and optimistic view of the (male) self, unfortunately, could not sustain itself at the turn of the century after the self-isolated Chinese society had been forced open by the Western powers and as "Chinese norms" began to break down. With the influx of Western ideas, the Confucian norms were not only unable to prop up the (self-contained model of the) self, they also came to be seen as the very cocoon that was suffocating the self who was henceforth to be seen as an individual. Precisely because of this, when the self turned up in May Fourth discourse, it became the voice that demanded social change and reform. In the language of the modern, this is the modern Chinese self that, under the influence of the Western humanist notion of the individual, emerged from the traditional hierarchy, whose concern was no longer first and foremost to perfect the self but to free and liberate (him)self from the grips of that tradition. The difference between the Confucian self and the modern self, in this sense, lies in the fact that the former emphasizes an unchanging and always self-referential concept of the self, whereas the latter departs from the former in response to history, or as the result of history. The liberation (and later, the split or besieged) motif in the modern self, that is, comes not from the iconoclastic attacks of the May Fourth intellectuals but is historically conditioned.

The important question one must ask in relation to modern Chinese history (a question Tu's and other contemporary Confucianists' charges against the May Fourth intellectuals are vague about) is this: Where and what was the self to be perfected at the turn of this century? That is, why did not the May Fourth intellectuals seem concerned with "the cultivation of the self"? One can even ask, along this line of argument, why in the late nineteenth century, when Kang Youwei attempted to revive the "origins" of Confucianism (which, again, based its belief in the perfectibility of the self), his efforts ultimately failed?[8] What is it about his thinking that did not manage to revive Confucian philosophy? Was Western influence too strong to fight against? Perhaps, but why? Also, why, while searching for the self, did the modern intellectuals refuse to revive it through Confucianism? The real irony lies in the very fact that, like the Confucianists then and now, the May Fourth intellectuals were actually concerned with the self and many were obsessed with its "crisis" status. The self, that is, was actually central to the minds of the May Fourth intellectuals when they took on traditional Chinese culture represented to them through Confucianism. Unlike the Confucianists, however, the May Fourth intellectuals rejected the self-referentiality embedded in the tradition and responded strongly to new ways of perceiving the relationship between the self (or, more accurately, the individual) and community (family, culture, society, etc.). To characterize the May Fourth intellectuals' rejection of tradition as a simplistic response to the West is to forget that we can only understand history "after the fact."

In some recent discussions, critics have (re)examined the emergence of the (writing) self in May Fourth literature.[9] They do so in a context in which, as they argue, modern Chinese intellectuals were increasingly confronted by, among other things, their own anxiety over a (lack of modern) Chinese identity. In her article "Text, Intertext, and the Representation of the Writing Self in Lu Xun, Yu Dafu, and Wang Meng," Yi-tsi Mei Feuerwerker writes, "By presenting history in the form of the diary entries of a designated madman, Lu Xun inserted into Chinese literature a new kind of problematic self, a self in a state of crisis over its own identity. The madman's sanity is at stake as he struggles to sort out his relation to the external world, but he must also learn how to reinterpret the traditional texts that had hitherto defined that world for him."[10] In foregrounding this "new kind of problematic self" in Lu's "A Madman's Diary," Feuerwerker shifts critical attention from the familiar interpretation of the story (it is the first Chinese fiction written in vernacular Chinese with an iconoclastic attack on traditional Chinese culture represented by Confucianism) to the "writing self," namely, the narrator/writer. This writing self in Lu Xun's story, as Feuerwerker reads it, is simultaneously embodied by the first-person narrator who provides information regarding the existence of the diary, and the first-person narrator—the "madman"— who is the author of the diary. As the "new kind of problematic self," he is symptomatic of a time when Chinese men of letters were forced to confront the inscriptive power of tradition as well as their own "weakness" mirrored back to them at the threshold of modernity.

In examining Yu Dafu's "Sinking," Feuerwerker argues that the "I" in the story is different from that found, intertextually, either in Sima Qian's "affirmation of the self" or in the "Daoist recluses . . . in discarding both of these textual traditions and the ideological codes they carried."[11] The protagonist "is imprisoned in a spiraling structure of voyeurism, masturbation, and paranoia, with self-destruction the only way out" (181). At the same time, Feuerwerker cautions that, "in spite of its obsessive focus on the subjective self, 'Sinking' is not the single-minded or one-dimensional work it is often taken to be" (182). The "writing self" is not the same as the "imprisoned" protagonist, and the difference between the two suggests, and this is implied in Feuer-werker's argument, the emergence of a modern male subject who will con-tinue to struggle between a "paranoid view of the world and the 'objective' situation" (182). This split is echoed, according to Lydia Liu, by the split self in Juansheng, a character in Lu Xun's "Regret for the Past."[12] As a man, Juan-sheng is both a liberator and one who abandons the woman he supposedly liberated, a paradox that signifies far more complexity than Juansheng's own plight. As a "modern" man, he can act as a woman's liberator because of his access to "new" ideas and the possibility that they provide him as a man. At the same time, this male position is also limited because it is a marginal one itself in relation to the tenacious traditional power structure and in the face of China's lack of a powerful modern identity.

Both Feuerwerker's and Liu's readings of the writing self in modern Chi-nese literature reveal the complexity of modern (male) subjectivity. As part of the psychological ramifications of China's encounter with the West, this "new kind of problematic self" is "a self in a state of crisis." It is a mental state often commonly known as *youhuan yishi* (an anxiety complex), which has accompanied China's century-long struggle to come to terms with moder-nity.[13] Seeing the modern writing self in terms of the problematic self, Feuer-werker and other critics provide one important dimension for our under-standing of the historical condition of the modern Chinese male self and its manifestations. Indeed, one can argue that part of Chinese modernity constituted the emergence of a consciousness—sometimes in the form of anguish, sometimes uncertainty, and sometimes declaration—that accom-panied the rapid social and cultural changes or were a result of those changes.

Here, an additional example of such a modern male self conveniently comes to mind: Qian Zhongshu's novel *Weicheng* (The besieged city) and its portrayal of the male protagonist Fang Hongjian.[14] By convenient, I refer to the coincidental (or perhaps not so coincidental) use of the word "besieged" in the English translation of the title. Even though the novel (published in 1947) was written decades after the May Fourth movement, when China had gone through the Resistance War against the Japanese and was facing a new set of social and political circumstances, it nevertheless offers proof that the crisis of the modern male self continued even beyond the days of the May Fourth movement. For this reason, I would like to dwell a bit longer on this example.

First, let me briefly recap the story line. Set in the 1930s, the novel *The*

Besieged City is about a young man's life after he returns to China following a few years of studying abroad. It opens with the homecoming journey of Fang Hongjian, the protagonist, on a ship back from Europe. As the French *Vicomte de Bragelonne* slowly approaches China, the author takes the time to introduce to us the background of his protagonist. Fang Hongjian comes from a southern gentry family. When he was still in high school, his family betrothed him to the daughter of a friend of his father's. The girl died before they could get married, which conveniently got Fang out of a situation he did not like but had little willpower to break out of. His luck continued when his deceased fiancée's father decided to support his study abroad. During his four years in Europe, however, he changed his major from one subject to another, finally ending up in the department of Chinese literature.[15] Still, he failed to obtain a degree. By the time he was about to return to China, though, he managed to purchase a spurious degree. At least in name, Fang Hongjian returns as Dr. Fang, having first sent home photos in which he posed in a doctorate gown.

Meanwhile, the opening section of the novel focuses on the sexual tension between Fang and two young women on board the ship: Miss Bao, a seductive woman from Nanyang (referring to Southeast Asia, or the Malay Archipelago, the Malay Peninsula, and Indonesia), and Miss Su, a woman from Shanghai with a legitimate doctoral degree in literature received in France. Miss Su appears to be interested in Fang, but he falls for the sexy and seductive Miss Bao, leaving the former with a sour taste (which will come back to haunt him later). When the ship arrives in Hong Kong, however, Miss Bao jumps into the arms of her fiancé and disappears from Fang's life for good after their one-night relationship. At that moment, all Fang can do is watch her disappear, feeling used and useless. The next thing we learn, however, is that he responds to Miss Su's somewhat sour remarks by offering to accompany her sightseeing in Hong Kong. Told in a typical Qian Zhongshu style—funny and sarcastic—this rather embarrassing anticlimax to Fang's romance with Miss Bao is symbolically revealing: as a man, Fang appears uncertain about what he does, and does not know what he wants. Throughout the rest of the novel, he is unable to transcend this uncertainty.

Because the novel centers on Fang's experience after his return to China and particularly on the failures of his relationships with women and his marriage, most critics have interpreted the title of the novel as suggesting the paradoxical nature of marriage; that is, marriage is like a castle under siege:

those who are outside want to get in and those who are inside want to come out.[16] If we read the opening section of the novel carefully, however, we find that the "besiegedness" is also from the very beginning linked to the *psychological condition* of the main character; his own life can be seen as a castle that part of him wants to stay in and part of him wants to exit. The novel is about a man who is placed in a perpetually ambivalent position, and in that sense, is himself besieged.

This more psychologically oriented interpretation of "besieged" is made by the author himself. In Qian's own words, behind the humor and the sarcastic tone of the novel's voice (something that has fascinated more critics) are "two years of concerns for the world and human life." During these two years, he wrote *Weicheng* because he was particularly concerned about "part of modern Chinese society and a certain group of people in it" with whom he was also particularly familiar.[17] Meanwhile, I believe that the humor and sarcasm also indicate a self-awareness that is symptomatic of the split of the writing self as interpreted by Feuerwerker. Indeed, toward the end of the novel, the voice of this writing self takes over as the story winds down, leaving the protagonist in a state of uncertainty.

By the end of the novel, Fang Hongjian has gone through various hardships and adventures, including getting married to Sun Rojia and then finding the marriage in shambles. The two often argue, and their last argument turns into a fight, causing him to leave the house and her to leave for her parents'. Hours later, when Fang returns home, Qian ends the novel this way:

> He fell asleep. At first, the sleep was light. Hunger kept snapping him back from falling into a slumber. . . . His subconscious tried to stop the sleep. Gradually, it became blunt, and his sleep could not be stopped. It became a slumber with no dreams and no feelings. The most primal example of human sleep is at the same time a sample of death.
>
> That grandfather clock began to sound the hour unhurriedly. . . . "Dang, dang, dang, dang, dang, dang" six times. Six o'clock was five hours ago. At that time Hongjian was on his way home determined to be nice to Roujia . . . , while Roujia was waiting for Hongjian to come home for dinner hoping he would make amends with her aunt and agree to work in her factory. In giving the belated time, this time machine inadvertently revealed the ironies of life, a revelation deeper than any language or any ridiculing can achieve.[18]

The irony of the *belatedness* here echoes the opening part of the novel, where Fang *belatedly* meets Miss Bao, a woman engaged to be married, and then *belatedly* turns to Miss Su after making a blunder. Symbolically, this belatedness becomes a sign of male uncertainty (hence weakness); it echoes the dilemma of the Chinese modern condition as it is perceived by Chinese intellectuals: time has never been on the side of China's quest for modernity. Temporally, China always seems to lag "behind" (hence, is "backward") or suffers from "bad" timing. The bad timing has "crippled" men like Fang Hongjian, whose existential being is like a castle under siege: spatially frozen, not knowing whether it is better to go in or to get out. When he does make a move, however, he always suffers from bad timing. Ending the story with the irony of time, the narrator/writer evokes the writing self, who, to repeat Feuerwerker's words, continues to struggle between a "paranoid view of the world and the 'objective' situation."

Together, both the problematic self and the besieged existence of Fang Hongjian help make one thing clear: the "new" kind of self-awareness that emerged at the turn of the century and that continued to occupy the consciousness of intellectuals marks the modern individual's departure from a pursuit of cultivation of the self to grappling with a desire to *search* for the self. It is a self, I might add, whose definition was mostly based on Western humanism's emphasis on human individual interests, desire, and sense of well-being.[19] This search motif has since become the magnetic point toward which modern and contemporary Chinese intellectuals have always turned. In this sense, one can also suggest that even efforts by Kang Youwei and Liang Qichao to revitalize the Confucian self can be considered an early step in China's search for its modern identity, for they were partly motivated by the perceived threat from the outside (especially Western) world. The search motif constitutes the subjectivity of modern Chinese intellectuals. It is a subjectivity that was and still is deeply conditioned by modern Chinese history, a history full of political and ideological conflicts and filled with a sense of crisis and a desire to find a way out.

(Male) Desire and Chinese Modernity

Such a desire resurfaced in the early 1980s with the emergence of a debate over the notion of subjectivity. Though in many ways the debate has been seen as political in essence,[20] it nevertheless signified the continuing concern on the part of intellectuals about the role of the individual and its philosophical implications. The leading critics in this debate, Li Zehou and Liu Zaifu, applied a humanist/classical Marxist-based theory to their discussions in which they argued, each in his own way, for an abstract notion of subjectivity. However, because they themselves are rather overly affected by the "sublime" nature (i.e., what is the essence of the subject and subjectivity, or what is the "correct" Marxist interpretation of subjectivity) of their concerns, these critics ironically showed little concern about the psychological complexity (or, to some, the "mundane" issues) of being an individual, especially the question of desire and its significance in the understanding of subjectivity.

To be sure, the question of desire is by no means mundane as such. In fact, in the context of my discussion, one can say that the notion of desire is anything but mundane. It pertains, to repeat a point made earlier, to the "historically precipitated but psychologically specific" aspects of the question of Chinese male subjectivity constructed within the complexity of modern Chinese history.

Hegel links human desire to the notion of consciousness (the mind) and brackets it in history; desire, according to Hegel, must be understood as part of the human psyche (i.e., the mind or consciousness) constructed contextually (i.e., historically).[21] At the same time, Hegel also contends that "history" does not always provide a clear passage to the "knowability" of human desire. This paradoxical relationship between consciousness and the unknowability of desire opened up a range of new paradigms for investigation in the twentieth century, among them the psychoanalytical study of the unconscious, which speculates on, among other things, why desire, to introduce another of its characteristics, is "unsatisfiable." Meanwhile, however, Hegel, according to Juliet Flower MacCannell, suggests that there is one form of human desire that is "satisfiable": "human desire is capable of achieving its own self-certainty through relating to the desire of an other, human, historical desire."[22] In psychoanalytic terms, such desire can be defined as "desire-as-recognition"; "self-certainty" is achieved when the self is recognized by the other; without that recognition, self-certainty cannot be achieved and desire cannot be satisfied (even though the self here is itself problematically imagined as the "whole" self).

To further understand this point in the context of my discussion, we must first separate desire from its Chinese equivalent, *yu* or *yuwang.* Although new meanings can be injected into these words, for the most part, *yu* or *yuwang,* as they are understood in modern Chinese, suggest sexual desires, insatiable want, or desire for something one does not have. These connotations mark the tangibility of the objects of desire and hence the mundane implication when used in Chinese. In both Confucianist self-cultivation and Taoist escapism, *yu* or *yuwang* is something one must learn to control or eliminate.

This corresponds to the earlier Christian teaching (pre-Protestant) in which God is the only object of one's desire and "involvement[s] with objects of desire apart from God are errors."[23] The correspondence here, of course, does not exist on a content level; it exists on the relational nature of desire and its "good" and "bad" objects. Traditional Chinese teachings—those loosely mixed with Confucianism, Taoism, and Buddhism—are largely social theologies aimed at warning against letting loose one's desire or directing one's desire at a "wrong" object. The retribution dogma illustrates this point best: if one does not channel one's desire in the "right" way, one will accumulate "debts" for which one will eventually be punished in one way or another.

Briefly stated, by the late nineteenth and early twentieth century, the cosmic order on which such teachings were based had been challenged and fundamentally shaken when China, as Jonathan Spence puts it, saw, and its elites realized on a profound level and highly ambivalently, that China was merely part of a larger world. Even though Chinese literati put up much resistance to the influx of new ideas by insisting on *zhongti xiyong* (a Chinese system combined with Western technology), the historical events were to put on trial the Chinese belief system of *sangang wuchang* (one that corresponded [patri]lineally and hierarchically with the order: Heaven to emperor, emperor to ministers, and father to son) at the turn of the century, further complicating what I would call the (Chinese) traditional order of desire as well. Along with weakening national standing in the face of the Western powers, Chinese modernity emerged in this context with the question Why was China left behind? hovering over the minds of intellectuals and over the Chinese Enlightenment movement at the turn of the century.

In the West, "the century of Enlightenment," according to Tom Rockmore, "was a period of optimism with respect to the possibilities of reason to emancipate us from prejudice of all kinds in order to direct and to perfect human life."[24] Such an agent of Enlightenment as Kant, in particular, believed that a theory of reason could transcend ignorance. In the Chinese Enlightenment, the corresponding response (although not necessarily in the same optimistic spirit) from the intellectuals also converged on the word *qimeng,* or enlightenment. Along with the politically significant rallying word *jiuguo,* or saving the nation, the Chinese Enlightenment was aimed at transcending the *yumei* (ignorance or lack of ability to reason) of the masses. There is, however, a major tension in modern China between issues of Enlightenment and the struggle for China's national standing, with the former focusing on the importance of reasoning (in the sense of developing intellect and the ability to question) and the latter insisting on the conviction of one mission—saving the nation—as more important and sacred than any other. This tension, incidentally, echoes that between faith and intellection which Hegel (and Kant) had to confront facing the French Revolution two centuries ago.

In any case, the Chinese Enlightenment at the turn of the century reached its highest point during the May Fourth movement, when language, education reform, and the vehement attacks on Confucianism were all part of the efforts to transform *yumei* (ignorance) into *lixing* (reason). The major part of the effort to "ascend to reason" at the time was *zhengtuo lijiao de jiasuo* (to break free from the shackles of Confucian ethics). Such a freedom also meant, ideally, to free oneself from the traditional way of thinking and, I might add, from the traditional order of desire.

Even though most of what I have just described is already part of the general understanding of China's encounter with and its various responses to the West, what I am specifically trying to make visible is, once again, the development of a modern psyche (or mind) that accompanied the process of these changes. As agents of Chinese Enlightenment, modern Chinese intellectuals were more than messengers of Western ideas. As messengers, they were also spoken by the messages they tried to spread and, consequently, by the entangled dynamics of (Western) Enlightenment in the process of introducing it into modern China.

This point harks back to an earlier part of my discussion concerning the problematics of the self. What is also at issue is not just the emergence of a split and an anxiety in the self at the turn of the century; it is the changing/changed dynamics of desire. And it is such a dynamics of desire, I believe, that has effected the split and anxiety in question.

If, as I mentioned earlier, desire according to Hegel can be understood as recognition, the point made by Jonathan Spence becomes relevant here: at the turn of the century, China was compelled to fully realize that it was merely part of a larger world. Such a new recognition of the modern world was, of course, forced on China and its elites by the Western powers. Nevertheless, it can also be understood as China's emerging as a modern subject, becoming aware of the other whose existence in relation to China can no longer be framed within the traditional order of the universe—the traditional framework of the universe being China at the center with various tributary entities on the peripheries and with (Western) "barbarians" occupying the yonder and "uncivilized" territories. The collapsing of this traditional view of the universe undoubtedly constituted a "new world (dis)order" for China, within which recognizing itself as one part of a larger world in turn generated a desire to be "recognized." And this desire to be recognized (by the West) is what was to become a major component of Chinese elites' (and later, intellectuals') quest for modernity.

The genesis of modern (Chinese) desire, one can argue, came about not through the Protestant-like reversal of the God and human relationship (God made *us* the object of *his desire,* and gradually the desire becomes unknowable) but through secular human conflicts between us (the former center of the universe and the civilized: China) and them (the former barbarians: the West). With the Chinese door forced open in the mid–nineteenth century, the presence of the other, I repeat, also forced Chinese elites to become aware that not only were there different worldviews, there were also nation-states that appeared to be stronger and more powerful. A conscious desire to "strengthen" things Chinese was generated in the face of such a threat. But once again, such an awareness is not only about strengthening per se, it is also about winning recognition. In the spirit of Hegel's definition of modern human desire—which is psychoanalytically translated as "desire-as-recognition"—this Chinese desire is aimed precisely at achieving (cultural and national) *recognition.* Desire in the modern Chinese context, in other words, entails efforts to win recognition and to identify with things modern: new knowledge (Western ideas, technology, etc.), new ways of reasoning (including challenging the traditional cosmic order), and, above all, "new" China as a nation-state. In modern China, the identification of one's desire with these "objects" would prove forever entangled with dissatisfaction, and the dissatisfaction—as part of the desire—would continue to be part of the sensibility of Chinese modernity.

In the context of the Chinese Enlightenment, the object of desire has transformed itself from a cultivation of the self with a clear object of achievement—ideally, to become a "better" or sagelike person, and practically, to be successful in one's quest for officialdom—to a struggle for achieving self-certainty (both individually and culturally/nationally) through gaining recognition of (a new) other. This new order of desire, however, over the last century has remained unsatisfied or unfulfilled for Chinese intellectuals (in particular), especially when China as a modern nation has constantly faced uncertainty in its national standing. As such, it has also become, one may suggest, the principal (archetypal?) desire that has precipitated in the psyche of modern Chinese intellectuals. The problematics of the (modern Chinese male) self (to adapt Feuerwerker's phrase) can, in this sense, be understood as both a search for *identification* and a struggle for *recognition*.

Perceptions of (Modern) Chinese Men

Instead of moving directly to the issues of identification and recognition, I would like at this point to take a detour by introducing some existing perceptions of Chinese men, a move that will return the discussion back to those issues.

Even though the question of what it means to be a modern Chinese man has not been a popular one among most historians or other scholars either within the PRC or in the field of Chinese studies in the United States, there are some (though very limited) attempts that have explicitly tackled this question and offered interesting and sometimes conflicting views. Collectively, these discussions indicate that, regardless of whether or not there is critical attention, issues of masculinity surface when the Chinese male subject position is challenged and questioned as China continues its quest for modernity. In the following, I outline two different but representative perspectives: Sun Longji's criticism of Chinese men's "wombnization" (or their need to sever their "umbilical cord" from their mothers) and his theory of why Chinese men are not "real men" yet; and Wang Yuejin's intertextual reading of the film *Red Sorghum* and his positive view about what he calls "the

femininity complex" of Chinese men. I then offer a discussion of these perspectives and speculate on the ways we can expand our understanding of the
question of Chinese male identity.

Chinese Men and the "Umbilical Cord"

One of the attempts to understand the (modern) Chinese male ends up
attacking him. In his " 'Mutaihua' zhi jingsheng xianxiang xue" (the psychological phenomenon of 'wombnization'), Sun Longji (Lung-kee Sun) draws
materials from the May Fourth literature and studies conducted by (American) sociologists between the 1950s and 1970s, mostly in Taiwan, on the acculturation of Chinese men to critique the "lack" (an important word to keep
in mind) of "modern male traits" in Chinese men (*zhongguo nanren*). It is
significant, incidentally, to note the generalizing term "Chinese men" that
Sun employs here. Even though the sociological data he refers to were drawn
from studies on men outside the PRC, his critique of "Chinese men" *assumes*
their counterparts on the mainland. Today, this assumption seems to coin-
cide with the emerging geopolitical paradigm of the "Greater China" enthusiastically mapped out by some Chinese elites in China and China specialists
in the West. Still, I must point out, the different histories within are such that
they should always caution us against generalizations.

In any case, at least in his article, Sun is very critical of "Chinese men."
According to him, in the limited scholarly attention given to the study of the
acculturation of Chinese men,[25] or fashionably put, the "construction" of
Chinese male subjectivity, most findings suggest that because of the specific
Chinese familial structure, Chinese men's acculturation does not entail the
kind of separation from the mother, either realistically or figuratively, assumed in the Oedipus complex model. Chinese men, as a result, are believed
to be closer to their mothers than are their Western counterparts. If such
findings do indicate the existence of differences in male acculturation, does
this Chinese model constitute a better alternative for the construction of
male subjectivity than the model of the Oedipus complex? Not according to
Sun. He characterizes the Chinese model as "abnormal." Chinese men, he
argues, have long "suffered" from a close relationship with their mothers, a
phenomenon he calls *mutaihua* (being wombnized, or men having yet to cut
the umbilical cord). Discussing some literary representations of men in modern Chinese literature, Sun contends that these male characters are represen-

tative of Chinese men's failure, at their entry into the "symbolic" (to borrow a well-known psychoanalytic term), to separate from their mother. Citing a number of male characters from that literature, Sun focuses on their failure to have a "normal" relationship with women. According to his reading, many male characters in the May Fourth literature share one thing in common: as men they are still dependent (mentally and/or psychologically) on their mother, and this makes it impossible for them to deal successfully with heterosexual relationships.[26] They have a tendency to turn relationships between men and women into mother-son or father-daughter relationships.[27] Although I am not sure why he includes father-daughter relationships while all the time discussing mother-son relationships, one thing is clear: Sun argues that Chinese men's inability to be independent persons with adequate social skills (especially for relationships with women) is symptomatic of their relationships with their mother. He claims that the characteristics of Chinese (male) subjectivity include the *lack* of a complete "separation" (*fen li*) and "individualization" (*geti hua*), especially when compared with Western men. Contrasting the "lack of (a complete) maturation of the Chinese male child" with that of boys in the "modernized West," he concludes that Chinese men have to "dewombnize" themselves, first for them to become modernized and second for Chinese culture to come to terms with modernity.

It is obvious that Sun's criticism of Chinese male acculturation is based on the premise that for China to modernize itself, Chinese *men* must be modernized first. Because, for Sun, modernization equals Westernization and represents the future for the Chinese, a Western model for male acculturation is "naturally" better than the Chinese one.[28] If Chinese male subjectivity continues to remain different from that of its Western counterparts, it is this very difference, according to Sun, that keeps a Chinese male from becoming a modern man. If Chinese men are to be modernized, also according to Sun, they must first "dewombnize" themselves, and furthermore, the womb must be shown as suffocating. This is what Sun's analysis of "weak" Chinese men finally leads to: modernity understood in Sun's sense puts the mother on trial for preventing the male child from becoming a real man. The weakness of Chinese men, according to Sun's logic, is symptomatic of the lack in the mother.

Even though in critiquing Chinese men's continuing "wombnization" Sun does not examine the nature of the Chinese father-son relationship, one can infer from his argument that his criticism of the Chinese mother is based on his acceptance of the Oedipus complex as a better model: for Chinese men to become real men, they must first learn to sever their close ties with their mothers in order to locate their real identities as individuals; to do so they must also learn to become the son of the father (so as to transcend the fear of castration). Sun's Oedipal-based alternative, therefore, requires a transference to take place, which, once again, is aimed against the mother: to return the pathological condition to the mother and sever the umbilical cord linked to her. Such a severing is assumed to be the first step to help the boy be reborn as a real man.

Chinese Men's "Femininity Complex"

On a more theoretical level, we encounter a different perspective on the "problem" of Chinese men: Wang Yuejin's discussion of Chinese men in his article "*Red Sorghum:* Mixing Memory and Desire." Wang takes a far less critical approach than Sun Longji in discussing the question of Chinese men and the notion of masculinity.[29] In fact, he is responding to criticism coming from a different direction that accuses the filmmaker of *Red Sorghum* of representing a masculinist stance, and he attempts to debunk the criticism made of Zhang Yimou's film concerning its representations of men and male desire.

Reading the film allegorically, Wang perceives it as "a cinematic milestone that proposes a powerful Chinese version of masculinity as a means of cultural critique," and "a return of the collectively repressed, an evocation of the cultural unconscious, a remembrance of the forgotten, and a tapping of intertextual memories."[30] Masculinity as represented in the film is "a self-deluded state," which the film is "both parasitical and critical of" (87). By way of an intertextual reading, Wang traces a trajectory in traditional Chinese writing to lay out a "culturally rooted" difference when it comes to notions of femininity and masculinity, suggesting that what constitutes the configurations of modern/Western masculinity may not be the configurations of masculinity in China. Traditionally, he argues, Chinese mainstream culture, one controlled by the literati, favors the soft, gentle, and "sober" state of mind in men. A man with masculine traits, on the other hand, is a hero with a flawed character and without much possibility of becoming a major player at the higher levels of the power structure. Wang argues, "Instead of being afflicted by castration anxiety, the problematic of the lack is quite reversed in the Chinese cultural context. *It is man who lacks*" (83, my emphasis). "If anything," he continues, "a femininity complex would be a more appropriate form of the unconscious in the Chinese psyche" (83). One is advised, therefore, not to be trapped by (Western) psychoanalytic assumptions about gender configurations that are centered around "male castration anxiety."[31]

This advice cautions against a simplistic reading of the representations of Chinese men found, for example, in such a film as *Red Sorghum* and in many other texts that share a similar tone. Meanwhile, echoing observations made by other critics regarding the "feminine" nature of the traditional Chinese male, Wang also quite convincingly points out that when a Chinese man appropriates the "feminine space," women do not figure in that space—the feminine space, that is, is not necessarily a space for women. Consequently, femininity does not equate to womanhood either. This point acknowledges the complex relation between femininity and masculinity within the (traditional) Chinese context: the feminine space is often the site of enunciation for "disempowered" men rather than for women.

One can infer from Wang's article a sense of what constitutes (contemporary) Chinese male subjectivity. And the sense seems to be that, figured more prominently as a femininity complex, Chinese male subjectivity is fluid and comfortable with its own lack, a picture in clear conflict with that sketched by Sun Longji. Whereas Sun measures Chinese men against an unquestioned notion of modernity (which assumes the "right" model for male acculturation), Wang complicates the picture via a different equation in which the Chinese (male) psyche, though situated at the opposite side of the Western model, is nevertheless comfortably (or at most ambivalently) related to a femininity complex rather than completely at odds with it.

Questions, however, still remain: How does history figure in Wang's intertextual reading of the femininity complex of Chinese male subjectivity? Does Wang suggest that throughout Chinese history there has been an unbroken trace of this femininity complex and that the traditional gender configurations (if there was a consistent set) have not undergone any significant change nor faced much serious challenge in modern times? Measured against what does one define or qualify the Chinese (male) psyche as having a femininity complex? Also, is this "soft, gentle, and sober state of mind in [Chinese] men" necessarily less masculine than, say, the Kantian self, a Western model that is traditionally said to be advocating reason as well? Is the femininity complex an actual traditional model, or is it one whose traditionality is actually informed more by modernity than by the entity called tradition? What, above all, does it mean when this Chinese and traditional mode of manhood is evoked? I will return to these questions shortly; for the moment, it suffices to say that Wang's discussion does not fully address them.

In spite of their differences, both Sun Longji and Wang Yuejin suggest there is a culturally specific Chinese male subjectivity reminiscent of the "deeper" structure of traditional Chinese culture. In relation to the West, modern Chinese male subjectivity is represented by the two as being on the margins; in one case, man is yet to sever his umbilical cord, and in the other, he is dominated by a femininity complex. Either way, masculinity does not figure strongly in nor does it occupy the center of Chinese male subjectivity. For Sun, this marginal position is problematic for Chinese men, whereas for Wang, the position is not necessarily marginal within the Chinese context; it is only called into question when measured (wrongly) against the West and when the latter is used as the criterion for gender configurations.

Male Lack, the Femininity Complex, and Chinese Masculinity

At this point, I would like to return to Wang Yuejin's suggestion that "it is [Chinese] man that *lacks*" (my emphasis). If, as I pointed out earlier, there is a lack of history in Wang's tracing of the intertextual trajectory of the femininity complex of Chinese men, how do we reevaluate this notion of (Chinese) male lack within the complex history of modern China?

Psychoanalytically, lack is a term derived from the notion of the castration complex. "In its most literal sense," according to Elisabeth Bronfen, the castration complex "means that the girl must accept her definition as inferior, because she is anatomically castrated, lacking a penis, while the boy must accept the father's castrating 'no' to his incestuous wish for the mother, i.e. must accept that he is temporarily inferior to the phallically more powerful father."[32] On this literal level, if we recall both Sun Longji's and Wang Yuejin's analyses of Chinese male subjectivity, we can see that they each (coincidentally) emphasize a different aspect of the castration complex. Sun's attack on Chinese men hinges on his impatience with the boy not being able to turn into a man by transcending his "incestuous wish for the mother." That is, Sun identifies the Chinese male problem—*mutaihua,* in his words—with the male child's inability to identify more strongly with the father. In this sense, if he also seems to suggest that "it is [Chinese] man that lacks," for Sun the Chinese male lack will remain real (and therefore bad) until the boy/child grows into a man. For Wang, on the other hand, the male lack is identified more with the girl—the lack is *inherent* (and therefore inherently Chinese). Given the anti-Western hegemonic implications in his identifying Chinese male lack with the feminine, Wang appears to suggest that such a lack is neither good nor bad. What is more, within the context of trying to debunk a certain criticism of Chinese men, his argument for the Chinese male lack registers a highly positive note in defense of Chinese men.

There is, however, one essential detail that Wang has neglected. In identifying the Chinese male lack as a femininity complex, the critic appears to understand lack and castration complex as feminine in essence. And, as long as lack and femininity are identified as one, Chinese male subjectivity can even be suggested to be better than the "masculinity-driven" Western model. What is more, as I pointed out earlier, when Wang's argument fails to take history into consideration, it also appears to suggest that the fluid (i.e., the feminine) nature of Chinese male subjectivity is a stable entity solidly preserved throughout history. Both theoretically and historically, however, the notion of lack has more implications than what is suggested here.

In Lacanian psychoanalytic terms, lack, as the English translator of Lacan's *Four Fundamental Concepts of Psycho-Analysis* explains, comes from the French word *manque,* which "is translated here as 'lack,' except in the expression, created by Lacan, '*manque-à-être,*' for which Lacan himself has proposed the English neologism 'want-to-be.' "[33] Lacan designated the notion of the lack as *manque-à-être* or want-to-be in order, he claims, to speak "of the function of desire" (29). In his efforts to explain the formation of the subject, Lacan identifies the lack as a psychological component that enables the subject to help the ego cope with the nothingness that is not represented as such and to come to identify with the "locus of metaphor—one object for another" (103–4).

In the evolution of Lacanian psychoanalysis, especially in its ambivalent relationship with feminist theories, the notion of lack has been made almost synonymous with that of femininity and sometimes with the position of the female. Such an identification is largely due to Freud's belief that femininity constitutes, among other things, penis envy, which assumes that women, due to their permanent lack of the male organ, are always reduced to the position of envy and of lack. This identification of lack with women, however, does not seem to be the focus of Lacan's discussion of the subject (even though, as some feminist critics have pointed out, he operates ultimately within the framework of the Law of the Father because, for him, phallocentrism is a given). Still, Lacan's notion of the lack does not have to be identified only with women.

Wang's claim that "it is [Chinese] man that lacks," on the other hand, seems to be based on what I would call the feminization of the lack. Although such an identification is significant in making visible the marginal positionality of the feminine, or more accurately, of women in relation to the order of (Western) patriarchy, it also limits the notion of the lack too much to what Lacan identifies as the oral level, and thus indirectly resubjects women to the position of less than full subjects. It leaves women on the penis envy level without taking into account other levels of their subjection and identification. Similarly, it also amplifies the dichotomy between femininity and masculinity without getting further into the realms of desire and identification, and without taking into consideration what lack means to Lacan: its want-to-be-ness.

This may explain why Wang, while identifying the femininity complex as culturally specific to the "Chinese [male] psyche," dismisses the manifestation of male desire in the film *Red Sorghum* as no more than a carnivalistic act of the "repressed," amounting to no more than an intertextual play with gender configurations. Men like "my Grandpa," Wang suggests, are merely reminiscent of the criminal outcasts in traditional texts, whose masculine traits are "nonphallic" (Kaja Silverman's term) and therefore not threatening to the dominant power structure. Because his discussion focuses on the femininity complex of Chinese men, the display of masculinity in the film *Red Sorghum* is effectively seen as degendered—carnivalized—and this degendering of the masculine in turn helps sustain his femininity complex theme. To identify Chinese men's lack with the femininity complex, in other words, the critic does not consider the desire or the want-to-be-ness manifested in the performative acts of carnival in the film.

The purpose of my emphasizing and foregrounding the want-to-be aspect of the notion of lack is simple. I want to point out that the "Chinese [male] psyche" does not exist *passively* to be imprinted (into a femininity complex) by the power structure, nor does the (Chinese male) femininity complex—as understood by Wang—necessarily entail a male embracing of his own marginality. Unlike the marginal masculinities whose "libidinal politics" is hailed by Silverman in her book, in which her intention is to undertake a "theoretical articulation of some non-phallic masculinities,"[34] I argue that the marginality of Chinese masculinity, like the (Chinese) mother's umbilical cord, does not necessarily guarantee a nonphallic libidinal politics. Although the male subjectivity represented in contemporary Chinese literature may occupy marginal spaces both in relation to the dominant power structure in China and to the West, its articulation does not entail either acknowledging or embracing "castration, alterity, and specularity." More often than not, the contrary is true. Many literary representations of men in recent Chinese literature, as we will see later, have manifested a desire to return to the (imagined) "masculine space." This, it seems to me, constitutes the specificity of the libidinal politics of Chinese male subjectivity at the moment: men voicing their libidinal desires for an unfulfilled (modern) heterosexual masculine space in which they can find their own masculine image, while they continue to slip back to the margins.

Given all this, I argue that the specificity of the modern Chinese male subjectivity in fact consists of, as I identified in my introduction, a male marginality complex. It is a male psyche predominantly manifested through Chinese (male) intellectuals' preoccupation with the weakness of the country, the culture, and Chinese men. In this sense, the complex is also a male desire, a desire to overcome marginality and to search for (masculine) identity.

To better understand modern Chinese male subjectivity, therefore, we need to move beyond focusing only on Chinese men's gender—masculine or feminine—traits and recognize that at issue is a modern male subject with a strong desire for, among other things, *identification* and *recognition*. If, as Judith Butler argues, to become a man (or a woman) entails an identification of some sort, we need to ask with whom the Chinese man ultimately desires to identify.

In her examination of the notion of masculinity, Butler argues that the relevance of her analysis of drag (performances) is that "drag exposes or allegorizes the mundane psychic and performative practices by which heterosexualized genders form themselves through the renunciation of the *pos-*

sibility of homosexuality. . . . Drag thus allegorizes heterosexual melancholy, the melancholy by which a masculine gender is formed from the refusal to grieve the masculine as a possibility of love."[35] Her point is illuminating: if the unsettling nature of the drag performance of a man dressed as a woman exposes heterosexual performative practices, it also helps us realize that there is something unsettling in the paradoxical nature of Chinese male subjectivity. Whereas the (male) preoccupation with male weakness signifies an anxiety over male lack, the anxiety itself may well be a reiteration of a set of norms, and the naming of male lack is itself (to echo Butler) a melancholy that in fact refuses a male identification with the lack (the feminine, in the Freudian sense). More important, rather than suggest that the male lack is the position identified by Chinese men, it is more logical to see it as a *rejected identification,* which suggests "wanting" on the part of Chinese male intellectuals rather than their being content on the margins and even "acced[ing] to castration."[36]

In other words, if Chinese male subjectivity is in the end a marginalized subjectivity (by the West, by the state power structure, or even, according to some people, by women), it does not necessarily follow that such a position is embraced by Chinese (male) intellectuals. More often than not, we find the inverse is true. The psychologically specific ramifications of the historical trauma, brought about by China's century-long quest for modernity and the political oppression during the first thirty years of the CCP's rule, have created a sense and a fear of lacking (or of not being a certain way) and a desire to want. What is more, if part of Chinese men's acculturation is deemed feminine, the debate over Chinese male traits—whether or not they are more feminine than masculine—is in fact itself part of the modern discourse that, to use Slavoj Žižek's term, "names" the traits "retroactively" and via a comparison with the West. The modern Chinese (male) preoccupation with male weakness—the male marginality complex—has less to do with a celebration of its femininity and everything to do with its being perceived as pathological and with a constant frustration over an inability to be recognized as strong, hence masculine.

Or, put differently and using Butler's model of a "melancholic formation of gender," it has to do with an "unfinished grieving" over the loss of (a retroactively named) male self. For, as Butler argues, "melancholic identification permits the loss of the object in the external world precisely because it provides a way to *preserve* the object as part of the ego itself and, hence, to avert the loss as a complete loss."[37] In this sense, we can say that the modern Chinese male preoccupation with male weakness is itself the very point where an identification with *what is not weak* is originated, preserved, and established as the object of (male) desire. The supposed close relationship between (Chinese) mother and son, therefore, does not necessarily mean that the son is not traditionally taught to follow in the steps of the father; in many ways, the mother herself steps in as a surrogate father and makes the son identify with him in his absence. Nor does it follow that the son fails to identify with the father, even though his route of identification may be different from that of the Western male.

What is more, briefly returning to Qian Zhongshu, if his portrayal of Fang Hongjian makes visible the *ganga* (literally, embarrassed, but more accurately, ambivalent or ambiguous) nature of the modern (male) existence, Fang's *ganga*, at the same time, can also be understood as a "melancholic" moment that saves the male self from being completely lost. In an indirect but highly relevant way, therefore, Qian's portrayal of Fang anticipates contemporary Chinese (male) writers' desire to move out of this temporospatial stalemate: to fanatically "catch up" by, among other things, searching for a desirable male identity. Unlike Fang, then, contemporary Chinese male writers, critics, and intellectuals appear more anxious to transcend their "besieged" dilemma.

With this, my discussion has arrived at the point where I can suggest that the sense of besiegedness is itself a form of masculinity deeply ingrained in the psyche of male intellectuals, and that, as I demonstrate in subsequent chapters, this state of mind continues to engage the intellectual elites of the 1980s in a powerful and yet ambivalent way.

The question now is how this male sense of besiegedness gets reproduced and thus in essence resurfaces and remains as a form of Chinese masculinity in the post-Mao era. That is, if besiegedness specifically suggests a man's ambivalence over his own position and maleness is to be understood historically, what is also there in recent Chinese history that keeps producing anxiety in intellectuals and simultaneously turns it into a form of masculinity? These questions return my discussion to the role of history in our understanding of Chinese male subjectivity. In what follows, I turn to recent Chinese history for an investigation into the historical implications of the CCP's own quest for modernity and its impact on the contemporary pursuit of masculinity.

Masculinity Revisited: The Post-1949 Quest for Modernity and the Myth of *Yinsheng yangshuai*

Speaking of Yinsheng yangshuai

As I mentioned earlier, *yinsheng yangshuai* as a public perception emerged after the Cultural Revolution (1966–1976), and in its own way echoed Sun Longji's concern over the (lack of) quality in Chinese men. It can be summed up this way: After years of Communist rule, Chinese men had become too weak and Chinese women had become too strong; known in Chinese as *yinsheng yangshuai xianxiang,* the myth literally means "the phenomenon of the prosperity of the feminine and the decline of the masculine." Though it helped bring gender difference back into public discourse, it did so with an implication that the gender difference was wrongly balanced.

According to the general and popular understanding of the "norms" of the traditional Chinese cosmic order, *yin* and *yang* should intertwine with each other in a harmonious way, with each occupying its "designated" position. Although many scholars have argued that the "original" implications of the *yinyang* order do not imply one (*yang*) more powerful than the other (*yin*), nor suggest that they have a simple correlation to men and women, in the 1980s, the two words were used in direct correlation to gender relationships and configurations. In fact, the term *yinsheng yangshuai,* when used in this particular context, was no more than a euphemistic expression denoting gender relations and configurations affected by the CCP's dominant ideology, linking woman (rather than the feminine) directly with the *yin* in the notion of *yinsheng,* and man (rather than the masculine) directly with the *yang* in that of *yangshuai.* In this sense, the phenomenon can be simply translated as the "women-are-too-strong-and-men-are-too-weak phenomenon."

In the literature of the 1980s, as I briefly mentioned in the introduction, there was also, corresponding to the *yinsheng yangshuai* phenomenon, a growing interest in the subject matter of "searching for 'real' men." The search was connected with the concern over the (lack of good) quality in men and came to be named as such via the title of a play, *Xunzhao nanzihan* (Looking for a real man) by male playwright Sha Yexin, and more specifically, via the disappointment demonstrated by the woman protagonist in the play in her not-so-successful quest to find a "real" man to be her future husband.[38] Her disappointment was meant to be seen as representative of public sentiment over the lack of real men in contemporary China. Whether or not the sentiment reflects reality is subject to debate, but it certainly is represented as if it were a reality recognized by those concerned, and further begs the question of what led to this perceived reality. To answer this question, a brief review of history is in order.

Before I do so, however, I must make an observation vis-à-vis our understanding of the history of the Mao era. As of now, many aspects of the first seventeen years of that era are yet to be fully studied and understood, especially with regard to its connection with issues of modernity. For the most part, because issues of modernity have often been associated with (Western) cosmopolitanism—modernism, for example—and because post-1949 China has been perceived to a large extent as an antithesis to this association, studies of this period have been almost exclusively political.[39] Little interest and therefore attention have been given to the more complex relationship between the CCP's desire to modernize and the cultural issues it had to tackle on various concrete levels. Although recent publications such as Wang Ban's *The Sublime Figure of History* and Zheng Shiping's *Party vs. State*[40] have begun to present a complex picture of the Mao era structurally, politically, and culturally, much remains to be studied and understood. Given the limited scope of this discussion, my brief account of this part of Chinese history is sketchy, mainly aiming at foregrounding aspects of that era that we need to take into consideration when studying male issues.

Masculinity and China's Post-1949 Quest for Modernity

In the 1980s, the manifestations of desire for real men came to be embodied by Rambo, Takakura Ken, and the rural man from China's northwest. Ironically, however, even though they appear as individuals with strong masculine features, these body images are not entirely new to the post-Mao era. Indeed, if we look into the Mao era, we find that similar images of men—as heroes—were also created. If contemporary male intellectuals demonstrated a strong critical position against the CCP's ideology, in many ways their desire for a strong male identity is also the product of the CCP's own quest for modernity. That is, the desire for masculine identity does not come only from the protesting self but also from, to echo Adorno, an "overlapping" construction. In that overlapping construction, furthermore, there was a collective participation in the CCP's pursuit of modernity and in the construction of what I call a Chinese national—collective—masculine identity.

To be sure, participation here does not mean wholehearted and proactive participatory activities (although such activities did take place among certain groups of intellectuals). However, as the Chinese scholar Huang Ping argues, there is something peculiar about the experience and behavior of Chinese intellectuals that raises questions regarding precisely their role and position within the structural and discursive changes in post-1949 China. Huang contends that there is an unresolved, puzzling question about Chinese intellectuals: "Why is there a lack of consistency between the words and behavior of Chinese intellectuals today and their behavior in the past [i.e., prior to the post-Mao era]?"[41] To answer this question, we must realize that "structural control and subjective behavior are not necessarily exclusive or oppositional. On the contrary, it is the very relationship between the two and the ways they intertwine with and condition each other that constitute the true picture of the social life" (38). Using this premise, Huang proceeds to tackle the question raised above by examining the relationship between the CCP and intellectuals as China went through unprecedented structural changes that, in Huang's words, effectively "de-intellectualized" the latter. The CCP's structural and discursive pursuit for a strong China is a case in point.

Though the jury is still out on the verdict of the first thirty years of PRC history, most of the historical accounts so far have been highly critical of the political oppression and psychological repression inflicted on the Chinese people by the CCP through various political campaigns. Few studies, however, have given a full account of the sociocultural environment and its psychological effects during the years prior to the Cultural Revolution (during which the most high-handed control and the worst violence took place). Even fewer studies have examined the various other sociocultural factors at play that contributed, at the time, toward the construction of notions of gender, romantic love, sexuality, and what it meant to be a man and a woman.[42]

Although all of this requires extensive study, briefly put, the founding of the PRC under the Chinese Communist Party led to significant structural and discursive changes, and those changes were to contribute significantly to the (re)shaping of, for lack of a better word, the psyche of the Chinese people. On the structural level, along with the Western blockade led by the United States after the founding of the PRC, the CCP's regime purged much of the foreign (Western, to be exact) presence in China, and followed (at least initially and in some major ways) the Soviet Union's model in its restructuring of society. Although the "revolution" in industry and agriculture did not take place overnight, the setup of the Party-state paved the way for China's future revolution and reconstruction. In cities, the government created jobs for the poor, who began to enjoy various benefits. The majority of the working poor in urban China began to have their basic needs—food, shelter, and health—taken care of. In rural China, land reform not only fulfilled the CCP's promise to Chinese peasants but also brought (a sense of) liberation to them.[43]

Structural changes brought about changes in social relations and profoundly affected men and women of different social sectors and classes. The emphasis on class struggle (*jie ji dou zheng*), both structurally and discursively especially, impacted individuals in their newfound and externally defined social positions and relations. With regard to gender relations, the Communist Party introduced its gender-equality policies, called on women to participate in the socialist revolution and socialist construction, and wrote and implemented policies for women to become active participants in the workforce. With that, other changes occurred.

On the cultural level, signs of modernity existed in ostensible and obscure ways depending, of course, on the whims of the CCP's official ideology. For the most part, at least in the first seventeen years prior to the outbreak of the Cultural Revolution, certain Western cultural products and artifacts coexisted with those from the Soviet Union, as well as those produced domestically by early-twentieth-century writers and artists or in the more dogmatic and propaganda-prone post-1949 era. Even though much of the official interest in Western culture was limited mainly in its premodernist literature and art, especially that produced during the nineteenth-century Romantic and Realist literary movements, such an official interest nevertheless provided opportunities, especially for the young, for access to ideas and sentiments that would resurface years later (and part of the resurfacing would be what we find in the literature of the 1980s). Although more studies are needed to fully examine the mixed baggage of the CCP's cultural legacy and its impact, it is safe to suggest that the mixture conditioned the complexity of the contemporary male writer intellectuals.

In addition to structural and cultural changes, the CCP maintained the desire to modernize China, a desire that was informed and constructed both by its own utopian vision and by the mixture of historical and cultural baggage it consciously or unconsciously inherited. In his book *In Pursuit of Wealth and Power,* Benjamin Schwartz argues that, for early intellectuals such as Yan Fu, the ambition was simple: China must emulate the West to search for wealth and power.[44] As long as China was willing to learn from the West, Yan seemed to believe, according to Schwartz, China would be capable of both wealth and power enjoyed by the west. Yan, Schwartz argues, was not introducing Western ideas as a colonial subject. Rather, he was borrowing them in the hope that one day China would become strong and powerful as well. That is, Yan would not mind if China imitated the West, so long as it became wealthy and strong. In this sense, according to Schwartz, Yan should not be identified as a colonial subject in spite of his enthusiastic efforts in translating major Western texts into Chinese. Schwartz's insistence on a distinction between colonialization and Westernization in modern Chinese history can be understood as not only a recognition of the complexity and specificity of modern Chinese history but also a willingness on his part to grant agency to modern Chinese intellectuals in their efforts to come to terms with modernity.

In a rather indirect way, Yan Fu's call for China to become strong and powerful was echoed both by modern Chinese intellectuals and by the CCP. For the Party, the founding of the PRC marked the end of the semicolonial and semifeudal society and the beginning of the "real" pursuit of wealth and power for China. Even though the CCP's definition of wealth and power is different from Yan's, the spirit behind Yan's quest is to a large extent shared by the CCP in its quest for a strong and industrialized China. At least at the beginning, therefore, the founding of the PRC appeared to help stop an anxiety shared by intellectuals: as a modern nation, many of them believed, the PRC was to lead China out of its weakened position. The era in which the Chinese were looked down upon as the "sick man of the East" (*dongya bingfu*) was declared to have ended.

Indeed, in the ensuing Mao era, one symbol that stood out in sharp contrast to that of the *dongya bingfu* and in close connection with China's pursuit for wealth and power is that of steel and iron (*gangtie*), symbolizing the CCP's resolve to industrialize the new China. In the 1950s, Mao was repeatedly quoted as saying that China should and would catch up with the United States and Great Britain in about fifteen years (when China would be able to produce a certain amount of steel).[45] Whether or not it was realistically possible, this was certainly an indication of Mao's ambition for a modernized China. Indeed, at least for the first ten years after the founding of the PRC, the CCP followed the blueprint of the Soviet model in building big factories, turning all the major cities, including Shanghai, into industrial enclaves. In the 1950s, cities engaged in the Great Leap Forward by trying to churn out more steel (only, of course, to have useless metal come out of crudely made furnaces). Making steel became the symbol of China's ambition for power and potential wealth. Meanwhile, it also became an important symbol in the production of a new "bodily integrity" for subject formation and hero making in that era.

Most Chinese growing up in the Mao era were familiar with one definition regarding what it meant to be a communist, a definition the CCP borrowed from Stalin, who was quoted to have claimed that "a communist is made of special material." The special material was further defined by a Soviet novel titled, in its Chinese translation, *Gangtie shi zenyang liancheng de* (How the steel was tempered).[46] The novel is about a young working-class man, Pavel Korchagin, and his journey toward becoming a "real" communist, a man made of special material. As the protagonist in a novel (and film, shown in China in the 1950s)[47] highly promoted by the CCP, this Soviet-made young revolutionary came to embody the CCP's ideal hero: a "flawed" human being turned into a strong and firm-hearted man with only one devotion.[48]

As Pavel Korchagin's story demonstrates, to become a communist or a revolutionary, one must turn against one's own body; individuals were expected to "leap forward" out of their bodies and to become steel-like heroes. It was a utopian subjecthood without individuals' own bodies—humanity/subjectivity—acknowledged. Such a subjectless subjecthood indicates a fear of the body made of flesh and blood, a fear that is at the core of the CCP's utopian ideal, whose "bodily imaginary," whose understanding and interpretation of the body, is more akin to a religious puritanism than anything else. With a "bodyless" self as its ideal subject, it was almost natural for the CCP to call on the Chinese to emulate Korchargin-like heroes: to become self-less (*wusi* and *wangwo*). For the CCP regime, to create wealth and power for China, individuals must themselves be turned into steel-and-iron beings that function, ironically, like "little screws" (*xiaoxiao de luosiding*). The symbolic implications of steel, selflessness, and the "little screw" here embody a quintessential paradox in the CCP's ideology: it wants people to treasure their self-integrity, but they can do so only by becoming self-less. As such, the ideology became repressive and foreshadowed an eventual fall into meaninglessness to the very people for whom such a "new self" was meant.

To further complicate the issue—so as to better understand post-Mao male anxiety and the notion of masculinity—however, even though the steel-like male body was revealed as no more than an empty signifier after the collapse of the CCP's official ideology, the void left by the disillusionment neverthe-less generated a stronger desire for a new cultural (and male) identity. In the post-Mao era, as mentioned in my introduction, such a desire was in part responsible for the literature known as *xunzhao nanzihan,* or the "search for manly men" literature. One of the interesting twists in the male representa-tions of men in the literature of the 1980s, therefore, as I will elaborate later, is that in trying to occupy the void left by the collapse of the officially estab-lished male image, it is the "suffering" male, who embodies both the weak-ened image of the Chinese (men) and the strong desire to transcend the weak position, who emerges as the new hero. Meanwhile, this new hero is himself entangled with the CCP's official ideology because, also as I will argue, the latter's collapse leaves not only a void (of strong men) but also strong im-prints that continue to condition the meaning of that void and the ways the oppositional discourse desires to fill it. For even though the steel-like male was rejected as a hero, its implication of strength nevertheless remains.

Indeed, what was valued in those male images (i.e., Rambo, Takakura Ken, and the Chinese version of the Western man found in post-Mao popular culture) continued to be their strength, either physical or mental. In this sense, these seemingly new images of men blurred the boundaries between the individual male identity that was supposedly being pursued in the post-Mao era and the collective masculine identity imagined by the CCP. In this context, when the question of male identity was turned partly into a matter of *yinyang* disorder and partly into a return to the "natural" order between the sexes, the essence of the collective masculine identity managed to sneak in through these (pinup) images of strong men and with even stronger ap-peal than before. Issues of masculinity resurfaced.

Speaking of Yinsheng yangshuai *Again*

Although the *yinyang* disorder became part of the public discourse in post-Mao China and although in recent years there have been studies in the West of whether or not the socialist revolution has benefited Chinese women, few studies have been conducted regarding Chinese men; one can only infer from many of the existing studies a general picture of where men might be situated in relation to various social and political changes, and to women.[49] Historians and feminist scholars of modern China differ in their views on the structural and discursive effects of the CCP's gender-equality policies on Chinese men and women; for some, gender equality for Chinese women was in fact not fully realized under the leadership of the CCP, and for others, it was Chinese men who got the short end of the stick.

Indeed, given the context of recent Chinese history, no one can deny the political implications underpinning this public woe over the status of men. Meanwhile, some of the strongest criticisms of Chinese men, as I briefly mentioned in my introduction, have come from Chinese women writers and critics. Zhang Jie's *Fang zhou* (The ark), for example, provoked controversy when it was published because of her strong criticism of the male characters for being selfish, vulgar, and chauvinist.[50] Many women critics both in and outside China have also questioned the images of men and women represented by Chinese male writers of both modern and contemporary times.[51] Through the lenses of these women writers and critics, we find that the issue is not whether or not men are "weak" and suffer from being "feminized." Rather, it is that men are still more powerful than women, and that male chauvinism is still very much a part of Chinese male subjectivity and is still dominant in Chinese society at large.

How do we make sense of these contradictory perceptions with regard to the positions of men and women affected by the first thirty years of the CCP's regime? To answer this question and the historical ironies embedded in the post–Cultural Revolution myth of *yinyang* disorder, let us examine an important discursive marker of the CCP's regime and ideology: *tongzhi* or comrade (whose ubiquitous presence and usage, at least during the first thirty years of PRC history, would subsequently, and ironically, obscure its discursive impact toward the end of this period). This word carried with it a range of social and political implications and functioned as the most important political (and self-)identification marker.

As part of its power consolidation, the Communist Party's official discourse managed to command its formidable presence through linguistic cleansing. Words used for individuals' public identification, such as *xiansheng* (Mr.), *taitai* (Mrs.), *xiaojie* (Miss), and *nushi* (lady), were soon to become obsolete as the communist dominant discourse introduced the word *tongzhi* or comrade. It is a word (of address and identification) borrowed from the international communist movement for its correlation to the "collective good." The word, therefore, was intended to erase or make less visible the identity of other traits of an individual, *geren* in Chinese, labeled a bourgeois concept riddled with class implications. *Tongzhi,* on the other hand, offered a clear political identity to those who were referred to as comrade and those who were not. At the same time, *tongzhi* itself is not gendered and thus needed gender markers, hence *nan tongzhi* and *nu tongzhi* (man comrade and woman comrade) came into use. *Nan tongzhi* and *nu tongzhi* not only provided gendered identification to individuals, but, because of the specific politically charged implications in the word *tongzhi,* their use also had a cleansing effect against the sexual connotations carried by such words as *nanren* (man/men) and *nuren* (woman/women).

As they came to be addressed as *nu tongzhi* and as they became part of the socialist work force, women from both urban and rural areas were (at least theoretically) expected to be recognized as on an equal footing with their male counterparts. Indeed, even today, most Chinese still remember the famous slogan coined by Mao Zedong: "Time is different now: what men comrades [*nan tongzhi*] can do, women comrades [*nu tongzhi*] can also do."[52] *Tongzhi,* in this sense, became the marker that went on to signify the gender equality envisioned by Mao.

If this declaration entailed women's being "liberated" from their homes to become active participants in the public domain, it also meant that both men and women had to share the same footing, publicly, in a politically charged environment: they were subject to a high-handed political system that subsumed individuality as part of the collective good and thus effectively suppressed individuality's expression. For men as well as for women, to be kept within the category of *tongzhi* meant to be safe from being ostracized; the desire on the part of most people was to try to maintain that status. In this sense, if we pose a reverse question concerning men by parodying Mao's slogan, "What must an ordinary *nan tongzhi* (male comrade) do that a *nu tongzhi* (female comrade) was also expected to do?", we may have the same answer. For both men and women, the answer would be, besides participating actively in the socialist revolution and socialist construction, perhaps not much else beyond what the Party wanted them to do: to be loyal to the teachings of Mao and the Party. Or to learn from Comrade Lei Feng (a revolutionary hero set up by the CCP) to turn oneself into a "little screw" of the "socialist machine." In relation to the power structure, the message to both men and women was loud and clear: to be selfless, self-sacrificing, willing to serve the people and to follow the Party line, and, above all, to be small and invisible.

Here, once again, my earlier question becomes relevant. If both men and women (as revolutionary *tongzhi*) were expected to be selfless, to serve the people, and to be loyal to the Party, why after the Cultural Revolution was it women who came to be seen as (abnormally) stronger than men, and what does it mean when such a perception caused the myth of *yinyang* disorder to emerge as a perceived reality?

On the one hand, critics attempt to trace the answer to the specificity of Chinese (traditional) patriarchy and its "residues" found in the CCP's policies on women.[53] They point out that traditional Chinese gender power politics used to allow men to occupy both the masculine and the feminine, leaving women with no space for enunciation or articulation. The *yinyang* order in traditional China, in other words, did not really function in the interests of women. Women as real people have traditionally been excluded from that order; the feminine speaking subject, that is to say, usually was not a woman. When she did speak, her subjectivity tended to be identified not as feminine as such, but as her being an exceptional woman: either a matriarch (who still would rule by following the existing order), or a woman warrior who fought disguised as a man, or a woman poet who wrote as men did. Women with "masculine" traits were often rewarded precisely for not being the feminine speaking *subject*. In this sense, even though the CCP's policies on women were believed to have been implemented against the grain of tradition, the underlying logic may not be that far from this tradition; instead of taking the feminine space back, Chinese women seemed to be given a masculine space within which they were encouraged to be "like men."

On the other hand, some historians question the assumption that Chinese women were even offered the opportunity to share the masculine space. As Elisabeth Croll notes, as early as the 1920s, the CCP began to "nurture the women's movement as part of an overall strategy to build anew a nationalist and revolutionary movement in China."[54] Meanwhile, Croll points out, the women's movement and the CCP revolution did not have an easy relationship to begin with, nor all the way through the CCP's quest for state power, even though the Party managed to incorporate women's (especially peasant women's) interests into the revolution.⁵⁵ After the founding of the PRC, the women's movement continued to be controlled by the CCP and its insistence on incorporating women's needs and roles in its own political, social, and economic agenda. The women's movement in China, in the words of Margery Wolf and Phyllis Andors, was either "postponed" or is "unfinished."⁵⁶ Such claims, of course, have encountered criticism that questions the authors' ethnocentric standards in measuring women's liberation in China and argues that for many women in China, the liberation has brought about important changes in their lives, changes that Western feminists have mistaken or underestimated.

Nevertheless, a rather obvious contradiction arises here between the concern over *yinyang* disorder and Western feminist scholars' critique of the CCP's relationship with Chinese women; the former suggests that Chinese women have exceeded their (feminine?) boundaries and thus broken the *yinyang* balance, whereas the latter maintains that Chinese women's liberation has been co-opted by the CCP for its own political agenda, which to a large extent failed to address the "real" issues concerning women. At the same time, as we can see, the two positions point in the same direction for blame: the Communist Party, either for "overempowering" women or for "usurping" the women's movement and undermining women's liberation. The contradiction lies in what each side blames the power structure for and how each identifies Chinese women in relation to that power structure. At the same time, however, another irony also exists. The *yinyang* disorder argument identifies women with the CCP's power structure; through this identification, the argument puts the empowerment of women in question because the empowerment was made possible by the CCP's power structure, a power structure that is viewed negatively by many intellectuals. *Yinsheng,* or the rise of the feminine, thus takes on a clear political implication; it is problematized because of its perceived close link with the CCP's gender-equality policies (hence with the CCP regime and its ideology). In this sense, the "prosperity of the feminine" or *yinsheng* does not really refer to women's acquiring actual power (of their own), but to women's acquiring an *image* that is negatively identified with the illegitimacy of the dominant ideology. *Yinsheng,* therefore, as we can see from various explicit and implicit treatments of women's images in contemporary Chinese literature and culture, is already politically dispensable; with *sheng* indicating an undesirable overgrowth of something, *yin* (women, to be exact) must be checked. Meanwhile, *yangshuai* turns out to be the "real" issue at stake: it comes to signify "the repressed," and, somewhere in the process, becomes allegorical.

Thus, in post-Mao China, *yinsheng yangshuai* became a term denoting the abnormality of gender balance resulting from the first thirty years of the CCP's rule. What is more, when the "feminized condition" of men was brought to the fore in this context, it was considered a problem not only for men but also for the culture and the nation. The negativity to which this phenomenon is attached is reminiscent of Mary Ann Doane's comment on the relationship between femininity and patriarchy, that "femininity within a patriarchal culture is always constituted as a pathological condition."[57]

Indeed, given today's Chinese context, Doane's observation is quite poignant. When China once again opened its door to the rest of the world and began to strive for modernization, the emergence of cultural concern over the so-called *yinyang* disorder indicates a worry about men's weakened (hence feminized) positions. When perceived in a reversed gender order in which the male power is supposedly on the decline, the idea that "Chinese women are too strong and men are too weak" is precisely meant to be seen as a pathological condition that contemporary China suffers from. The desire to correct this condition, then, serves as, among other things, a natural license for men to "desire as men."

This constitutes the essence of the contemporary male desire to transcend the perceived *yinyang* disorder and the male sense of besiegedness. Against the historical trajectory I have just laid out, our understanding of such desire can help us better comprehend the complexity and the specificity of the supposedly besieged Chinese masculinity.

In what follows, I examine some of the manifestations of this desire by focusing on male representations of men in the literature of the 1980s. Through textual and intertextual readings, I explore such matters as representations of male sexuality, marginality politics expressed through a creation of "new" heroes, male desire for a "strong man" (masculine) identity, and the roots-seeking cultural movement as a male search for an alternative cultural and national identity.

Chapter 2

Sexuality and Male

Desire for "Potency"

In the early 1980s, following the end of the Cultural Revolution, two literary texts addressed some then-taboo subjects, and thereby played a significant role in the reemergence of personal expressions of love and desire in literature: Zhang Jie's short story "Ai, shi buneng wangji de" (Love must not be forgotten; 1979), and Zhang Xianliang's novella *Nanren de yiban shi nuren* (Half of man is woman; 1985).[1] As the first post–Cultural Revolution short story that directly discussed the dilemma of marriage without love and love without "legitimacy" (e.g., love for/of a married man), Zhang Jie's "Love Must Not Be Forgotten" questioned the lack of moral grounds for marriage as a social obligation separate from love. It was not until the publication of Zhang Xianliang's *Half of Man Is Woman,* however, that the subject of (male) sexuality and its emotional perspective was openly dramatized.[2] And in spite of criticism from some women writers, the story was read by many as a political allegory.[3] After the initial discomfort, the story was also gradually accepted as a bold stroke that brought sexuality as a major subject back to Chinese literature.

Of particular interest in Zhang Jie's story and Zhang Xianliang's novella, though, is a peculiar discrepancy between the two, which has eluded most critics: the question of what it means to be a woman is addressed through examination of issues of love and marriage, whereas the question of what it means to be a man is linked to sexuality.[4] At least in the early 1980s when themes of an erotic and sexual nature appeared in contemporary Chinese literature (along with the resurgence of humanism in the post-Mao cultural movement), it was male writers who tended to take more interest in these subjects than women writers, and Zhang Xianliang's novella functioned as a harbinger marking the beginning of this renewed public interest.[5] Even though there have been women writers (such as Wang Anyi) who have tackled the matter of sexuality since the mid-1980s, the initial discrepancy mentioned here remains a point yet to be addressed.[6] Is the difference merely accidental?

In discussing Chen Kaige's film *Yellow Earth,* Esther Yau offers a historical interpretation of the (contemporary) Chinese matter of sexuality. She states that, "with an integration of socialism with Confucian values, film texts after 1949 have often coded the political into both narrative development and visual structures, hence appropriating scopophilia for an asexual idealisation. In the post–Cultural Revolution context, then, the critique of such a repressive practice naturally falls on the desexualizing (hence dehumanising) discourses in the earlier years and their impact on the cultural and human psyche."[7] Yau argues that it is within the context of the desexualizing and therefore dehumanizing practices of the CCP that post–Cultural Revolution films ought to be understood, especially those made by the fifth-generation directors. Of course, the CCP's desexualizing practice, as Yau suggests, was not limited to the domain of filmmaking. Hence, if we expand her argument into the realm of literature and if we take note of her equation between desexualizing and dehumanizing, we can see this underlying argument: the sexual overtones found in recent Chinese literary and cultural production are a reaction against the "desexualising (hence dehumanising)" practices of the CCP; to (re)sexualize, therefore, is to humanize. To humanize, in this context, is also to be oppositional politically.

To be sure, the historical context of (re)sexualization in post–Cultural Revolution China correctly reflects a general perception about issues of sexuality in post-1949 China and conveys a stance held by many critics, in China and in the West, about the official dealings with issues of sexuality in the first thirty years of the PRC. Still, this commonly held perception does not address the question I raised earlier concerning the discrepancy between men and women writers regarding the subject of sexuality. Why, once again, is it male writers who feel compelled to explore the question of sexuality? Did the sexual repression or the desexualization practices of the CCP happen only to men? How do we account for this division along the gender line?

To address these questions, we not only need to understand the revived subject matter of sexuality in the public discourse as a return to humanism with strong political (as in politics) implications, we also need to pay attention to the less examined issues such as the relationship between the subject matter of sexuality and the strong male interest in it and the relationship between the post-Mao male search for masculine identity and Chinese (male) intellectuals' continuing quest for modernity. To better examine these links, we need to first discuss what is meant by sexuality and how we understand it in the Chinese context in relation to the general perception of sexual repression in contemporary Chinese history.

Sexuality, Repression, and Chinese Male Desire

In modern Chinese, *xing* is the word often used to mean "sex," and because of its specific usage, both as a noun and as an adjective, it can be translated as "sex" and "sexual." Unlike the word *yin* (or *se* and *yu*), which is traditionally used to mean things or behavior of a sexual nature as decadent, sinful, and even dirty, *xing* in modern Chinese tends to carry a more "scientific" weight; it is a word that conjures up the biological meaning of human sexual behavior that the word *yin* does not. In classical Chinese, on the other hand, *xing* is hardly used in this modern sense but rather in reference to the nature of people or certain things (e.g., *ren zhi chu, xing ben shan,* or "human nature is originally good"), and this implication is still found in modern Chinese, where *xing* is used as the suffix of such words as *nuxing* (female), *nanxing* (male), and *renxing* (human nature), bearing with it a (Western) humanist connotation.[8] In fact, in modern China, such a combination carries with it a humanist implication strongly influenced by the nineteenth-century European formation of the notion of sexuality in which, as Foucault's genealogy of sexuality indicates, human identities came to "naturally" hinge on their sexual propensities (I will return to this issue shortly).

By and large, however, within the first thirty years of the CCP's dominant discourse, *xing* (sex/ual), except in the category of science and in conjunction with human reproductive issues, gradually became a synonym of *yin,* and because of this connection, when used in a cultural or social context, it was often used negatively or mainly for the purpose of educating the masses to guard against the danger of seeking sexual pleasure. Indeed, in this sense one can argue that to the CCP, *xing* was anything but natural; it was considered contaminated—in the sense of *yin*—and therefore had to be controlled, regulated, and, if possible, rendered silent.

Meanwhile, because the modern word *xing* was always closely related to the scientific meaning of human sexual behavior and was part of the word *renxing* or human nature, when the CCP's sexually repressive practices were challenged as a violation of human nature in the post–Cultural Revolution era, *xing* (sex/ual) reentered the public discourse with a strong appeal as part of the return of human nature (*renxing de huigui*). After its return, the conflicting and entangled connotations of the word, as I have quickly summarized above, continue to exist, signifying the complex history it embodies.

The English word "sexuality," on the other hand, does not have a ready Chinese equivalent; the intricate implications of the concept of *xing* are not the same as those connected with the notion of sexuality. From the various ways the concept of sexuality has been examined and interrogated in the West, we find that the meaning exceeds what the Chinese word *xing* can convey, and that because the word *xing* in Chinese has yet to be fully interrogated, such a translation (i.e., sexuality means *xing*) does not automatically entail an understanding that sexuality is more than just human nature conditioned by human biology. To translate "sexuality" into Chinese, more than just the word *xing* is needed. To convey the notion of sexuality, *xing* needs to be combined with other words as a prefix to mean sexual, such as *xing xingwei* (sexual behavior and act), *xing gainian* (concepts, ideas, and notions regarding sexuality), *xing guanxi* (sexual relationships), *xing yuwang* (sexual desires), and so forth. Indeed, these are the terms now commonly used by contemporary Chinese sexologists (such as Pan Shuming) in their efforts to help the Chinese "better understand" sexuality, an endeavor, I believe, that is strongly influenced by modern Western sexology. In spite of the fact that contemporary Chinese sexology is perceived by many as a (new) science, translating "sexuality" into Chinese in this way nevertheless helps us see more clearly the social and cultural components of the notion of sexuality. As those compound words indicate, the notion involves social structure, norms, and discursive practices. It is also in this sense that the various critical discourses on sexuality in the West become relevant to my discussion here.

Ever since Freudian psychoanalysis placed human sexuality on the map of the social, issues concerning sex and sexuality have been frequently subject to theoretical interrogations in the West. In recent years, even though there is an ongoing debate over the cultural/natural dichotomy in discussions of sex and sexuality, sexuality has in many ways been defined by various feminist theorists and cultural critics as socially and historically constructed. Nancy Hartsock argues, for example, that "sexuality must be understood as a series of cultural and social practices and meanings that both structure and are in turn structured by social relations more generally."[9] Psychologists such as Ethel Person contend that "the meaning of sexuality will always be linked to nonsexual meaning because of the infantile intertwining of sensuality and object relations. . . . Sex qua sex, without these other meanings, is an impossibility. Sex will always be permeated with meanings that attach to individual and social parameters."[10] On the notion of sex qua sex, Hartsock adds a reminder that, "because sexuality is commonly seen as rooted in an unchanging human nature and biology," it is important to point out that "human activity or practice has both an ontological and an epistemological status."[11] Although the division between ontology and epistemology is often subject to further debate, Hartsock's point functions to suggest the constructed nature of sexuality, namely, the epistemological status of our understanding of human sexuality.

On this very notion, critics such as Judith Butler, by revisiting Foucault, take a fresh look at the notion of sex and argue that "sex is, from the start, normative"; it is what Foucault has called " 'a regulatory ideal.' " In this sense, she continues, " 'sex' not only functions as a norm, but is part of a regulatory practice that produces the bodies it governs."[12] Sex, according to Butler, is itself a construct. In her analysis of Foucault, she further points out:

> For Foucault, the body is not "sexed" in any significant sense prior to its determination within a discourse through which it becomes invested with an "idea" of natural or essential sex. The body gains meaning within discourse only in the context of power relations. Sexuality is an historically specific organization of power, discourse, bodies, and affectivity. As such, sexuality is understood by Foucault to produce "sex" as an artificial concept which effectively extends and disguises the power relations responsible for its genesis. (92)

It is the discourse of sexuality, in other words, that functions to produce the concept of sex as a natural or ontological category (supposedly) prior to so-

cial construction. By making visible the relationship between sex and sexuality, Foucault's argument points directly at the relationship between sexuality and various power relations.

In describing sexuality as formed by nineteenth-century Victorian conventions, which continue as the norm in the twentieth century, Foucault
presents a version of the Western history of sexuality not as merely "refined,
mute, and hypocritical," as others have charged it to be, but as being controlled and regulated discursively.[13] In modern Western history, it is not,
according to Foucault, repression (via silencing) that renders sexuality in
"order"; rather, it is precisely through talking about it that sexuality gets
shaped, regulated, and "normalized." By examining the discursive practices—
in medicine, in science, in education, and so forth—that constantly define
and redefine human sexuality, Foucault manages to demonstrate the constructed nature of a culturally specific understanding of sexuality.

The answer to the question What is sexuality? in this sense is an open-
ended one culturally determined by, once again, "the historically specific
organization of power, discourse, body, and affectivity." To understand issues
of sexuality, therefore, one not only needs to understand them as part of the
social and the historical but one also needs to recognize the power and discursive mechanisms at work within a specific locale socially and historically.

In the spirit of Foucault's argument and this open-ended comprehension
of sexuality, how do we now understand the "historically specific organization" that affected sexuality in modern and contemporary China? The answer lies partly in the concept of repression (which Foucault downplayed)
and partly in how we understand it in the Chinese context, where, as I have
mentioned, repression has been the major focus of contention.

Freudian and Lacanian psychoanalysis and various Western theories (feminist or otherwise) influenced by them assume a notion of repression different
from that understood in the contemporary Chinese context. What is meant
by repression in these theories is oriented around a psychoanalytically comprehended notion of desire. Whether advocating or challenging it, most
Western theorists share one premise in their debate: in the relationship between desire and its repression, which provides "an occasion for the consolidation of juridical structures," desire "is manufactured and forbidden as a
ritual symbolic gesture whereby the juridical model exercises and consolidates its own power."[14]

When used in the Chinese context, however, the relationship between desire and repression needs to be understood somewhat differently. On the one hand, the word "repression" tends to be charged with political implications and is often used interchangeably with the word "oppression." Indeed, in the wake of the Cultural Revolution, "sexual repression" is generally used with reference to the ten years of heightened political control in which the power of the state was exercised in personal lives more than as just a symbolic gesture. To understand Chinese sexuality in post–Cultural Revolution China, one has to consider that in recent Chinese history (especially during the Cultural Revolution), sex and other related matters were in many ways rendered taboo and banned from public discourse (except when mentioned negatively).[15] Repression in this sense did not mean just the repression of original sexuality but was a constant reminder that sexuality was taboo. Repression, in other words, existed in this context precisely in removing sexuality from public discourse, in rendering the notion unspeakable and secretive, and in efforts that projected the body as publicly asexual. All was made possible, once again, not through normative discourses, but via sheer political power. Repression in this sense, therefore, cannot but conjure up the notion of oppression.

On the other hand, as Harriet Evans argues, sexuality in post-1949 China also existed discursively in the official public discourse, especially in the pre–Cultural Revolution years, and sexual repression in China must be understood in a more complex way than it is generally perceived.[16] Evans questions the assumption that issues of sexuality in contemporary China were silenced, and she uses the CCP's official discourse on sexuality as evidence to demonstrate China's post-1949 discursive formations of the notion of sexuality. It was through discursive practices, Evans argues, that particular kinds of social mores on issues of sexuality were established and practiced. And she cogently maintains that without a better understanding of the earlier (i.e., of the 1950s and 1960s) official discourse on sexuality, one cannot fully understand the complexity of issues of sexuality in the post-Mao era. Sexuality in post-1949 China, as Evans demonstrates, is far more than a simple matter of repression; it is one of regulation and construction.

I find Evans's argument compelling and share her line of questioning in this study. Nevertheless, I want to add a cautionary note by suggesting that we still need to recognize the political context of the era and acknowledge the coercive nature of the public discourse—in the sense that the state openly demanded conformity to the point of being oppressive—and the fact that the coerciveness was often compounded by various political campaigns, big and small, and has been manifested in literature accordingly.

In short, we can say that the complex existence of issues of sexuality in post-1949 China lies in the fact that, although sexual repression in the Chinese context inevitably conjures up the notion of oppression, such historical specificity does not obviate the necessity of considering whether the Chinese version of sexual repression (as the commonly held perception understands it) does more than just oppress. Although political oppression has played a crucial role in the recent history of Chinese sexuality, sufficient attention needs to be given to how or in what ways that role has been played. We need to understand issues of sexuality in contemporary Chinese literature not only in the context of sexual repression, but also along with the fact that repression, or, to echo Evans, the CCP's discursive regulations of sexuality, has also shaped Chinese sexuality. And in this sense, we need to ask whether the male interest in sexuality mentioned earlier is simply a political gesture against sexual repression and a matter of restoring sexuality to Chinese men.

Indeed, one can further argue that, during the Cultural Revolution, it is precisely because every individual was perceived as a sexed and (hetero)sexual person prone to the decadence of *yin* that suppressing public interest in sex and sexuality would make sense to the dominant ideology. In the contemporary Chinese context, including Zhang Xianliang's *Half of Man Is Woman,* many stories have appeared in which the subject of sexuality comes back with a vengeance. Such a return reveals the presence of individuals' dealing with sexual matters and their various ramifications during the zenith of sexual repression (and as such, their presence can be understood as a form of resistance to the repression). Also, because sexuality under repression is shown in a way that is often characterized by critics as *xing niuqu* or "sexually twisted" and therefore abnormal, the focus of these stories lies, ironically, not in the nonexistence of sexuality but in its presumed abnormality.

Now, if we come back to Yau's point discussed earlier, I suggest that the CCP's desexualization practices should be understood as a construct in that the practices functioned as normatives materialized within a particular historical context and, when the political situation changed, came to be charged as abnormal. What is more, the desexualization practices did not entail a production of "unsexed" or "desexed" subjects. That is, when the prefix "de" is used to indicate the CCP's sexually repressive practices, it does not mean that the repression is to be understood as an erasure of sex and gender as constructs. If anything, the prefix "de" can be understood as a construct that functions in its negativity, rather than through erasure. In fact, if sex/uality was taboo during the Cultural Revolution, its existence was preserved in that negativity that, ironically, became the guarantor for the "purity" of issues of sexuality in the Chinese critical discourse of the 1980s. What is more, when the CCP's sexually repressive practices simply stigmatized sexuality as decadent, sinful, and dirty, they also rendered an understanding of the issue itself impossible, thereby, perhaps not so ironically, keeping many patriarchal assumptions concerning sexuality unquestioned and unchallenged. Regulating sexuality in the first seventeen years of PRC history and later silencing it during the Cultural Revolution, therefore, did not entail a revolutionary understanding of the issue.

Indeed, the coercive nature of the public discourse on sexuality and the oppressive practices later on during the Cultural Revolution were often conducted with the assumption that it was female sexuality that was potentially dangerous. The gender-equality policies of the CCP, for example, though providing women with more opportunities to gain relative independence in the public domain, were produced with some of the most gender-biased conventions (e.g., women equal sex) unquestioned. A good example comes from the public humiliation conducted against women that was especially common during the Cultural Revolution, a practice literally conducted against a woman's body (e.g., putting a string of old shoes on her neck both as an insult to her and as a public reminder of sexuality's being taboo).[17] Many of the practices not only reinforced the deeply rooted and heterosexually oriented traditional notion of *nannu shoushou buqin* or prohibition of any physical contact between men and women in public, but also assumed the traditional stereotypes of male and female sexualities. When sexual repression was openly challenged after the Cultural Revolution, the pendulum swung to the other side but the stereotypes remained intact.

If "the forming of subject requires an identification with the normative phantasm of 'sex,' "[18] in post–Cultural Revolution China there cannot be, as I have suggested, an un- or presexed subject waiting to be (re)sexualized, nor can there be a prerepression sexuality to be restored. The evocation of sex/uality in Chinese literature, specifically in male representations of men, therefore, cannot be simply about returning sex as an identity to men. What is at issue, that is, is not so much whether Chinese men should (re)claim their sexual identity as what kind of identity they desire to reclaim and why.

All of this brings me back to the questions raised earlier and more: When sexuality reemerges in public discourse after the Cultural Revolution, from whose experience are the effects of sexual repression represented and qualified as "twisted and abnormal"? Why does the subject matter seem to fall "naturally" to male writers? If "looking for a real man" for women writers means to find men with a strong and "upright" character and a caring personality, what does it mean when male writers associated the real man image "naturally" with male heterosexual potency and with a voyeuristic (or scopophiliac) male desire? And what, above all, does it mean when much of the energy of the male concern and search, as we will see later, appears to be oriented around the question of whether or not Chinese men are "potent" (and therefore "manly") enough?

Potency, the Phallus, and Chinese Male Sexuality

Given the sheer volume of the Chinese population, we must realize (either jokingly or seriously) that the issue of male potency in contemporary Chinese literature cannot be of mere biological consideration. Indeed, even as Zhang Xianliang's *Half of Man is Woman* demonstrates, the male lack of potency as a dominant theme is used mainly to symbolize one point: the protagonist's lack of potency—when he fails physically to possess his own wife—results from political persecution to which he has been subjected. Additionally, as discussed elsewhere, the politics of representing a male lack of potency (and the struggle to regain it) in this story is deeply entangled with a male ambivalence toward his own sense of suffering.[19]

Conversely, just as the protagonist in Zhang Xianliang's novella fights to regain his physiological potency, the biological connection is nevertheless what the male representation of the male concern over the lack of potency hinges on. In the story, when male impotence is shown as a threat to his identity, his desire to regain potency and hence a "real" man's identity is naturally represented as both human and politically correct. With its simultaneous anatomical and metaphorical implications, the word "potency" in this sense resonates with what in psychoanalysis Western critics term a penile/phallic connection, an issue related to the study of masculinity. Because of this resonance and because there have been numerous discussions of this connection among critics in the West, before I discuss Chinese male desire for potency in textual examples I will first take a detour in the following. I will briefly trace the discussions related to this connection to see in what ways the debate and dialogue among critics concerning the issue of masculinity can be of use to the discussion at hand.

As a psychoanalytic term, "phallic" is often found in Freud's writings, where, according to David Macey, Freud uses it "with reference to the symbolic phallus of antiquity." That is, he uses the notion of phallus as "a representation of the erect male organ and a symbol of sovereign power."[20] In Lacanian psychoanalysis, however, the link between the phallus and the male organ is transcended when "the term 'phallus' is used to emphasize the symbolic significance taken on by the penis is intersubjectivity and in the process of accession to the Symbolic. In this sense, the phallus is said to be an abstract signifier which is not to be confused with the biological organ" (318).

Western feminists, in their discussions of male and female subjectivities in conjunction with Freudian and Lacanian psychoanalysis, have indicated a strong ambivalence toward the notion of the phallus, especially the Lacanian one. Some emphasize that the notion enables feminists to examine the acculturation of gender differences in the patriarchy and the construction of male and female subjectivities in relation to that. Others, however, have argued that the Lacanian phallus is not an empty symbol: the phallus is not and cannot be totally separate from the signified that it replaces. Because of this, it is crucial for feminists to question the relationship between the two and its effect on those who have the phallic signified and those who don't. Jane Gallop, for example, contends that it is not enough to celebrate the notion of phallus understood as a way of allowing theorists to see the constructed or the cultural implications in the phallic signified and to demystify the account of the naturalness of sexual differences.[21] The Lacanian phallus, she insists, is itself gendered in that its seemingly genderless neutrality as a symbolic signifier actually functions to veil its penile reference, and it is the penis-phallus connection that allows the phallus to function on a symbolic level in the Name of the Father.

Many recent debates over the notion of phallus perceive the penile-phallic connection in a more complex and less clear-cut fashion. In his efforts to examine "masculinity and the 'exchange of women' " in conjunction with the phallus, Jean-Joseph Goux posits the notion's "veiling effect" and argues for the necessity to "unveil."[22] Goux revisits Lacan's use of the myth of Isis and Osiris to see how it functions as an ancient account of how the phallus comes to be the object of a cult. According to the myth, the phallus is erected in place of a missing penis and is an object put up for worship in place of the "real": "[It] is the myth itself which interprets, as if we had reached a core beyond which deciphering cannot go, a center which drives all deciphering. This myth, which exposes the fate of the divine initiate, presents and displays the dramatic relationship between the 'real penis' threatened by castration, and the 'phallus' now a symbol, a simulacrum, the signifier of rejuvenation and sexual pleasure" (42). The erection of a simulacrum in the place of the missing penis is, according to Goux, used by Lacanian psychoanalysis to "rediscover, 'unveil,' a phallic function that our culture had forgotten" (42). Psychoanalysis "does not stop at the penis as organ; rather it redefines the phallus as that 'simulacrum . . . ' and unveils what was veiled" (43). It demystifies the equation between the penis and the phallus by revealing the simulacrum function of the phallus and the lack that it veils. Also, however, there is an important difference between the ancient and the modern and even postmodern phallus. "The modern phallus," Goux argues, "is a deciphered phallus." It "is rediscovered, but [is] no longer the same. It is unconscious and structural" (45). It is deeply embedded in structural and discursive practices that, among other things, function to construct gendered subjectivities. It functions on an "unconscious and structural" level in which the "veiling" of the male lack continues to take place (in the Name of the Father) while the effect of the veiling continues to equate the penis with the phallus, which further functions to buttress the Law of the Father. For Goux, in short, the phallus cannot sustain its power without a penile reference, but at the same time, it takes the place of "the real" and functions to veil in the name of the missing male organ.

Goux's argument is intriguing because even though he focuses on the symbolic meaning of the "missing" penis or the male lack, he does not fail to engender the phallus. The Law of the Father, according to him, cannot function without a constant equation of penis and phallus. Nor does his argument about veiling the lack necessarily entail a lack of penile reference; covertly, he insists that the penile reference itself is already culturally constructed, an argument forcefully supported by Butler's reassessment of the category "sex." The lack, that is, is not an actual lack of the penis, but the lack of an all-powerful image of the male organ veiled by the phallus. And what the phallus veils is not the missing penis but the missing or lack of, once again, an all-powerful image of the penis. This argument points toward the paradox of the penis-phallus equation and the fact that the lack effected by this paradoxical equation is always already part of the construct of male subjectivity (Chinese or otherwise).

Returning to the issue at hand, I argue that in the Chinese case, the penile-phallic connection exists on a similar paradoxical level and can be found in many male writers' works in which the major concern is male anxiety over potency or the lack thereof. It manifests itself through a dilemma with which Chinese male writers continually struggle to come to terms: although it is important to reveal the male lack of potency as a political protest against the CCP's dominant ideology, it does not entail a male identification with that lack. Rather, the male lack is identified with the oppressive power structure, while at the same time there is a search for a real male identity that is not suffering from the lack and can be restored, first and foremost, in the realm of sex/uality.

Put differently, this (Chinese) male lack of potency, or, more accurately, the male preoccupation with a lack of potency, does not necessarily entail a "kind of reconciliation with . . . femininity," as Kaja Silverman would argue,[23] nor does it, as I have already argued, equal what Wang Yuejin terms the Chinese male femininity complex. Rather, it is a (desiring) male subject position whose paradoxical nature is, in part, poignantly captured by Rey Chow in this way: Chinese men are "woman" to the West but "father" to Chinese women.[24] In essence, it is this paradoxical (and therefore often ambivalent) position that I examine in my discussion of male representations of male sexual desires.

In what follows, I present two texts, *Xiguan siwang* (Accustomed to death), a novel by Zhang Xianliang, and *Dong zhi men* (Winter's gate), a novella by Liu Heng. I choose these two because of the writers' impassioned interest in representing their male characters as sexual beings and in exploring the complexity of their male characters' positions as such. Zhang represents a relatively older generation (who came of age in the early 1950s) and is in many ways fixated on the sexual aspects of men who, like him, have experienced political persecutions. Liu comes from a relatively younger generation of men (who came of age during the Cultural Revolution) who are not that fixated on their own personal experience but are nevertheless immensely interested in exploring similar issues. Although they differ in many ways, they have given strong voice to men as sexual beings. In reading these texts, I focus especially on the ways men are portrayed as sexual beings in conjunction with a constant presence of anxiety, and on how this anxiety manifests itself through an entanglement of a desire to be and a fear of not being potent and strong, hence masculine. I examine this paradox in conjunction with what I have called the Chinese male marginality complex and with the historically specific implications of this Chinese male subject position.

Sex, Death, and Politics in Zhang Xianliang's *Accustomed to Death*

Zhang Xianliang is a writer best known for his stories of the Chinese gulag, especially *Lu hua shu* (Mimosa; 1983), *Nanren de yiban shi nuren* (Half of man is woman; 1985), and the novel *Xiguan siwang* (Accustomed to death; 1989). As the male writer who broke the ground for the taboo subject of sexuality in the wake of the Cultural Revolution, Zhang has not exactly been the darling of many Chinese critics.[25] At the same time, however, as someone who is known for his portrayal of male desire, Zhang's vested interests in the subject matter embody many issues that have yet to be fully addressed.

Narratively, one common aspect of many of Zhang Xianliang's stories is the protagonist Zhang Yongling, a former political prisoner. Although in the novel *Accustomed to Death* the protagonist remains nameless, given its subtexts, it is not difficult for us to tell he is none other than Zhang Yongling. (Given the author's own personal experience, Zhang Yongling's stories also bear the inevitable marker of an autobiography.) If we follow the chronological order of these three texts, we can see a gradual change on the part of the protagonist in his experience as a political and then a former political prisoner.

In *Mimosa,* Zhang Yongling suffers from lack of food, both literally and metaphorically. He experiences the shame related to not having enough to eat and witnesses how everybody in prison is reduced to the level where all they think of is how to get more food whenever possible. His physiological hunger is relieved by Ma Yinghua (Mimosa), a local woman, who nurtures him back to health and also encourages him to study. Although the story suggests that the protagonist and Mimosa become lovers, the emphasis falls on the nurturing nature of the woman (both for his hunger for food and for encouraging him to study), and thus their story is presented with a strong touch of a mother-son relationship.

In *Half of Man is Woman,* the physiological focus shifts from hunger to sex. This time, the protagonist suffers from a sexual hunger due to his impotence, which further reinforces his sense of suffering. With the phrase "half of man is woman," the writer suggests that only a woman can restore a "half man" to completeness. But the story also clearly indicates that the woman on whose body he eventually proves his potency is not the right woman for him, not only because she is of a different social and cultural status, but also because she has too much desire of her own. In this story (and later in the novel *Accustomed to Death*), impotence is a metaphor for victimization by political persecution, but in the end the metaphor is invariably transferred onto women's bodies, which in turn function mainly as a constant trope for the author to evoke his protagonist's past suffering.

When *Accustomed to Death* was published, it turned out to be another book that shows Zhang Yongling's struggle with two themes: sex/uality and political persecution. The major difference in this novel is that it breaks up the linear way of telling the story by mixing time and space, past and present, and various geographical boundaries. The new style, however, does not stop the author from sneaking back into the novel the major components of the other two stories; he essentially rewrites the story of Zhang Yongling according to the milieu of the time when the novel was written. At the same time, the author also attempts to revise the image of Zhang Yongling, making him a man with a strong sexual drive but no longer driven by sexual hunger. It is this repackaging of Zhang Yongling as a sexually driven man that is interesting to me.

Here, let me give a brief description of the novel. In *Accustomed to Death,* time and place have changed as far as the protagonist's social and political status are concerned. He has become famous for having written about his experience of political persecution and impotency, and he is now traveling around the world giving lectures, meeting other writers, and going from one woman's arms to another's, not only no longer impotent but also seemingly more potent than he himself can bear. At the same time, however, the protagonist continues to experience moments of mental terror (fear of being shot to death, for example), and the terror occurs every time he has a successful sexual encounter with a woman. The constant erosion of his pleasurable moments, which suggests that he is constantly facing an imminent threat, constitutes the essence of the repetition. As the last piece in the trilogy of Zhang Yongling's life, the novel attempts to offer a more complete psychological profile of the reemergence of an oppressed man. Even though the self re(dis)covered in the end is still troubled by memories of his past, he is at least a highly potent man. The journey of his physiological sense from hunger to sex and to sexual relationships with many women is meant to indicate the growth of Zhang Yongling from a "half" to a "complete" man.

The parallel between his physiological fulfillment and his growth into a complete man is important to keep in mind here: it emphasizes a man's journey from the political margins to success both in his career as a writer and in his life as a man, already linking anatomical potency with that of metaphorical potency on a symbolic level. The question, however, is why a seemingly triumphant conclusion of a man's experience from both literal and metaphorical impotence to potency is represented in the shadow of death. If the shadow of death implies the potential danger of the return of political oppression in China, why is its occurrence almost exclusively mixed with moments of his sexual ecstasy? If it implies that he is a man who suffered from political oppression in the past and that the oppression has become part of him to the extent that it constantly overshadows his pleasurable moments in the present, what else can the metaphor of death indicate? Finally, what is the correlation between death and women's bodies in the moments of his sexual ecstasy?

From "He" to "I"

Unlike most of Zhang Xianliang's other stories, *Accustomed to Death* is written in an "experimental" style, alternating between the first-person narrator and the third-person narrator, with the protagonist being represented interchangeably with the pronouns "I," "he," and "you." Chronologically, the narrator (wearing the "split self" on his sleeve as "I," "he," or "you") first travels to America, where he encounters several women: Jinghui, a middle-aged overseas Chinese woman who lives alone in San Francisco (because her husband lives in a different city and, according to the narrator, has affairs with other women) and who puts him up in her house; his former lover from China, who now lives with an American man in the States; and his translator, a Taiwanese woman with whom he ends up in bed. Then he goes to France and meets Natalie (in Chinese, Na Ta Li) and has an affair with her. After that, he returns to China and visits the woman who reminds the reader of Mimosa (though the author does not offer her identity). His experience with these women is represented in a stream-of-consciousness way, full of free associations in which he also remembers his first lover, his current wife, and his mother. The temporal and spatial clashes of present and past events are meant to present the struggle of a male self who tries hard to be both complex and coherent.

At the same time, all of these (either implicitly or explicitly) sexually charged relationships signal one clear message: the man is physically potent. Indeed, throughout the novel, the selling point of most of these relationships is sexual, centering around his own "gaze"—depictions of these women's bodies or their seductiveness or lack thereof—and hinging on his own reflections and memories of sexual encounters with these women. It is as if the sheer number of women and the daring depictions of his sexual relationships with them are hard evidence proving that this man is now sexually savvy and sophisticated. This penile reference, however, though sufficiently narcissistic, does not stand alone in the novel as its focus.

As if in accordance with its title, the novel introduces the death theme from the very beginning. It does so with the help of the experimental style by "splitting" the protagonist and setting up the tension between past and present, with "he" representing the past and "I" the present. It goes like this:

> I don't remember when I started thinking of killing him. Of course, that must have been after I left him. At the time when I was studying [examining] him, however, I did not feel that way. It is only later on that he made me feel increasingly unbearable.[26]

Three lines later, we find that this "he" is none other than the "I," the narrator himself:

> His wish and mine eventually became the same one. When I decided that he should die, he willingly agreed. It made things much simpler for me; I didn't have to worry too much. (2)

The "I," in preparing the "killing" of "he," recounts the political oppression by suggesting that "he" himself once wanted to end his own life as a way of protest. "He" did not succeed not because, according to "I," "he" did not have enough courage to do it but because he was prevented by nature (as the tree on which he was going to hang himself "screamed"), which seemed to be more human than human beings themselves:

> The scream of the tree woke him up. He looked up and found that his head was overgrown with bristlegrass and that he had sat on a stone roller for years. At the same time, the moonlight was shedding its bluish light, and the land was immersed in a blue ocean; water gently touched his hair like a mother's hand stretching from the invisible air. (6)

Instead of putting his neck into the noose, he drags himself back to the prison. Ironically, however, "I" goes on:

> At that very moment, I split from him. I saw some trembling smoke coming from behind him and immediately disappear in the darkness. That was his cowardly hesitation. From then on, he was clouded in that smoke, for that failed attempt completely destroyed his courage. (6)

The ironic twist here is meant to provide a logic to "I's" split from "he" and to shed a more favorable light on the former, who now occupies a position to further expose "he" as the deteriorated part that must be disposed of. Hence "I's" killing of "he":

> After that attempted suicide, he had been close to death several times. Each time, he was exhausted by it. From then on he became obsessed with the "meaning" of life, with flowery and pretentious words, mistaking such language as the fruit of human thoughts. Meanwhile, the reality outside the language continued to make him suffer. . . . So he often thought of dying [or death]. Death had become his habit. But he who was exhausted by death no longer had the power to die, or he became too lazy to die. This is when my help was needed. (7)

In ridiculing "he's" obsession with the meaning of life and with flowery and pretentious words, the author is apparently referring to his earlier stories in which he used "politically correct" language to relate his experience as a labor camp prisoner. With the creation of this new narrator "I," the writer indicates an intent to create a distance from that "old" Zhang Yongling whose voice is now identified as coy and whiny. To revise the image of Zhang Yongling, therefore, "I" must replace "he" in the act of killing.

In other words, with "I" as the newer (and better) self separating from the old "he," the split is employed to announce a shift of the narrator's point of view. This opening section of the novel functions as a declaration, claiming that this Zhang Yongling is different from the one in the other two novellas in the trilogy, *Mimosa* and *Half of Man Is Woman*. More specifically, this opening serves as a manifesto in which the author is anxious to tell everybody that he himself is different, and, like "I," is seeking a new recognition. In the rest of the first chapter, therefore, after "I" earnestly explains why "he" has to die, he goes on to state that "he's" death, like the death of Christ, is meant for the "new" self to live "more meaningfully" (12). For death, as he suggests, is in essence a salvation:

> At the very moment when he died, we merged and became one. It was the most pleasant moment, more so than any lovemaking with a woman . . . (2)

It is pleasurable because, as "I" explains at a different point in the novel when the same scene is repeated, "after a 'bang,' I saw Christ lying on a piece of cloud, naked and sexy" (12).

On a symbolic level, this opening section in which "I" is to kill "he" can be understood in several ways. The repeated attempts at suicide, first of all, symbolize the consequences of the political persecution "he" once suffered as a victim. But the "new" self is only ready to accept the old one for his suffering and insists on rejecting him for being weak (unable to go through with his suicide attempts), hence the killing and merging. Meanwhile, when these two seemingly paradoxical acts—killing and merging—in essence help produce the new self, his rebirth simultaneously manifests something else: the homoerotic implication in the quote above evokes the crucifixion of Christ, thereby identifying (male) victimization with the highest (and most moral) level of suffering. It is on that level where the narrative repositioning of the protagonist manages to acquire another layer of symbolic meaning suggesting that the new male self is both human (i.e., sexually potent) and morally superior. Here sexual desire is transformed into a figure of speech, indeed a simulacrum, signifying the penile-phallic connection present throughout the male search for potency.

What is interesting, however, is that throughout the novel, the moral superiority of this repositioning is, at the same time, peculiarly connected to a death motif largely manifested in conjunction with moments of the protagonist's sexual pleasure or, more specifically, with women's bodies. Throughout the novel, that is, whenever the protagonist's sexual encounters with women are depicted, the narration is always morbidly intertwined with a death motif. If the death motif implies the protagonist's moral function as a witness to political atrocities, what does it mean when it is so readily associated with women's bodies? For that matter, how do we understand this death-turning-into-a-new-self in conjunction with the protagonist's seemingly insatiable appetite for sex? Does this repositioning necessarily entail a Chinese version of masculinity embracing "castration, alterity, and specularity," as is suggested by Kaja Silverman in her discussion of masculinity on the margins?[27] Or is it in essence a male search for a powerful simulacrum and hence a more manly image of the self?

Sex, Death, and Woman

To address these questions, we need to return to the novel itself. Indeed, from the very beginning, as "I" reflects on the life of "he," the novel connects "he's" suffering with women and alludes to the link between (political) punishment and his undying (and ever so strong) sexual potency:

> I think that throughout his life he has been humiliated by other people; the only ones that he owes an apology to are women. He does not owe anybody anything except [apologies to] women's feelings. Therefore, the body part that deserves most punishment is his penis; also the best way to eliminate him is to start from there. But when I finally saw it, I had to chuckle: the punishment that the society has imposed on him has all gone to the wrong place[s].[28]

What is "wrong" about the punishment? No answer from the narrator, but one can infer from the rest of the story that it means the punishment has failed to "castrate" him; as a man, we are told, he is a "complete" sexual being (i.e., not impotent) capable of multiple heterosexual relationships. The (political) punishment inflicted on him, that is, has all gone to the "wrong" places (i.e., places other than his genitals) and has left him with "a large one." Apparently, his sexual potency is employed in the novel, at least in part, to demonstrate a defiance of the power structure and to suggest the coherence of his own maleness in spite of the suffering. Also, when he claims that he owes apologies only to women's feelings, the implication is clear, albeit in a converse way: he is too sexually potent (and too politically scorched) to be faithful to any of them; if Huang Xiangjiu, the woman character in *Half of Man Is Woman,* is supposedly deprived of her pleasure due to his impotency, in this novel where he has long regained his potency, a woman who comes into sexual contact with him can no longer have him all to herself. He is taking back what was taken away from him by political oppression, and the only place for that is on women's bodies (because his male potency is all he is left with). All of this suggests that when indulging in his penile reference, the narrator appears to assume that women's pleasure depends solely on his "potency."

This narcissistic view of the "large one" (once again, left to him as the result of the punishment having gone to the wrong places) is further enhanced when his sexual encounters also take on larger meanings aided by the death motif.

In the novel, the first occurrence of the convergence between death and women takes place at "the moment I took up the gun" to kill "he":

> I heard roosters crow from afar. I didn't yet have time to wonder how come a rooster in the city could crow so clearly, the gun was already automatically aimed at his groin. Just at that moment, the room was suddenly filled with noises of women's giggling, each giggle implying a unique style. The China pink flower in the room began to shake violently, its fluid gushing out and splashing onto the walls like drops of blood. On his face, however, there was a smile. At that moment, I realized that his smile was exactly the same as mine, so I pulled the trigger with an easy conscience. (12)

At the very moment of the execution of "he," women and death, both of which symbolize his suffering, come to be conflated. From this conflation in moments of Zhang Yongling's sexual (dis)pleasure, therefore, we will henceforth find the following formula at work: women's bodies + male orgasm + death theme = male sexuality. Formulated as such, this male sexuality is not only constituted of his sexual potency freely worked out on women's bodies, but has to be shown as constantly under the threat of death.

In the rest of the novel, whenever the narrator (no matter whether it is "I" or "he" or "you") remembers, describes, or free-associates various moments of lovemaking, he destroys each moment of pleasure via some deadly message. When he first meets the Taiwanese woman who serves as his guide and interpreter during his trip to the States, for example, he already sees death, in sexual terms, in this encounter:

> Following you, I was able to appreciate your waving waist and hips. The curves of your body flowed like water as you were walking, pushing the movement of the airport. The sunshine here was especially bright. . . . Later, when I was in rainy Europe, I often remembered this sunshine. And when I was flying in the sky, I always wondered whether or not the reason that I wanted to be executed in bright sunshine may have to do with the sunshine of that day. (86)

When they become lovers, the same motif repeats itself:

> I stared at the moon. Embraced by the moonlight, I lost my body and genitals, only a pair of eyes was left. . . .
> I began to realize that this horror resulted from that successful love-making we had a few hours before. No matter whether I make love to you or to other women, I will always remember the death of that day, especially on a night with shiny moonlight. (148)

Another telling example comes when the narrator is on the plane to San Francisco and remembers, among other women, one in particular and their lovemaking. He describes what her eyes look like when "he was like a truck driver merely watching his truck run over her." He connects three things here: a gun (pointed at his head), the horror in her look when they make love, and his desire to make love with her so as to find the gunpoint in her eyes. With the gunpoint in her eyes and the gun pointed at his head, though both exist in his imagination, the narrator wants to make sure that this particular convergence has its historical references.

The woman in the protagonist's memory, as it turns out, is his actress-lover, who has left China after realizing that the two of them could not continue together (because he is married). When he was in prison, she used to appear in certain frequently shown "revolutionary" movies in which she played such roles as a woman doctor or the head of a guerrilla team. In spite of the revolutionary message of the movies, her image on the screen became part of his sexual fantasies during his years in prison, even though the roles she played, according to his memory, were quite androgynous and her image was far from being desirable:

> Her face on the screen appeared in a collage with the slogans. When you stared at her face, you thought that she was too high and too re-mote to reach. . . . You thought that she was that woman guerrilla leader who would point a gun at the head of a class enemy or the woman doctor who would not save the life of an enemy. At that time when you [imagined that you] held her in your arms, it was not just a sexual fantasy or because her image reminded you of women whose images you had long forgotten. . . . You held her because you could feel a dark pleasure of vengeance. (40–41)

In his imagination, this "dark pleasure of vengeance" suggests his desire to punish such a woman by possessing her body even if only in his imagination. And the sign of the protagonist's liberation is that he can now run over her body like a huge truck, causing her to look exactly the same way he did when he was threatened with death.

This particular memory is very telling. Reminiscent of Zhang Yongling's struggle to regain his potency in *Half of Man Is Woman,* we find that the woman's body is once again used as the battlefield between the power struc-ture and an oppressed man. On a symbolic level, that is, the male protagonist shares a common ground—woman's body—with the power structure: her body serves either as a symbol of his liberation (when she becomes his lover and when his previous "dark pleasure of vengeance" is finally realized) or as a metaphor of the success of a revolution (the revolution that gave women power, which was acted out by the actress in the movies). Conversely, her body can also function either to symbolize the corruption of the power struc-ture (because it turned women into heartless creatures, as was shown in the movies) or to signify the oppression of individuals (because oppressed men do not have easy access to women). Either way, her body is turned into a trope of the struggle between the male subject and the power structure.

To be sure, this conflation of the death theme and women's bodies is, as I suggested earlier, highly allegorical. But, if the juxtaposition of death and his sexual potency is meant to question the power structure, to what extent is the power structure really challenged? In what ways, at the same time, does his challenge, realized through women's bodies, also become a narcissistic gesture and turn misogynistic? How do we understand the fact that a constant reevoking of the historical trauma results in representing him as a potent man on the one hand and in justifying (either consciously or subconsciously) a misogynistic view of women on the other? Also, besides the political implications—political persecution has deeply traumatized him—is it possible that the repetition of the death motif indicates not only a constant battle by the protagonist to recover from the trauma of oppression, but also a constant (counter)desire to remain with that trauma? If this is the case, how do we understand the relationship between the trauma and the male subject? I will come back to these questions after discussing the next story.

Death and Male Impotency in Liu Heng's *Winter's Gate*

Before the publication of *Winter's Gate,* Liu Heng had already written stories dealing with the sexual desire of men on the margins (or "male subalterns," as some critics would call them). In his *Fuxi Fuxi* (Ju Dou), the man is Yang Tianqing, nephew of an old man, Yang Jinshan, who is married to a young woman, Wang Judou, with whom Yang Tianqing has a long-term illicit relationship. In *Hei de xue* (Black snow), a story set in contemporary Beijing, it is Li Huiquan, a former criminal, whose sexual fantasies and desire are impaired by his own social position and a sense of alienation that he feels from the rest of the society. Though set in different times—one in rural China before and after the founding of the PRC, the other in contemporary urban China—both stories depict the protagonists' desires as painfully secretive and repressed in conjunction with their peripheral social positions and as uncontrollable given the intense nature of the repression. In many ways, these are tragic figures, each gripped with an intense hopelessness. At the end of each story both characters end up dead, one committing suicide and the other robbed and killed by hooligans.

In this sense, compared with Zhang Xianliang's male character, who ultimately manages to come out triumphant as a man, the characters created by Liu are men with no redeeming possibilities; they are men of tragic fate. If

Zhang's protagonist toys with the death motif in conjunction with sexuality, some of Liu's men will eventually meet their deadly fate without so much as a chance to even imagine it. If Zhang's male character tries to maintain his male identity via his gaining potency and winning over numerous women sexually to prove his manhood, Liu's male characters' sexual desires are denied precisely because they lack the position to prove their manhood. The fate of Liu's characters, in other words, comes from their seemingly unredeemably marginalized position.

In *Winter's Gate,* the author takes the tragic nature of such male figures one step further by intensifying the protagonist's marginality, his displaced position, and his never-to-be-consummated sexual desire for a woman whom he is simply not "man enough" to possess. And the intensity is realized by the chilly and grotesque nature of the representation of a man who is *sexually invisible to both men and women.* In discussing the implications of this character, I first map how the story shows that the male protagonist is sexually invisible to both men and women. I then discuss how the story uses the death theme to redeem the protagonist's invisibility and his lack of potency.

A Man Invisible to Both Men and Women

Winter's Gate is set during the Sino-Japanese War (1937–1945) in a northern rural region occupied by the Japanese. Gu Shicai is the main character; he works as a cook for the officers of a Chinese collaborating troop's battalion, which is stationed next to a Japanese battalion. Both troops are located near a small town. In this town lives Gu's adoptive father, who owned a food stall that went bankrupt and who is now an opium addict. As the adoptive son, Gu takes up the responsibility of helping the old man, whose only daughter, Shunying, had run away with a man years earlier. As the story begins, Shunying returns to her father after her husband has died and Gu sees her for the first time since he was a child. Awestruck by her beauty, he immediately feels ugly. Being small in stature and meek in manner, he is paid no attention by this adoptive sister of his, and yet he gradually realizes that he is filled with desire for her. Meanwhile, there are several men from both the town and the Chinese battalion who constantly and openly express their desire for her in front of Gu while ignoring the fact that he is a man as well. They frequent the food stall which has reopened after Shunying's return and where Gu often witnesses their desire being expressed crudely and openly, without Shunying's showing any sign of discouraging them from doing so. All of this fans Gu's desire for her, and in the last part of the story, he bluntly confronts Shunying and tells her not to let any of those men get near her and that she will belong to him. When in their last confrontation she rejects him, he stabs her to death. However, just as the reader assumes that Shunying is dead, one wonders whether the killing is not just in Gu's imagination. For when he talks with his adoptive father about her later, their conversation suggests that she has left town again, this time with the brother of her late husband. The story ends with Gu cooking up a poisoned banquet for the Japanese troops and their Chinese collaborators and walking toward the minefield afterwards, apparently to commit suicide.

In a style consistent with that of the experimental writers of the 1980s—using a sense of detachment that yet creates an intense effect that sends chills down the reader's spine—Liu's story succeeds in representing the relationships among a seemingly insignificant man, the world around him, and a woman he desires but cannot have.

What characterizes the tragic nature of Gu Shicai is his position as a man invisible to both men and women. His invisibility is both alluded to and openly stated throughout the story. It is employed as the quintessential element of Gu's tragic fate no matter and in spite of how hard he tries to make himself visible by asserting his sexual identity. In his first encounter with Shunying, for example, the reader is told that she does not recognize him even after he tells her who he is:

> He was so discouraged that he wanted to run away. No matter how beautiful she had turned out to be, he could still recognize her but she simply did not remember him! She stood there tall and well-built with her eyes covering all of him. He was unable to look up . . .[29]

As the story unfolds, however, this "looking" relationship—"her eyes covering all of him" and he "unable to look up"—changes as Gu becomes increasingly voyeuristic and desire-ridden and yet unable to command a returning gaze from Shunying, whom he desires with a fatal intensity. His invisibility is made acutely visible in one scene in the story when Gu tries to stand up to a few men from the nearby Chinese battalion who openly and crudely express their desire for Shunying. His heroic action, unfortunately, only results in more humiliation when these men push him to the ground, take off his pants, tie his head and hands in the pants, and throw him out in the back of the house with the rest of his body left naked. All of this is done in front of Shunying. As he is being roughed up by these men in front of her, the story describes how he feels in relation to her:

> He looked up and saw her legs, her stomach, her chin, and the un-
> fathomable look in her eyes as she looked down! . . . He wanted to tell
> her that it wasn't his fault and that he was not their equal to begin
> with; that he was small and thin, useless, and had been bullied by oth-
> ers for his whole life; that except for his adoptive father, every man in
> the world looked down upon him; and that not even a single woman
> had ever looked up to him and in their eyes he was worse than a dog!
> (10)

Shunying, meanwhile, coldly tells the men to "go out to play" and turns around to go into the house, essentially refusing to "see" him. Struggling to get loose, Gu realizes that the men had only made a slipknot. This makes him further realize that "whether treating him nicely or badly, people have never taken him seriously" (10). Those men did not punish him with all seriousness because they do not treat him as their equal. The point to keep in mind here, however, is that this latter realization is made visible only when he fails to make Shunying see him (I will return to this point later).

Forcing her to see him, as the story shows, will become Gu's major obses-sion, an obsession that is manifested in (none other than) death. The death motif enters when the men who have expressed their desire for Shunying are killed and when Gu starts to brag about the killings in front of Shunying. If bragging about the killings is Gu's effort to make Shunying see him, he fails miserably, for she refuses to believe him. The only way for Gu to make Shun-ying see him as a man, the story appears to suggest, is to turn the killing on her. Indeed, this last act supposedly happens toward the end of the story when Shunying refuses to believe his claim that he is the one who has killed those men who used to humiliate him. "He is going to kill his goddess," the story repeats several times, and finally, we read this:

> He knew it was this long and plump body of flesh that had been most
> harmful to him! . . . He bit her! He wanted her to apologize and beg for
> her life! For having looked down upon him! Heavens! He was going to
> kill his goddess! (19)

There is a long passage in this scene that leaves the impression that he has killed her:

> He knelt down, his hands holding her legs. Her smile gradually disappeared, and he started crying. She tried to move her legs but was not able to make him let go. She grabbed the hair that clung to her stomach and slapped his head with such force that the noise sounded like something was cracking open, but all of this was to no avail; his hold became even tighter. Suddenly, her body was touched by his teeth. She realized something terrible was going to happen but it was already too late! She panicked, while Gu Shicai himself could think of nothing else but the deepest humiliations he had ever experienced. He knew the one that had made him feel most humiliated of all was this piece of long and fleshy flesh! . . .
>
> She struggled with him, and they fell onto the ground. He took out a small knife that he had used to skin a sheep that day and placed it by her throat. He madly pressed his mouth onto hers and used his other hand to touch the eyes that he had been extremely thirsty for, which, upon his touch, closed in despair. . . .
>
> When her hands touched his neck, he frantically pushed that knife down . . . he knew that she had made him suffer and at this moment, he could not prevent himself from making her suffer. . . .
>
> He escaped from that door in which lay a big, fair, and beautiful corpse. She had sucked dry the body fluid in him and he had not a single tear to shed. (18–19)

At the end of this scene, we are told that Gu runs away from the house, leaving her body in the hallway. The violence in this scene is appalling and constitutes nothing less than an attempted rape and murder, the ultimate violence against a woman. Whether the slaying of Shunying has actually taken place or is only part of Gu's fantasy, the violence (fantasy) against the woman is the only one in the story that gets graphically depicted.

At the same time, however, the story immediately confuses these "facts" by telling the reader that when Gu is on his way to see his adoptive father again, he is told by someone else that his adoptive sister was seen leaving town with her late husband's brother. By internally interrogating the facts, the story in this sense is also on its way toward turning Gu into a mythic figure and completes the mythmaking by granting Gu a glorious act. At the end of the story following those "deaths," the protagonist meets his own death: when he finishes cooking a poisonous dish for the Japanese officers and their Chinese collaborators, he walks into a minefield.

From a Nobody to a Hero

In giving a synopsis of this story, I have focused on two points: how Gu Shicai is depicted as someone invisible to both men and women, and how he is also told to avenge himself by either imagining to kill or actually killing those men and the woman who is the unattainable object of his desire. From the narration, the reader has a clear sense that the second point—the violent killings—is justified by the first point, namely, Gu's *lack of recognition from both men and women.* It is his extremely marginalized position resulting in his invisibility that leads to an extreme reaction. At the same time, what actually triggers all of this, according to the story, is the woman. He may have always been invisible to both men and women, but what makes his invisibility visible to himself is when the woman comes into the picture "provoking" his desire; it is this heterosexual male desire that drives him to realize his invisibility to other men and to see any man who shows interest in her as his enemy. And it is his seemingly asexual identity—his invisibility as a man to both men and women—that he ultimately rejects, and violently so.

To be sure, the story takes care to place Gu's lack of a male identity in the historical context of his time: the downtrodden nature of men like Gu who are marginalized to the point of being deprived of their male identity. The story justifies the killing of those men by showing them as the most despicable human beings in modern Chinese history: Chinese collaborators with the Japanese invaders, killers of innocent Chinese people, men of the rich gentry class (a class on the enemy list of the Chinese Communist Revolution). Juxtaposing the woman against these men, however, the story manages to smuggle in another justification for Gu's attempts or desire to kill: he tries to save her from these morally corrupt and dangerous men. What problematizes this justification, of course, is the intense urge in him to possess her and the voyeuristic nature of his relationship with her. Therefore, when it comes to Gu's invisibility to women, the historical reference appears less relevant; to him, she is no more than an unattainable object of desire, guilty of complicity with those men's power to possibly possess her. Even though the story tries to demonstrate that, as a man, Gu is doomed both by his invisibility (even to the object of his desire) and by the intensity of his desire (which consumes him so utterly that the only way out for him is to destroy the object that he cannot possess), we find a discrepancy in the story's implications of his invisibility to men and women and of his violent reaction toward them.

Meanwhile, with the destructive power that Gu is finally given, the story also grants him a mythic and "heroic" status by way of his own death. As we remember, after poisoning the Japanese troops and their Chinese collaborators, Gu walks toward the minefields, clearly to commit suicide. And this is where a change in the narrative voice takes place in the story, which suggests the birth of a legend:

> No one knows since when and from whose mouth the Gu Shicai who dared not use a little more salt was turned into a killer, who hanged a man twice as big as he was, . . . and would kill anyone that he wanted to kill. (21)

With this we come to the very end of the story:

> But everyone from Beidacang knows that this wandering soul is always right in front of them. His fear-filled and wondering eyes searching for the next victim and saying, "Shall I kill you?!" The consulting tone of voice sends a deep chill down one's spine. But whatever your response to him is, this saddened soul will always already be filled with tears.
>
> Gu Shicai, where are you now? Old brother, if you are tired, please take a break; if not, please continue. We thank you for doing this. (21)

The last sentence in Chinese is "Bai tuo le," which literally means to thank somebody for doing what one wants that person to do. For the first and only time, the story shifts the narrative perspective by introducing the first-person narrator and addressing Gu directly. And this shift entails some interesting questions. Who, for example, are the "we" that thank Gu for killing? Why do "we" thank him for killing? What is it that Gu is asked to "continue to do" (*jie zhe gan*)? To dare to tell somebody to his or her face "I'll kill you" but in a meek manner? What does this mean, especially when we realize that Gu only utters this statement in the story to his adoptive sister, a woman? If Shunying's slaying is no more than an imagined one, how do we understand such a fantasy and its violent nature in relation to this direct narrative voice?

This last-minute identification with Gu Shicai—after he is dead—on the part of the narrator calls for further attention. Marie-Claire Huot comments on the death of Yang Tianqing in her reading of Liu Heng's *Fuxi Fuxi* (sometimes translated "Ju Dou") in this way: "Death . . . makes heroes out of men. . . . Chinese civilization has always catered not only to the elders, but also to the dead and is consequently a 'youth-killing civilization.' . . . An amplification of such an attitude enables youth to be recognized posthumously, to be recuperated once they are dead. Upon his death, Tianqing is turned into a hero."[30] It is interesting to note here that the same scenario is repeated in *Winter's Gate;* for Liu to directly embrace Gu (and his marginality) is an impossibility. The only way to embrace him is to destroy his marginal position and his inability to assert a sexual identity—through Gu's heroic suicide (along with killing all his enemies)—thereby turning him into a (dead) "hero." His death, in turn, becomes a revealing moment of truth regarding the question of male potency.

When the author grants Gu a mysterious role in the death of those powerful men and makes obscure whether he actually kills Shunying, Gu's killing desire is upgraded to a symbolic level indicating that his (masculine) power lies in the moment when his own desire finally comes to his consciousness and when he realizes his own invisibility. This awakening on the part of Gu adds yet another symbolic layer to the meaning of his death: after death, he is turned into a legendary figure; once a legend, his power as a potent man becomes a possibility; as a *dead* hero, in turn, his heroic death gets erected in place of his lack, thereby granting him the potency that he never enjoyed when alive. This, I believe, is the underlying logic by which the narrator's direct identification with Gu becomes possible. And it is in this way that, by turning a little guy (*xiaorenwu*) like Gu into a legendary hero, *Winter's Gate*'s celebration of little guys in essence becomes a celebration of the masculine—phallic—power. That is, the veiling—hence the simulacra—effect of the death of the little guy takes place when he is simultaneously eliminated as a weak man and erected as a male hero. Death in this sense carries a double meaning—indeed, the penile-phallic connection—that manages to secure the meaning of the power of the phallic. This echoes Huot's observation when she calls Liu's *Fuxi Fuxi* "an ironical celebration of androcentrism, in Chinese style," and points out that the author is in fact deeply concerned with masculinity: "his concern solely for masculinity can be read as consciousness of the continuing, endless supremacy of patriarchy in contemporary China."[31]

The last paragraph of *Winter's Gate* in which the narrator directly addresses Gu Shicai, thanking him for continuing the killing spirits, is yet another indication of such a consciousness.

Death (Drive) and Male Potency

From my discussion above, we can see one element Zhang Xianliang's novel and Liu Heng's novella share: their male protagonists' sexual (im)potency is represented in a deadly way. Male sexuality in both cases is directly tied to the question of (im)potency with a repetitive emphasis on the suffering of the characters. At the same time, we also see a difference between protagonists Zhang Yongling and Gu Shicai in terms of their sexual experience: the former succeeds in physically possessing women, whereas the latter fails even in his violent attempts. Narratively, of course, Zhang Yongling's "success" is portrayed as a kind of (dis)pleasure constantly overshadowed by an imminent death theme; having sex with women is like being executed. Regardless of whether this (dis)pleasure is in fact pleasure in disguise (after all, Zhang Xianliang wrote a novel exclusively about his protagonist's sexual encounters with numerous women), it is the looming death motif (as well as the sense of martyrdom) occurring in moments of the protagonist's sexual experience that gives legitimacy to Zhang Yongling's promiscuous sexual behavior. It is also this very motif that is strongly echoed in Liu's novella.

In a rather interesting way, the repetition of the death motif in both Zhang's novel and Liu's novella is uncannily reminiscent of the Freudian notions of the death drive and historical trauma, and his understanding of the construction of masculinity. According to Kaja Silverman's reading of Freud's death drive and trauma theory, "the death drive can perhaps best be defined as *the compulsion to repeat experiences of an overwhelming and incapacitating sort*—experiences which render the subject hyperbolically passive" (emphasis mine).[32] The Freudian death drive here does not fall on the notion of death (like the death motif in Zhang's novel) but rather on the notion of repetition. That is, what is repeated in Zhang's novel—the death motif—for example, should be considered "experiences of an overwhelming and inca-pacitating sort" resulting from a historical trauma; it is the compulsion to repeat this kind of experience that is at issue here.

If what is meant by "experiences of an overwhelming and incapacitating sort" refers to "experiences which render the subject hyperbolically passive," what constitutes the historical trauma in the cases of Zhang and Liu (or that of any contemporary Chinese writer) is none other than political persecu-tions that culminated in violence during the Cultural Revolution and the oppressive ideological control of the CCP's regime. What we have in Zhang's novel and Liu's novella, therefore, are several key ingredients for an almost perfect psychoanalytic reading: a compulsion to repeat, the repetition of "ex-periences of an overwhelming and incapacitating sort," and historically trau-matic events: the Japanese invasion and the Cultural Revolution. I believe these concepts can help us further understand some of the paradoxes that we have frequently encountered with regard to male desire for potency.

In her study of masculinity on the margins, Silverman tries to locate a space in which resistance (of the "dominant fiction" or "the law of the sym-bolic order") exists and is practiced. Among other things, she reexamines Freud's notions of the death drive and mastery in conjunction with the con-struction of masculinity. She points out that Freud tries (though not quite successfully) to distinguish the notion of the death drive from that of mas-tery. Freudian mastery emphasizes the coherence of the ego of the subject; as Silverman states, "Freud associates the ego [mastery] with psychic binding [or coherence], and the death drive with a radical unbinding [or incoher-ence]."[33] According to Silverman, the problem is that Freud cannot always sustain a clear distinction between the two. If, for example, construction of (male) subjectivity is inevitably entangled with historical trauma and a com-pulsion to repeat certain experiences, the death drive (as defined by Freud) refers to how such experiences "render the subject hyperbolically passive," whereas "mastery . . . results when those same experiences are *actively* re-peated—when they are linguistically rather than affectively reprised" (59). Freud seems to define the difference between the two as one being "passive" and the other "active." If they both work toward a coherence of the ego, according to Silverman, the distinction between the two becomes unclear; as a result, Freud "often conflates the two."

In trying to tease out a clear difference, Silverman argues that it is the "unbinding" energy in the death drive that, as "a force inimical to the coherence of the ego," challenges "Freud's assumption that the death drive leads to the evacuation of tension." She contends that "masculinity is particularly vulnerable to the unbinding effects of the death drive because of its ideological alignment with mastery" (61).

Here we can see that after her evocation of Freud's death drive and her challenge of his assumptions, Silverman's discussion arrives at another level of this theoretical model: she argues that Freud's inability to distinguish death drive and mastery is clearly due to his failure to see the death drive as inimical (and therefore a threat) to the coherence of the ego. The presence of the death drive, in this sense, contributes to constantly undermining masculinity. Linking this point directly to the two texts in question, one sees that, although through a linguistic repetition of traumatic experiences they seem to be an active response to historical trauma, the death drive actually and constantly undermines the coherence of the ego or the self that the male subject attempts to rediscover. The death drive manifested in the texts, in other words, makes it impossible for the protagonists to be turned into masculine subjects (hence their "male subaltern" status, in Huot's terms?).

The problem, however, remains: Silverman's is an attempt to exonerate a masculinity at the margins that does not search for the coherence of the ego, that is not threatened by the "unbinding effects" of the death drive, and that is, above all, capable of embracing its own marginality. But in the case of the two stories in question, the marginalized male does not necessarily embrace his marginality. This is where my argument differs from Silverman's. I return to the conflation of the death drive and mastery found in Freud, because what the conflation suggests is a centrifugal tendency or movement on the part of the marginalized male, a move that should be further understood within its (respective) historical context; the death drive does not necessarily lead to a rejection of the coherence of the ego.

The death motif in Zhang's novel and Liu's novella manages to create two heroes. The difference lies in the fact that in the novel, Zhang mainly toys with the death theme while allowing his protagonist to fulfill his sexual desires (or in psychoanalytic terms, his pleasure). The repetition of the death motif, then, becomes somewhat pretentious. As a result, the male protagonist has a difficult time reaching the level of a "real" hero. In Liu's story, on the other hand, the protagonist eventually dies and what is then repeated is not the death motif itself but his alleged heroic acts and the deadliness of his marginalized position. Incidentally, in celebrating this little-guy-turned-hero, the story continues to subordinate the role of women by making them ultimately responsible for the destruction of the men on the margins. Female sexuality, at the same time, is also (once again) revealed as dangerous to those men who do not have sexual power to succeed.

The extreme repression of sexual desires and the excessive indulgence in sexual pleasure are the two ends of masculinity with which the protagonists continue to struggle. At the same time, by constantly destroying sexual pleasure via a death motif and by turning the little guy into a hero via death, the two stories have managed to put death in place of (the lack of) potency, thereby reestablishing a Chinese masculinity in the image of (dead) heroes. The male martyrdom or the death motif, in other words, becomes the simulacrum for a perceived lack of potency. The death = phallus formula functions simultaneously to veil and unveil the lack of, to use Goux's term, an "all-powerful" image of the male organ.

Coming back to the discrepancy between women writers and male writers in their relationship to the subject of sexuality, we can now conclude that the male preoccupation with sexuality is primarily a man's preoccupation with male potency. That is, when sexuality is understood mainly as a question of (the lack of) male potency, when male identity is directly linked to a potent masculinity and Chinese men are perceived as weak (symbolized by the lack of potency), sexuality appears to be the natural place toward which the search for male identity (and for real men) gravitates. This is perhaps why the sexuality encountered in these stories has very little to do with exploration of sexual relationships but almost everything to do with male anguish, fear, and uncertainty, all of which are mixed with a misogynistic tendency and an anxiety to regain potency. This is also perhaps why, although full of protest against the power center, self-absorbed male sexuality is nevertheless stuck with its own mirrored image of that center ready to respond (*xiangying*) to the latter's desire by struggling to be viable—indeed, potent—in the modern world.

Chapter 3

From Heroes to

Adjuncts, Nobodies, and

Antiheroes: The Politics of

(Male) Marginality

Part of the significance of the previous chapter lies in showing to what extent male sexual anxiety exists in contemporary Chinese literature and how we can interpret its implications. As my discussion demonstrates, Chinese male sexuality and male desire for potency are intertwined in such a way that they are turned into yet another version of a life-and-death issue. As such, this particular life-and-death issue, its political implications notwithstanding, points toward how the deadliness of a male lack (of potency) can, at the same time, be turned into something of a "sublime" quality capable of eventually redeeming this lack and turning it into a form of masculinity. Indeed, as is shown in Liu Heng's *Winter's Gate,* the only way for the male lack to resolve itself is for the impotent man first to die. Only then can the dead be turned into a hero, thereby qualified to be "erected," posthumously, as a man whose image in turn veils his lack. Toward the end of Liu's story, Gu Shicai is thus immortalized by the narrator speaking directly to his "soul," thanking him for still being around and for (allegedly) continuing to carry out his killing spirits.

This immortalization of Gu Shicai is in fact reminiscent of the emergence in Chinese literature of the 1980s of a new and popular form of hero: the marginal man, a male figure who is portrayed as a misfit wherever he goes. Especially with the reemergence of modernism, it became a rather fashionable practice among male writers to cast a marginal figure as their major character. To the extent that the implications of such a marginal figure are yet to be fully understood, this new hero is the focus of my discussion in this chapter.

I begin with a brief historical account placing the emergence of the marginal male figure as new hero in its historical context. I then undertake an analysis supported by three stories. Because I believe that a better understanding of representations of the marginal figure must exceed the familiar Jamesonian allegorical interpretation, the focus of my discussion will be more closely on the dynamics of the representations themselves; my interest lies in the contradictions and mutual implications they share. More important, I am intrigued by the extent to which they manifest what I call the marginality politics collectively (and subconsciously?) engaged by many contemporary Chinese male writers, and the link between such politics and the position of male intellectuals.

"This Hero" Is Not "That Hero"

In the first half of the 1980s, when searching for manly men (*nanzihan*) was becoming a cultural trend, some male writers responded by creating new heroes. One such writer was Zhang Chengzhi, who based a series of stories on his experiences as an "educated youth" in the minority regions of China's northwest. He is best known for such novellas as *Hei junma* (Black stallion), *Beifang de he* (Rivers of the north), and *Huangni xiaowu* (A yellow-earthen hut).[1] His protagonists are noted for their masculine traits: tough, staunch and unyielding, upright and principled, resolute and steadfast, brave and unconstrained; they detest any "feminine" side of themselves and are determined to stay "manly."

One such manly man is the protagonist in *Rivers of the North*. He is a filial and responsible eldest son, a conscientious student, a tough-minded man, and above all, a person with strong patriotic feelings. In the story, the hero retraces the path of his youth by returning to the northwest, visiting the major rivers in the region, and dreaming of visiting rivers in other parts of the north. Toward the end of the story, the rivers of the north converge and become a powerful metaphor in his dream, in which he stands by the frozen Heilongjiang River and asks it to melt for him and to send him to where it meets the ocean so that he can step out into a new life:

Please melt, Heilongjiang! he cried out. You have been in a slumber for over half a year since last November. You should wake up now that you have gathered enough strength through this mysterious northern winter. Crack open your white armor, blow up the thousand-mile-long ice, utilize all your magic power, and take me to the ocean! I fell in love with your character when I was standing by the Erqisi River and with your perseverance when I was next to the Yongding River. . . . I came with my love for you, and with my life and my youth. Please melt for me![2]

Although the Chinese word *he* ("river") does not have any linguistic link with the English word "he," it is amusing to note that in the context of this story, "he," the protagonist, is almost exclusively identified with *he,* the rivers, especially with their masculine characteristics. Falling in love with the rivers, the protagonist falls in love with himself; through invoking the masculine traits of the rivers, he sees himself happily reflected in them as a manly man.

In the prologue of this story, Zhang connects this new image of men with the need to combat the "weakened" spirit of the Chinese:

I believe that there will be a fair and deep recognition of our generation: only then can the uniqueness of our struggle, our thoughts, our footprints, and our choices become significant again. We may continue to feel sorry for our naïveté, our mistakes, and our limitations, and wonder how to start anew. . . . but as a country with a vast territory and long history, our future will ultimately be a bright one. It is because within this motherland [*muti,* which literally means "mother's body"], there exists . . . a creative power which will enhance the delivery of a healthy baby whose happy cry will bury the moaning and groaning of the weaklings. (65)

Zhang's protagonist is one such new baby whose manliness is upheld as the hope for China.

Although the depiction of this protagonist would amount to an urgent call for new heroes in post-Mao China, Zhang's representations of such heroes ironically have failed to capture the imagination of many of his fellow male writers. For one thing, his protagonist bears the heavy imprint of the heroic models created by the CCP and continues to remind one of the *gao, da, quan* figures (men of upright and unfailing moral character) found in the CCP's didactic literature. There, as mentioned in chapter 1, the image is based on the Stalinist notion of what constitutes a communist: a man "made of iron and steel." Zhang's belief in heroism shares with the CCP's doctrine an *excessive romanticism* regarding human nature, a romanticism that relies on subliminal slogans and grandiose visions, such as the Motherland, nature, cultural heritage, and nationalism. In his efforts to recreate heroes in post-Mao China, Zhang failed to recognize or acknowledge the changes taking place in the psychological condition of the Chinese, a condition resistant to an immediate return of a heroism too reminiscent of that created by the CCP based on the principle of its "revolutionary romanticism."[3]

By the post-Mao psychological condition, I refer to a deep and prevalent disillusionment among many Chinese with the ideals upheld by the CCP, its teachings, and its power structure. It was a sentiment that resulted from an estrangement, indeed, an alienation, between the ruling ideology and the people who had been taught to believe in it. This sense of alienation was publicly expressed in the wake of the Cultural Revolution. As early as 1978, Wang Ruoshui, one of the disenchanted official intellectuals, initiated the debate in his article "Guanyu 'yihua' de gainian" (About the concept of "alienation").[4] Situating his argument within the framework of the young Marx's thought on the relationship between social issues and human conditions, Wang challenged the lack of concern for "human nature" in Mao's doctrine and argued for recognizing the importance of humanism as part of Marxism. Seemingly discussing Marx's concept, Wang's actual object of interrogation was China's social and political reality thirty years in the making. Although Wang was quickly criticized for "twisting" (*waiqu*) Marxism and the debate was stopped by order of the CCP, the concept of alienation was here to stay in China and would manifest itself in other forms of expression. Besides carrying strong political overtones challenging the CCP's dogmatic interpretation of Marxism, Wang's argument also touched on an issue central to Chinese modernity and yet still without a proper place in it: the role of the individual and his or her relationship to/in the collective. This alienation debate, though brief and suppressed, signified the beginning of contemporary Chinese intellectuals' renewed concerns over issues of Chinese modernity or the nature of the human condition in twentieth-century China, which had been ignored while the CCP was preoccupied with developing the collective.[5] It also functioned as a public declaration that named the psychological condition of the Chinese—the fact that people began to feel at odds with the doctrine they had been told to believe in—by the time the Cultural Revolution ended.

It is within this generally acknowledged historical context that a post-Mao Chinese modernist movement in literature and arts (better known in China as *xianfeng wenxue,* or avant-garde literature) emerged, reacting against the CCP's "revolutionary romanticism" (and, though indirectly, against Zhang Chengzhi's heroism). Such a departure resembles in part the major transition in modernism that took place in the West early in this century, which is described by Art Berman as a transition "during which modernism yields its romanticism and adopts a critical formalism."[6] Briefly put, if Western Enlightenment philosophers such as Kant resorted to reason and the sublime as a way out of human dilemmas, under the CCP's leadership it is the collective good that was upheld as a way out of the disappointments of the human condition.[7] The problem arose, of course, when the CCP mistook its own vision as *the* vision of the collective good and upheld and romanticized it to the extent that it became oppressive. As a result, by the end of the Cultural Revolution China was virtually begging for a way out of its ideological (and to some, suffocating) grip. The critical formalism adopted in Chinese modernist literature after the Cultural Revolution functioned to critique the idealistic romanticism in the CCP's dominant ideology by reevoking, among other things, the notion of subjectivity (*zhutixing*) and a renewed intellectual interest in the relationship between the collective and the individual (*geren*).[8] In the post-Mao Chinese context, modernism was not so much "both a critique of modernity . . . and an example of it,"[9] as it was in the West (where the reaction was against Kantian romanticism). Rather, it was more like a Chinese *nalai zhuyi* (borrowing and making use for one's own purpose) that would enable a reentry, via new forms and styles, into the forbidden paradigms of the CCP's regime, such as the realms of human nature and the question of individual desires. Because of this, one must also note that Chinese modernism is not constrained within the boundaries of Western high modernism. Because of their flexibility, Chinese writers often play with different styles and forms of expression by juxtaposing modernism with some of its unlikely bedfellows, such as realism.

Just as high modernist literature had developed in the 1920s in Britain and the United States and in the 1930s in China, formal changes in post-Mao Chinese literature also created new images of characters. Among them, new images of men emerged that differed not only from the lifeless heroes created by the CCP but also from the manly men created by such writers as Zhang Chengzhi. Along with the formal changes (some critics call it *wenti geming,* or "discursive revolution"), these new images symbolize the establishment of a new aesthetic order in literature. Within this new order, fleshless and larger-than-life heroes were replaced by marginal figures or individuals who existed on or exiled themselves to the fringes of society: paranoid individuals, mentally and physically deformed beings, good-for-nothing antiheroes, or "social dregs" such as hooligans (*liumang*). Although this foregrounding of marginal figures is reminiscent of the Bakhtinian celebration of the return of the repressed, what interests me are some of the inevitable follow-up questions: What happens after the repressed return? Where do they return to and why? Does a celebration of the return of the marginalized necessarily entail a celebration of the weak? Or is it a celebration of something else? If representations of such new images of men constitute an effort to reconstruct, what is it that is being reconstructed and why?

These questions, incidentally, echo one raised by Nan Fan, a Chinese critic, in his discussion of the father-son relationship represented in contemporary Chinese literature. Like many critics, Nan Fan perceives the representations of the father-son clash in contemporary literature as symbolic manifestations of the clash between old and young generations within the Chinese political context. He argues that "because [of today's Chinese context], it is very difficult for people to have a common sphere to discuss issues; real theoretical debate is impossible. Rather than making speeches, therefore, people tend to make face [*ban guilian*] instead [as a form of resistance]." Confronted by an all-powerful father, Nan Fan points out, "making face" and being irreverent and self-indulgent are the only ways for the son to differentiate himself from the father and at the same time not be destroyed by him. Although the son's resistance can largely remain on an emotional—carnivalistic—level and hence does not have the possibility of rising to the level of reason, a "revolutionary spirit," according to Nan Fan, "may well exist in their indulgence and irreverence."[10] Having realized this, however, "we cannot but also pursue this question: after the son dismisses the father with his practical jokes [*er zuo ju*], what happens next?" (73).

In what follows, I discuss three stories by Yu Hua, Han Shaogong, and Wang Shuo. Critics have categorized these writers differently and have focused mainly on their new narrative style and their "revolt in language" (*yuyan de fanpan*).[11] Generally speaking, Han represents the *xungen wenxue* or roots-seeking literature that emerged around 1985. Yu is of the experimental or avant-garde generation who emerged in the second half of the 1980s. Wang stands alone as a single-writer phenomenon: *Wang Shuo xianxiang* (Wang Shuo phenomenon). In their own ways—Yu for his paranoid self, Han for his mythical characters, and Wang for his "hooligans"—they "make face." And despite their differences, they are collectively recognized as writers who challenge the norms of the CCP's dominant ideology and discourse by writing "differently"—a difference that, to echo Howard Goldblatt, would not amuse Chairman Mao.[12] It is in this context that I examine another commonality shared by these writers: the marginal(ized) male found in their stories. And it is in conjunction with the ways such a figure is represented that I explore the question raised above: When the marginal male returns as the repressed, where does he return to? And in what ways can his point of returning also shed additional light on our understanding of the question of Chinese masculinity?

Beginning with the paranoid self found in a story by Yu, I will explore the implications of his highly symbolized male figure. If this character is modeled after the high modernist fashion, how is he to be understood within the Chinese context in which he is created? How do we understand the way his marginality is portrayed and played out? If marginality is the author's point of departure, is it necessarily his point of return? If not, why not, and how do we further understand the implications of the marginal figure? Integrating Han's and Wang's stories into my argument, I ask what, if there is a shared common interest among these writers in male marginality, links them in this interest? With these questions central to my discussion, I hope not only better to address the question I have repeatedly raised—Where do the repressed return to?—but also to explore this implication as well: When invoking the repressed, exactly whom are we talking about?

The Marginal Male Figure as Hero: Two Cases

The Paranoid Self in Yu Hua's "The April Third Incident"

Yu Hua is one of the experimental writers who emerged along with others such as Ge Fei, Ma Yuan, Zhaxi Dawa, and Can Xue in the mid-1980s. Stylistically, these writers are distinctively modernist in that they play with and disrupt the "normal" sense of time and space and create characters almost totally absorbed within their own world and consumed by a sense of fear and uncertainty. Many of Yu's stories echo the motif of speechlessness and the abjectness found in these writers by focusing on a kind of paranoid person who is locked within, sharing no common language with the outside world.

This formalist commonality among these writers, however, has been qualified differently by some critics based on the gender of the writers. Lu Tonglin, for example, has pointed out that one critic in China, though characterizing the woman writer Can Xue's works as manifestations of " 'the delirium of a paranoid woman,' " appears to believe that "the fear which in Can Xue's works earns her the name of the 'paranoid woman' can be transcended into Yu Hua's *masculine* imagination" (emphasis mine).[13] The qualitative difference between the two, as Lu also points out, is that the latter reminds this Chinese critic "of Robbe-Grillet's novels and Antonioni's films" (177), an identification that effectively places Yu on a higher level than Can Xue in terms of a modernist sensibility.

The deeply subjective perception of the world that is often depicted in Chinese modernism as "nightmarish," though revolutionary in the Chinese context of the time, is certainly not unfamiliar to those who understand the sensibility of modernist art and literature. If many of Yu's characters are in fact no less paranoid than Can Xue's, why can the seemingly marginalized figures represented by the former be seen as capable of transcending "the paranoid woman" in Can Xue and as being "masculine" (and therefore good)? What, in other words, is masculine about Yu's representations of paranoid characters? This question can be better answered after I examine Yu's short story "Siyue san ri shijian" (The April third incident) and the other two stories as well.

In terms of narrative, "The April Third Incident" is a story without a story line, a formal characteristic shared by many high modernist works. Therefore, there is no actual plot to summarize except to say that the protagonist is a young man who seems to be paranoid about the outside world, suspecting that everyone else, including his parents, his friends, and people he doesn't know, is conspicuously plotting to destroy him. April third in the title is the date the protagonist overhears his parents mention in their conversation and it is also when he finally runs away from home, believing that he has managed to prevent a conspiracy against him from taking place.

The story begins with the protagonist, a nameless young man in his late teens, standing by the window of his room, looking out. He puts a hand in his pocket and feels a key there. After the description of what the key feels like to him, we see the protagonist start free-associating the shape of the key with the difficult path he will be taking. He next thinks of various doors and what will result if one puts a key into a lock and the key turns. This key-door-lock-and-unlock theme at the beginning of the story signifies something voyeuristic about this character—his desire to unlock secrets as well as a fear of knowing them; he wonders about what will happen when "the key turns" and when the "truth" behind these doors is revealed to him. What follows is significant: he imagines that he is entering a door from outside, when his body does just the opposite: "very simply, he opens the door and goes outside."[14] This is the first clear indication of the split of the self, a recurring theme in this story (and reminiscent of the split self discussed by Feuerwerker, except Yu's is much more an "in your face" kind of split). From now on, with such phrases as "he feels," "he seems to hear his own steps," "he is watching a boy going away from him. . . . and the boy is himself," and "he feels he sees," reading the story is like watching an Antonioni film: one part of the protagonist is watching (through the camera) the other part of himself acting; the protagonist not only watches the outside world but also himself inside this outside world. This split, however, suggests the existence of a "he" who is situated behind the camera, watching, among others, himself. Who is this "he" behind the camera? Before we answer this important question, we need to take a closer look at how the split self is fully represented in the story.

The split motif—being "foreign" from within—is employed as the most significant metaphor emphasizing the *alienation* or estrangement this character will experience toward the outside world. Yu's story foregrounds this motif by separating the "normal" juncture of senses between one's—especially men's—internal experience (*neixin tiyan*) and the outside world, and does so by presenting the outside world via the protagonist's alienated senses. Spatially, for example, there are places where the protagonist recurringly finds himself wandering or forced into: doors, streets, his parents' home, other people's homes, and dead-end alleys (*hutong*). Like scenes in Antonioni's films, the "camera" follows the protagonist wherever he happens to be, but there is no necessary link or logical relationship between one place and the next. The random shift from one place to another, compounded by his constant delusional sense of hearing different voices, creates an inner space that separates him from the outside world. As a result, wherever he is, the spatial dimension is cut up largely through his sense of hearing. When at his friend's home, for example, "he hears Zhu Qiao or Hansheng ask. . . . Their voices sound strange. . . . He feels his own voice sound strange too. . . . He feels as if he heard Yazhou's voice; it came floating from somewhere. . . . He hears some of them getting up and moving about; after a while he can hear murmuring voices and muffled giggling coming from the balcony" (232). Similar scenes get repeated at home and at other friends' places, all symbolizing the existence of a gap between him and the outside world, a gap created by the voices whose "murmuring . . . and muffled giggling" symbolize the existence of things undiscernible, incomprehensible, and above all secretive. Such is the external world from which the protagonist wants to escape, and the only place he can escape to is his inner self.

On his eighteenth birthday, he stays in bed remembering his childhood. No one at home celebrates his birthday; he steals a cigarette from his father and smokes it in his own room. It is then that "he sees the boy disappearing from him" (226). This boy, clearly, "is himself and his past" (226). The experience of his eighteenth birthday is feeling "alone and with no one to rely on" (*wuyi wukao*). With that, he senses something changing: his eyes suddenly become cold. Another split is taking place here, manifested in the change of his view of himself within that outside world.

His sense of alienation and fragmentation is best illustrated by one scene when the protagonist sees himself through shop windows: "The shop windows are somewhat like mirrors. He walks back and forth in front of them looking at himself sideways. His movement obscures the reflection and the merchandise in the windows are blotting out his image" (238). When he stops in front of a drugstore, various boxes of medicine in the window distort parts of his body—shoulders, abdomen, and nose—although "his eyes are not blocked; he looks at his own eyes feeling as if someone else's eyes were looking at him." When he stands in front of the windows of a department store, where his body is once again divided by merchandise, he sees other bodies reflected there: "those distorted shadows make him feel something secretive is going on. He turns around and sees some people on the other side across the street standing there talking, pointing their fingers in his direction" (238).

If there is a strong touch of Kafka in this story, Yu seems to focus more on the inner self of the protagonist than on the paradoxical and incomprehensible world surrounding a character who is "metaphysically innocent" and whose lack of knowledge as an outsider (such as K in *The Castle*) brings out the strangeness of a world people assume they know. In Yu's story, the absurdity of the outside world does not come from one level of comprehension clashing with another; rather, it comes from the protagonist's subjective feeling toward the outside world, of being alone against the rest of the world. In short, this is someone who has withdrawn into the shell of the self, focusing only on himself. Like the narcissist, he meets his own gaze through reflection, but the difference in this case is that the reflection is fragmented.

To be sure, one has to take into consideration why the reflection is fragmented, which brings us, once again, to Fredric Jameson's well-known view of reading "Third World" literature allegorically. The fragmentation of the self reflected in the mirror is historically significant in that it signifies both the terror brought about by the political campaigns before and during the Cultural Revolution and the breakdown of value systems in China in the wake of the Cultural Revolution, all of which resulted in a sense of alienation. The paranoia of the protagonist is apparently meant to symbolize what the writer perceives as the craziness of an environment that most Chinese were once and are still condemned to live in. This political implication is also shared by the other writers mentioned above. Together, they stage a strong critique of the power structure, not, in their case, by painting the bloodiest pictures of this world but by making visible its dark and absurd dimensions. The sympathy, at least in the case of Yu's story, appears to be invested in the protagonist, who is portrayed as being driven to constant paranoia and fear by a strong sense of alienation.

However, this political commonality does not explain the gender-based difference between Can Xue and Yu Hua (and implicitly, other male modernist writers) characterized by the Chinese critic mentioned earlier. Apparently, what is implicated in his comment exceeds the realm of politics.

The Split Self: What Does He Split Into?

Why is reading Yu Hua's stories like watching an Antonioni film? Because both make the reader-viewer aware of the presence of another self. If we visualize the story with the help of the film analogy, we can see the protagonist as the one standing behind the camera and watching himself through it. In the seemingly schizophrenic presence of the paranoid self in the story, as this analogy indicates, we simultaneously sense the presence of the other half of the self capturing and showing, through the "camera," his own existence in a fragmented state in a senseless world. This split recalls the moment in the story when the protagonist stands in front of the shop windows looking into the mirrorlike glass, seemingly situated outside of the world in which the alienated and fragmented—the paranoid—self exists. Who (or what), then, is this seeing or gazing self?

The mirror motif employed in Yu's story is a useful point of entry into this question. By way of a linguistic overlapping, this motif conveniently leads to the well-known Lacanian notions of "mirror stage" and "symbolic stage." I recognize the potential pitfalls of what may seem to be a random borrowing of concepts like these. But because the mirror motif employed in the story clearly suggests a relationship between the seeing self and his own reflection, the implications of this relationship as they are studied in these Lacanian concepts—the dynamics of one's sense of the self in relation to the social, the cultural, and the political—merit the borrowing. A brief digression into these notions can thus be instrumental in further illuminating the issue at hand.

According to Lacan, the mirror stage pertains to an early stage of developing a sense of one's self: when looking into the mirror, one learns to recognize one's self reflected there, an important step for self-recognition. Additionally, the mirror stage helps the "normal" self develop not only a sense of the self but also a sense of one's own wholeness, which is guaranteed by accepting the reflection as the true image of the self. In the symbolic stage, however, according to Lacan, the sense of one's self is achieved through more than the self watching its own reflection and recognizing it as such. In this stage, the sense of one's self is gained, via language, through a recognition of views made by *other* than the self, which in turn causes the self to see the reflected image of the self in a way different from a strict mirror reflection. The seeing subject, in this stage, has learned to see with the eye of the symbolic—or the superego, or, in Silverman's words, the "dominant fiction"—that signifies additional meanings about the reflected self. One typical example is Oscar Wilde's portrait of Dorian Gray. In that story, what is reflected in the "mirror" (i.e., Gray's own portrait), though distorted, is taken seriously by the self seeing the reflection. Put differently, it is the perception of the seeing self that affects the image in the portrait to apparently change from bad to worse. Regardless of the actual content behind Gray's worsening views of himself, this scenario suggests that the split of the self is, once again, effected by other (the other) than the self. There, we must add, the seeing self is presumably also a knowing subject. And it is the knowledge embedded in the seeing self that affects his or her perception.

In this sense, we can say that Yu's protagonist is different from Kafka's K; whereas K's metaphysical innocence is employed to challenge the metaphysical implications of knowledge itself, Yu and other Chinese modernist writers tend to focus their attention on creating characters who, albeit marginal, nevertheless "know better." Therefore, unlike K in *The Castle,* whose lack of knowledge in his traveling to and stay in the village gives rise to a constantly uncanny experience on the part of the reader, an experience generated by a conflict between the state of metaphysical innocence on the part of K and the "knowing" villagers, the seeing self in Yu's story appears to have already transcended the state of metaphysical innocence by knowing ahead of time (literally, in the story) what might be happening to him. Furthermore, if we read this knowing ahead of time in a reversed way, treating it as a flashback, what we have is in fact an articulation of an existential crisis in relation to a historical context: it is the maddening political campaigns and movements that make individuals paranoid and fearful; the otherwise normal and complete self is fragmented (wrongly) by political movements and oppression. The self found in the context of such an environment, though seemingly marginalized by others, is ultimately the one who *knows* better, whose escape can be thought of as an awakening from a bad dream, an awakening that hopes to reunite with the paranoid self in the mirror into one and the same—whole—self.

Now, the gender-specific difference noted by the Chinese critic regarding the experimental writers can be reexamined: it must be his recognition of such a subject position and his own identification with it that make it possible for him to claim that there is a basic sanity—a "masculine imagination"—in Yu's stories in spite of their seeming senselessness, and to perceive it in a positive light. And it is this masculine sanity that holds together the seemingly fragmented images of the self, preventing the seeing subject in front of the mirror from disintegrating completely, like Dorian Gray, or from being like the "paranoid woman" in Can Xue. Indeed, this is what the critic states: "[Yu Hua] seems to be very good at capturing the sensibility and psychology of adolescent or young men, and then turning the psychological evolution of people of this age group into a sense shared by the whole of humankind. If we interpret 'The April Third Incident' to be a story of fantasy, we will be able to recognize the *sublime quality* of the paranoid [young man]. Such interpretation can also help change the nature of the story" (my emphasis).[15]

Several points can be noted here: although it is a story about a young man, it is actually a story of universal significance; there is something sublime about this seemingly absurd and plotless story; and the sublime implications in turn change the nature of the story from a simple one about a young man to one far more complex than his paranoia alone could produce. The importance of this story, the critic suggests, lies in its metaphorical or symbolic implications. Although he does not elaborate on what he means by the "sublime quality" capable of changing the meaning of the story, his emphasis on this point suggests that he not only recognizes that the underlying theme in Yu's stories exceeds the paranoia of his young characters, but also, and more important, that he perceives the split self as a knowing subject—indeed, a desiring male subject—capable of transcending his seeming senselessness.

In the end, we realize that the seemingly split self may not have been split to begin with, and that is why Yu's representation of the paranoid self is capable of signifying a masculine imagination to the critic, who in turn sublimates the (male) paranoid into a universal wholeness. And this wholeness, as I have argued, is sustained by the presence of the knowing subject that Yu's story ultimately hinges on. Because of this, the paranoid self, the split senses of the world, and their seeming chaos that we find in the story all exist primarily on the surface, between an external fragmented world and an internal whole self. The split in question, in other words, does not come from a split within the (male) self and his self-knowledge. Rather, it comes from, yes, a romantic imagination that resists seeing himself as fragmented, split, and decentered, and that prefers to see himself as the knowing subject capable of eventually returning to the center of an orderly world.

Binzai the Adjunct in Han Shaogong's Bababa

Han Shaogong is best known as the first writer to use the term *xungen* or "roots-seeking" to characterize the kind of literature he was interested in writing (an issue I explore in chapter 5). After the publication of his famous *xungen wenxue* "manifesto" "Wenxue de gen" (Roots of literature),[16] Han produced a series of stories often featuring an "abnormal" figure as the main character. Such stories include "Gui qu lai" (Return), "Lan gaizi" (Blue lid), "Lao meng" (Old dream), "Bababa" (Dad Dad Dad), and "Nununu" (Woman

woman woman). Except in the last one, every major character in these stories is a male who suffers from either complete retardation or a serious degree of schizophrenia and who exists on the fringe of society, often as a result of political persecution. My analysis concentrates on the main character, Binzai, in the story "Bababa," one of the first post-Mao stories that tackles issues of cultural and individual identity and alienation mainly through representation of a deformed and retarded male figure. Unlike Han's other stories with marginal male protagonists, this one does not link Binzai's marginality directly with political persecution. It contains instead a more explicit attempt to tackle those issues on a seemingly mythical level. And this makes the character Binzai an interesting subject for discussion.

Collected in *Xinxiaoshuo zai 1985 nian* (New fiction in 1985), the story was praised by the editors this way: " 'Bababa' is an enormously rich text. It is like a lock with many keyholes in it that can be opened by different keys. Both its language and symbolic implications exert a stupendous effect on its reader. . . . Behind each proper name, key word, and phrase looms a history whose depth casts a long shadow over modern times, signifying to us that the soul [of the past] is still with us. . . . Although the story is narrated in a heavy, cold, and emotionally detached way, we can still feel a strong energy for life mixed with a profound epiphany and anxiety."[17] So characterized, together with other stories published in 1985, "Bababa" signified a new direction taken by the young writers in their efforts to search for new and different narrative styles, and, importantly, in their renewed efforts to reexamine the meaning of Chinese culture.

The story is set in a rural area in Hunan Province. Although the time frame in the story is not historically concrete and the writer makes it appear mythical by mixing the past with the present, one can assume that it is set in rural China where time past and time present are not clearly marked.[18] Narratively, "Bababa" also does not have a strict story line; it is, as the editors have suggested in their comments, a story of myths about the fictional Jitouzhai Village, where the villagers are constantly concerned about their own identity, especially the origin of their ancestry. The characteristics of their dialect, the long history of their feud with another village, and the rituals they perform to cope with natural disasters are some of the recurrent subjects the story describes. Thus, critics read this story as a symbolic challenge to the power of the Han or mainstream Chinese culture, which has overshadowed other regional cultures and identities such as those represented by this village. At the same time, if we use another key to unlock the story, it can be read as one about the people of a marginalized culture (symbolized here by the villagers) searching for and asserting their identity, and how their efforts are manifested through the songs they sing, the dialect they speak, the beliefs they hold, and the rituals they perform.

If it is a story about a marginalized people in search of identity, what seems to be peculiar, then, is the character Binzai. Binzai is someone who exists on the furthest fringe of this marginalized group as a doubly marginalized figure, and yet at the same time he occupies the center of this narrative. By doubly marginalized, I refer to the fact that, unlike everyone else in the village, Binzai does not speak, except for two phrases. He is someone who, in psychoanalytical terms, fails to enter the Symbolic order. As such, he exists on the extreme periphery of the affairs of the village. Nevertheless, the author names the story after one of the only two phrases Binzai utters, *bababa,* and puts his presence everywhere in the story even though for the most part Binzai merely floats through those affairs as a half human being. This narrative strategy—giving a ubiquitous presence to Binzai, who is but a peripheral figure, and centering the mythical quality of the village around Binzai, who is nevertheless completely oblivious to village affairs—clearly indicates the symbolic status of this character. Before we address the implications of this doubly marginalized figure, however, let us first take a brief look at the depiction of Binzai. The story begins with his birth:

> When he was born, he slept for two days and two nights, drinking and eating nothing. He looked as if he were dead, which frightened his relatives, and it wasn't till the third day that he burst into a loud cry. When he was only able to crawl, the villagers started playing with him, teaching him how to be human. Very quickly, he learned to say two things: one was "Baba," the other "F——k mama." Although the second one was rude, when uttered by such a small child, it did not have much of a meaning.[19]

When he starts to speak, the first two things that the villagers (rather than his mother) teach him are two phrases: baba, and f——k mama. In the case of Binzai, however, there is an irony: although he does not have a father, he is taught to say the word *baba* first; though he does have a mother, instead of learning to say *mama,* the phrase he is taught to utter is a very bad curse on his mother.

Binzai's linguistic achievement, we are told, stops at the two phrases; he is mentally retarded and stops growing both linguistically and physically. For the rest of his life, he remains the height of a child, physically deformed, and utters only the two phrases. Moreover, the grotesque appearance of this character is compounded by questions concerning the legitimacy of his birth and, of course, the character of his mother; no one in the village knows who his father is. As a result, when he utters the word *baba* to any man in the village, his utterance always causes a problem: he inadvertently misidentifies the person (even though the identification is actually made by those other than the one who utters the word) with his own illegitimate status and brings to the surface some related assumptions. For the person on the receiving end, that is, Binzai's utterance names him wrongly as his father, and thus (temporarily) throws the person's identity into question. As a result, Binzai is always punished for being the cause of such a misidentification. Its absurdity notwithstanding, this repeated act shows that even as a peripheral figure, Binzai nevertheless causes interpretations and reaction. On the one hand, he suffers verbal abuse from and at the hands of the villagers, who treat him as a completely marginal figure; he is noticed only when he is in the way. On the other hand, his abjectness does not prevent the villagers from reacting to him. Consequently, this becomes a constant paradox throughout the story in which his peripheral position functions to make visible and/or highlight the absurdity of the villagers' efforts to interpret.

Although Binzai is incapable of understanding the notion of *baba* or dad and therefore never would engage in the act of searching for his real father, the villagers have tried to figure out who his father is and have arrived at several possibilities: someone who was "unhappy with the ugliness of his wife, who gave birth to an ugly child and left the mountain area to trade opium," or someone who "was killed by bandits," or someone who used to engage in some small business in town but squandered all his money on prostitution and was seen begging on the street of another town. No one, however, could be sure who Binzai's father was. This constant uncertainty about the identity of Binzai's father is always coupled with misogynistic remarks about his mother, her ugliness, her being an outsider herself to the village, and her "loose" character.

Given the central theme of this story, we gradually realize that, even if Binzai's real father were to be found, the latter's identity would not change the fact that Binzai would continue to utter the word *baba* to any man in sight. The identity of Binzai's real father and the character of his mother matter only to those other than Binzai himself. On a more symbolic level, therefore, the villagers' interest in finding out the identity of Binzai's father actually signifies their own struggle for identity and their discomfort with what they see in themselves. Also symbolically, however, as I discuss in the next section, Binzai functions as more than a manifestation of the villagers' search for their identity. Furthermore, when the nonexistence of the father and the obsessive search for him on the part of the villagers indicate a ubiquitous acceptance of the importance of his identity, Binzai's seemingly nonsensical utterance of *bababa* comes to represent this collective unconscious that is obsessed with its original father figure.

Similar to Yu Hua's paranoid protagonist, what we have in Han's story is someone whose birth and daily existence are shrouded both in mystery and in misery. What we find in these stories are two concrete examples of the new hero in question: two anomalies, one paranoid and the other retarded. On a symbolic level, the representations of these characters are meant to be understood and hailed as an allegorical critique of the maddening nature of an oppressive power structure. But the symbolic implications do not end there. If we understand allegory in the way Walter Benjamin understands it, as the "symptom of imagination,"[20] we can further ask: Besides being an allegorical protest against the existing power structure, what else are these marginal figures symptomatic of?

The Return of the Desiring Male Subject

Even though very few critics have argued this, I suggest that the presence of the desiring male subject found in Yu Hua's story can also be found in the representation of Binzai in Han Shaogong's story. In fact, represented as a mythical figure, Binzai is eventually sublimated to the level where his marginality is turned into an archetype, one, perhaps not so ironically, with a redeeming quality that fits a masculine imagination.

The villagers are particularly fascinated by the mystery of Binzai's father. Meanwhile, just as there are many versions of who Binzai's father is, there are also different stories about the origins of the villagers' ancestors: "some say from Shanxi (Province), others say from Guangdong." The villagers, how-ever, firmly believe that their ancestors came from somewhere else based on the fact that "their language is different from that of the villages at the foot of the mountain."²¹ The most detailed and authoritative interpretation of their ancestry exists in the songs passed down from the past; they call this kind of singing *chang gu* (singing of the past), which, incidentally, used to be sung by a man named Delong, who is thought by some villagers to be Binzai's father. The songs begin with "their father's generation" then move "to that of the grandfather, and from the grandfather's generation to that of the great grandfather, all the way up to 'Jiangliang,' " to "Younai," and finally to "Xing-tian" (8). This local version of their ancestry, however, as the author points out, conflicts with that of an official historian who points out that their an-cestor could not have been Xingtian, because Xingtian had been executed by the Yellow Emperor before he could foster any offspring.²²

As I have mentioned, critics have read all of this as Han Shaogong's crit-icism of the Han culture (which in essence, for him and other roots-seeking writers, is the CCP's dominant culture), which he believes to have margin-alized other (regional Chinese) cultures. And that he is also challenging the official version(s) of history and attempting to represent what is marginalized by and what is left abject in relation to the Han Chinese culture. His interest in "Xiang" or Hunan culture is not to rediscover the culture but to represent the absurd effects the mainstream culture has had on such a regional culture. Hence, we also see in the story that it is the "normal" villagers who speak and undergo a constant confusion effected by and through language. And they are the ones who are tragic-comical beings caught by the language confusion and by the need to interpret. In their bullying, or making fun of, or interpret-ing Binzai, that is, the villagers themselves are made to appear absurd and laughable.

To return to the implications of Binzai, let us now take a close look at the last part of the story. There, we learn that Binzai's village, Jitouzhai, is being defeated by Jiweizhai in a feud, and villagers of the former are frightened and worried. In their despair, they suddenly realize that something about Binzai is mysterious, and that perhaps he is the one who holds the secret to their success. Although at one point they wanted to sacrifice him to the God of Grains, this time they decide to treat him like a God. They carry him on a piece of wooden board to a temple, kneel in front of him calling him "master," or "celestial being," and stare at him trying to figure out the meaning of his facial expression and other gestures. When he finally points his finger to the sky and murmurs "Baba," the villagers believe that they have finally received the divine symbol. However, because it is still not clear what exactly Binzai has pointed to, the villagers argue over what the symbol means. Finally, the meaning is decided by those who have *huafen* or the right to speak: Binzai had pointed at *yan* or the eaves of a house; because the word sounds the same as *yan,* a character combined with two *huo,* which means fire (and not the *yan* that means to talk), it means that they should continue to fight and fight with fire. Although there is no logical end to this event, the story tells us that in the following battles with the other village, Jitouzhai continues to suffer heavy losses, so much so that the village begins to deteriorate. In the midst of all of this, Binzai's mother disappears and then Binzai disappears in search of his mother. The two villages, meanwhile, decide to talk and make peace. These events do not necessarily have a logical relationship, but their lack of a logical linkage may well be the very point that the author wants to make, to ridicule the act of interpretation taken seriously by the villagers.

When placed in this context, Binzai's abjectness begins to take on more meaning. His chaotic and senseless existence, which is woven into the story along with the activities of the villagers, raises the question of who may be more laughable and absurd, Binzai or the villagers. As I mentioned, in demonstrating the marginalized position of the village (which symbolizes the marginalized Xiang culture), the story focuses on Binzai, who exists on the margins of the marginalized village. If we understand the story as the author's critique of mainstream Han culture, however, how do we identify Binzai when his double marginality also seems to turn interpretations made by the marginalized villagers into questions?

For an answer, we need to turn to the very end of the story. There, Binzai reappears after having lost his mother and disappeared for some time. The story depicts his return this way: "Surprisingly, he didn't die." Moreover, he is not quite the same as before: he looks better and "even the running sores on his head are healed. He sat naked on the foundation of a wall using a stick to play with the water in a jar in front of him and stirring up rays of sunshine."[23] Although "very thin he has a huge belly button, which amazed the children in the village and made them worship it. They took a look at his belly button, kindly gave him some pieces of stone, and began to imitate him by clapping their hands and shouting 'Babababababa!' " (38). It is interesting to note here that Binzai's utterance of *baba,* though meaningless to himself, is picked up by the children. The ugly Binzai is finally at center stage after going through a kind of metamorphosis that places him in a particular kind of relationship with children, leaving us with further questions to contemplate.

What, for example, does the huge belly button mean in light of the story of Xingtian, who turns his belly button into his mouth after being beheaded, and the fact that the villagers believe Xingtian is their ancestor? What is the implication of both Xingtian's belly button and that of Binzai? If the former signifies the possibility of speaking in a different way, what language does Binzai's signify? Also, what is the relationship among Binzai, his huge belly button, his utterance of *baba,* and the children picking up his utterance and chanting *babababababa*? What does this transference from Xingtian to Binzai mean?

These questions point toward the need to take another look at the peripheral position of Binzai, especially the implication of his double marginality. The path that Binzai has gone along—from being mistreated as a fatherless idiot child, to being worshipped by the villagers in their desperate need to find an answer from the divine power, to being befriended by children—seems to suggest that as he functions as a sign read by others, his seeming abjectness becomes a constant that reveals the changes, the ugliness, the stupidity, and the danger of those who try to interpret. In this sense, at the same time, his abjectness becomes less and less abject. In fact, as the end of the story has suggested, Binzai is turned into a symbolic figure conflated with the villagers' (supposed) ancestor, Xingtian, whose belly button is presumed to speak everything that is beyond "normal" language that nevertheless constitutes the truth.

The truth, the story seems to suggest, exists beyond words and interpretation, and can always be resurrected through hope. Here, as we can see, hope is represented by the children who pick up Binzai's utterance and chant after him. In discussing the subjectivity of modern Chinese intellectuals in conjunction with the notion of hope, Rey Chow has argued that, "as a figure of wager, hope can . . . be redefined through 'subjectivity,' " and "the predominant subjectivity that surfaces in the May Fourth period . . . is not so much a dense psychic 'self,' impenetrable and solipsistic, as a relationship between the writer, his or her object of narration, and the reader."[24] What, then, is the relationship between hope and the "predominant subjectivity" that surfaces in the post-Mao period? It is perhaps still how to write, as suggested by Chow in her discussion; only this time it is manifested in a different way. Here, the hope appears to exist, paradoxically, in Binzai's failure to enter into language, which, as the story implies toward the end, does not have to be viewed as a failure; it symbolizes a philosophical aphasia effected by the hegemony of the CCP's dominant discourse that renders its subject speechless. By returning to the "real cultural roots"—Xingtian, symbolized by Binzai's belly button—China will have a new hope, represented by the children who (it is hoped) will speak a different language.

On this note, we can suggest now that the return of Binzai symbolizes the return of the Chinese (writer/critic) intellectuals, as the knowing and desiring male subject, who had been rendered silent by the CCP but (as they hope) have now found a different way to speak. In other words, Binzai's abjectness, like the fragmented self reflected back to the protagonist in Yu Hua's story, is identified with the oppositional Chinese intellectuals. And his abject position is transcended when, like the young children chanting after Binzai, the intellectuals return with a huge belly button to speak both with truth in hand and with cultural roots underlined. Put differently, when the end of the story turns Binzai into a symbol signifying Xingtian, the legend of this mythical figure also implies that he is a symbolic figure whom intellectuals like to envision as their own: as an embodiment of Xingtian, they return with, once again, truth in hand and cultural roots underlined.

Our examination of the return of the intellectuals, however, does not end here. As the identification of Xingtian implies, the return is accompanied by what I see as a strong desire to identify with a truth-making position and to speak with a different language. The irony, however (besides the fact that the language they try to speak may not turn out to be *that* different), is that in actuality what many writers and critics seem to be more fascinated by is often less a search for truth and more a search for identity (or for a better image of their own). Because of this, the point to which they return is highly conditioned by what I see as a masculinist tendency—a desire to become a kind of master—in that desire. A good place to examine all of this is the perhaps still entrenched intellectual celebration of another kind of marginal male figure represented by Wang Shuo: the hooligan.

Wang Shuo's Antiheroes: The Third Case and the Politics of (Male) Marginality

Wang Shuo Phenomenon

Compared with the highly symbolic nature of the split self represented by Yu Hua and Han Shaogong, Wang Shuo breaks out of the subliminal boundary and delves into the earthly world (or the common world of the ordinary people, *pingming*). Through playful representations of the "dregs of society" (*shehui zhazi*) as heroes, Wang celebrates "no-respect" (to echo Andrew Ross's book title) and manages to become one of the most popular writers in contemporary China.

Although Wang has publicly announced his retirement from writing, he has produced enough stories and has stirred up the contemporary Chinese literary and cultural landscape in such a way that he continues to exist both as a famous writer of many popular stories as well as somebody who remains famous by not writing (not to mention his active participation in the production of some of the best-known contemporary TV series and movies). Starting in the mid-1980s, Wang began to receive increasing popular and critical attention with his stories, which are characterized by clever lines, witty remarks, and parodying of the official discourse tumbling out of the mouths of his hooliganlike male characters. All of these characteristics exhibit a highly irreverent attitude toward authority (and sometimes intellectuals), which seems to be welcomed by the populace.[25] Packaged as such, Wang is hailed by many—and criticized by some as well—for being a *pingming* literature writer, a writer who writes for and about the common people. In the context of my discussion, the question I want to address goes beyond either praising or criticizing Wang's use of *pingming* per se. I am interested in to what extent we can understand his *pingming* characters as marginal figures, to what extent this conventional interpretation needs to be questioned, and, more important, why intellectuals seem to be so eager to welcome and, to a significant extent, profess to identify with such heroes.

Generally speaking, Wang's reception can be categorized in the following way. First of all, his witty parody of official discourse delights many of his readers. Especially in some of his earlier stories, such as "Wanzhu" (The operators), "Yidianr zhengjing ye meiyou" (Nothing reverent), and "Wanr jiushi xintiao" (To play is to be excited), Wang uses his seemingly offbeat characters to make fun of the official language. This is perhaps the most brilliant aspect of Wang's writing: his ability to poke fun at the emptiness and absurdity of the official language by having it spoken at the least revered moment, about trivial matters, and by the people least likely to use it. The comical effect of this, however, exists largely as an insider's joke; without being steeped in the milieu of the language and both the subtle and ostentatious reference points, the reader would have trouble getting the humor. His most successful secret thus also limits Wang's popularity; he can be extremely popular within China, but his humor tends to lose its meaning in translation. What makes him popular is, to a large extent, not translatable.[26] In this sense, Wang will always remain relatively secluded in the Chinese context. Oddly, his stories' not being easily translated may show, in a reverse way, some of the absurdity of the official language.

Second, many critics have celebrated the kinds of characters Wang brings to life in his stories, namely, the hooligans and "social dregs." In his "Wang Shuo and *Liumang* ('Hooligan') Culture," Geremie Barmé records the popular reception Wang received in China for writing about "the social stratum that [enjoys] a popular lifestyle . . . that contains violence and sex, mockery and shamelessness."[27] Barmé focuses exclusively on Wang's interest in *liumang* culture and takes care to place it in the context of modern Chinese history, where he separates Wang-style *liumang* from the political *liumang,* who "are merely waiting in the wings for power, their frivolous attitude a disguise for more ominous intentions,"[28] described as *zhengzhi liumang* (political hooligans), these often include various political parties and their struggles for power. Wang's fiction, Barmé argues, finds "its heroes within the underbelly of urban society, among 'potential criminals,' the idle and chronically unemployable," and "represents an anarchic 'unofficial' world" while rejecting "the heroic models of post-Mao literature—intellectuals, students, rustic (as opposed to revolutionary) peasants and sentimental soldiers—he even goes against accepted moral standards" (32–33). Throughout his description, Barmé does not mention the gender of these characters, nor do the people he cites in the article. Their gender, of course, is always already assumed: they are male. What makes Wang stand out among post-Mao writers, according to critics, is precisely that he creates heroes who "fight valiantly, if not cleanly, whenever faced with conventional society" (48). Conventions, in other words, are the enemies of Wang's heroes.

Third, many critics have celebrated the kind of hero found in Wang's fic-

tion, arguing that when he makes fun of the sublime, the elite, and the sentimental, this gesture helps raise questions about the "bad" that can be and has
been done in the name of the "good." In his article "Duobi chonggao" (Stay
away from the sublime), for example, Wang Meng places Wang Shuo's "blas-
phemy" in a historical context, arguing "that we must speak fairly [about his
blasphemy]. It is life itself that has blasphemed the sublime. Just remember
how many terrible and disgusting dramas were played out by Jiang Qing
[Mao's widow] and Lin Biao [Mao's once chosen successor]. And how many
times have the political movements made fun of such serious matters as *isms,*
loyalty, Party membership, honor and even life itself. It is they who first
started this cruel game of 'playing.' "[29] The sublime or *chonggao,* in other
words, was itself a blasphemed notion before Wang Shuo came along to play
with (make fun of) it. Contextually speaking, therefore, what Wang pokes
fun at is not really anything purely sublime and worthy of being taken seriously. In this sense, we can say that such critics as Wang Meng and many
others view Wang Shuo as a social critic who satirizes political, social, and
cultural hypocrisy. The Wang Shuo phenomenon, Wang Meng argues, "is a
very Chinese and very contemporary phenomenon" (16).

In the midst of all the praise, of course, there are criticisms, most of which
focus on Wang Shuo's lack of respect for anything serious in his creation of
those antiheroes.[30] More specifically, Wang's critics question the value of glo-
rifying hooligans, petty criminals, and "social dregs." They feel uncomfort-
able seeing such marginal social groups placed at the center of popular culture
and are reluctant to acknowledge the resistance value in Wang's writings.

For the most part, as we can see, writers and critics such as Wang Meng
celebrate and welcome the center-staging of Wang Shuo's antiheroes, taking
it as a free ride of their own in a Bakhtinian carnivalistic sense. Still, what is it
about Wang's hooligans that could have generated such a positive response
from these intellectuals? What do the latter recognize in them? Is it the vin-
dication of the *xiaorenwu* ("the little guy")? If so, who and what are those
"little guys" exactly? And what makes them appealing to the intellectuals
and hence identifiable? I address these questions in relation to one of Wang's
novellas, *Dongwu xiongmeng* (Animal vicious, or In the heat of the sun).[31]

Wang Shuo's (Anti-)Hero

The novella *Dongwu xiongmeng* was published in 1991.[32] Unlike many of
Wang's earlier stories, it is set during the years of the Cultural Revolution, and

it concerns a group of teenagers growing up during this period of political turmoil. Unlike many other stories set during the Cultural Revolution, however, this one does not directly deal with the political persecution and the horror experienced by older people, or the political fervor and disillusionment experienced by the Red Guards' generation. Instead, it is about a group of middle school youngsters living through the Cultural Revolution seemingly unaffected by it, while the content of their lives, in its own way, reflects the imprint of the time. Also, unlike many of his other stories, this one specifies where this group of youngsters comes from, that is, what their family backgrounds are. This is the first time in Wang's stories in which he finally situates the social status of his antiheroes, something he cannot avoid doing when he writes autobiographically about the Cultural Revolution.

On the surface, it is a story about the narrator's memory of his teenage years during the Cultural Revolution. More specifically, it is about the protagonist's (the narrator's) crush on a girl when he was a middle school student. It details something that most non-Chinese do not think existed during the Cultural Revolution: the turmoil of teenage years with the attendant peer pressure, rebellion against parents, and growing interest in sex(uality). The personal touch, however, does not come from the claims made by the narrator at the beginning that he "wants to be honest" about himself by telling the story of his past. Rather, it comes from the constant reflection made by the narrator retrospectively. That is, the narration of the story constantly evokes an awareness on the part of the reader of the distance between the narrator who is remembering his past and the "I" who is in that past. The personal touch, in other words, is to be found in the narrator's reconstruction of his past. The fact that Wang shows a difference between the "I" of the past and the "I" of the present is, at the same time, reminiscent of the split self found in the two stories discussed earlier in this chapter.

In that past, the teenage narrator rebels against everything he is being taught at school and at home, behavior typical of Wang's antiheroes. He hates school and constantly plays truant, hangs out with the people his parents forbid him to, joins gang fights, clumsily fools around with some young girls (and fantasizes about one in particular), and, above all, sneaks into people's homes with a master key he made. He is one of those "bad" boys who is made to appear not *that* bad, but only human. The "human" part of this boy comes particularly from his unsuccessful quest for love. The girl (Milan) he likes and fantasizes about does not return his feelings. Toward the end of the story, after much anguish, the narrator punishes Milan by assaulting her. As if to even the score, the story ends while he is in turn being punished by his rival who, together with the rival's friends, make him drink from the swimming pool.

This story has Wang's usual stylistic features: frankness, rudeness, crudity, and sarcasm. On yet another level, as I have already suggested, this story specifically situates the social status of the hooligans that Wang has been praised for representing. Both the spatial layout in which these young people are located and the spatial boundaries they move in and out of signify the social background of Wang's antiheroes: their families are those that are walled in and away from the ordinary city dwellers because they are from what is known as the "military courtyards" (*budui dayuanr*). Therefore, to understand Wang's versions of *liumang* or hooligan, one needs to understand the distinction between ordinary city dwellers in Beijing and the Chinese version of military brats, especially those from Beijing. In this story, Wang finally makes the distinction for us.

Throughout this story, the narrator's father is often absent. When he is at home, the father is portrayed as a tyrantlike figure who is extremely unhappy about his good-for-nothing son. As a result, the son shuts him out of his life almost completely, doing all the forbidden things behind his back while at the same time showing an obedient front. His defiance implies rejection of the values the father tries to instill in him. At the same time, his defiance does not necessarily mean a lack of identification with the father on another level; his defiance is made possible precisely by the privileged position resulting from the power of the father that he rebels against.

Such a paradox is embedded in and pervasive throughout the story. Early in the story, for example, the narrator reflects on why he does not like to go to school:

> I was not in the least worried about my future. My future was already decided: after high school, I would be joining the army and would eventually become a lower-level officer but wearing a four-pocket uniform. That was all my dream. I had no ambition in becoming a high-ranking officer, for in my mind those who occupied high-ranking positions were never going to die. . . . I did not have to do anything. . . . Once I became eighteen, it would be my turn [to join the army]. (133)

Obviously, the narrator is making fun of high-ranking leaders as well as his father, who will make him join the army, and expressing his disdain toward this kind of power. From a different perspective, however, this also indicates the narrator's privileged position in society. And it is precisely this privileged position that allows him to continue to play without having to pay for the consequences. The same is true with his playmates, whose privileged positions show through the narrator's seemingly sarcastic portrayals of them.

One day, on his way back from a meaningless parade with the school to which his parents have sent him so as to separate him from the bad boys in his old school, the narrator spots his former gang. He describes them as follows:

> More than ten of them, all wearing a military uniform and those old-man styled shoes. Some sitting on their bikes and others with their bodies stretching on the bike sitting on the back seat, they gathered in the middle of the intersection in front of the police stand. Every one of them was holding a cigarette. They were talking excitedly while puffing out smoke; they were an attractive crowd, looking as if they owned the corner of the street. When the line of students, who were their age, were passing by them they looked at them coldly with contempt, making the law-abiding students very uncomfortable and making the teachers pretend not to see them. (136)

It is clear that this hooliganlike crowd is not just any group of bad boys. They have markers that distinguish them from other youngsters: their uniforms and shoes. Although during the Cultural Revolution, military uniforms became fashionable outfits for youngsters, there are still detailed distinctions between them that can reveal one's social status. The narrator continues to observe:

> The young people who went there, regardless of their gender, all wore military uniforms. At that time, the sense of fashion and status that uniforms offered was beyond what today's famous brands can give. Only uniforms had more diverse materials and colors than the navy blue khaki and cotton materials worn by the ordinary people. The state had once ordered different uniforms for officers above the rank of majors. They came in dark yellow, light yellow, white and green and in dif-

ferent styles and included high boots made of good-quality leather. . . .
More than ten years ago, the young boys and girls wearing these different kinds of old uniforms looked particularly attractive in the then
colorless streets. They all felt very good about themselves and each had
some respect for the other. (142)

Wang is known for his scathing sense of sarcasm, but when it comes to these
youngsters, his pen is not as sharp. In fact, one can even sense a rather strong
touch of nostalgia in his depictions of these uniformed youth. Such nostalgia
is the very moment of his self-identification with youngsters who, even during the Cultural Revolution, continued to enjoy a sense of privilege and superiority. This sense of privilege is also the license that the narrator enjoys in his
petty criminal activities, in his other attempts to bend the rules, and, above
all, in his ultimate act of violence against Milan. These are no hooligans of
ordinary standing; these are *liumang* whose acts of violence and criminal activities do not cause them to suffer much in the way of consequences (which,
ironically, appears unnoticed by Geremie Barmé in his distinction between
political hooligans and Wang's social misfits). Wang's antiheroes have it easy
not because the writer makes them that way, but because they actually belong to a privileged class that guarantees an easy way out, something that, in
turn, ought to leave the marginality of Wang's "antiheroes" (and the notion
of *pingming* or ordinary city dwellers) in quotation marks.

The issue here, I must quickly point out, is not as simple as the privileged
social position of Wang's antiheroes. The concern is the masculinist overtone
that comes with the depiction of these privileged rebels, and, more important, how this overtone captures the imagination of the intellectuals. Let me
elaborate with a linguistic point. In Beijing dialect, there is a term often used
by men or to refer to men: *ye* (master or father) as in *da ye* (with emphasis on
both syllables) or *ye menr.* It has the implication of a man's being the master
of, superior to, others, and it is also a marker that implies a kind of male
attitude, which is cocky, self-assured, and sometimes rude. For the most part,
Wang's stories constitute a celebration of such an attitude, releasing, as many
critics have argued, the pent-up anger of the ordinary people toward the absurdity of the power system that itself has corrupted most of the values it
once preached. This *da ye* attitude, at the same time, does more than indicate
the tension between ordinary people and authority. Wang's stories glorify

this *da ye* attitude (in a seeming competition with that of *ye,* the father) as a male—masculine, to be exact—identity. And it is this *da ye* component that attracts the intellectuals to embrace Wang's hooligans.

In the film *In the Heat of the Sun,* which is based on *Dongwu xiongmeng,* there is a very telling moment that illustrates my point. Toward the end of the film, the scenes change to the present. In black and white, the camera presents a view of a modern-looking freeway intersection with tall skyscrapers looming behind. A luxury limo is driven into the scene, and as it comes closer, we see several men in their thirties standing through the sunroof of the limo holding in their hands what look like bottles of wine or beer, laughing and shouting, apparently rejoicing over something. As the limo moves toward the center of the screen, we recognize them to be the grown-up versions of those teenagers whose lives during the Cultural Revolution have been portrayed. Without their saying anything and with the camera following the limo that has passed in front of it, the film ends.

As we know, in PRC politics, only heads of state have been seen in an inspection limo, center-staged in massively organized celebrations. The resemblance between the two here may be understood as the former teenagers parodying the authorities in celebrating their own ascending power: it is no longer a political occasion that merits their inspection-style limo ride. Meanwhile, the approaching limo with the camera zooming in on it is also a return of sorts, as it is visually presented, with the limo carrying those formerly marginalized figures toward the center of the screen. This time, however, there is an irony. Complete with a limo, Western-styled suits, expensive wine, and the center-staging of them all, this return does not appear to be carnivalistic as such nor can it be simply called the return of the repressed (in its original or Bakhtinian sense). What is suggested is the once marginalized now seeing himself at center stage taking the place of the "father" in the limo.

This last scene, to be sure, does not really exist in Wang's novella. But the visual addition to the end of this story is nevertheless most telling. It shows that the filmmaker is himself curious about what happens next, after the son has made face and shown his irreverence to the father. To him, as is shown in the film, it is only natural that the former is to take the place of the latter, and this time the transition is to take place against the background of the triumph of modernization, Western-style. This new background is perhaps as revolutionary as showing the son now center stage, only this time, the defiance comes from the one who is identifying himself, almost unabashedly, with the power position of the father that he aspires to replace.[33]

Da ye: The Return of the Repressed?

It is clear by now that a celebration of the marginal male figure does not necessarily entail an affirmation (or a celebration) of his marginality. If his marginality is used to symbolize a critique of the existing power structure, the margins are certainly not, as I mentioned earlier, the point to which the male subject desires to return. More often than not, the opposite is true. As I have shown throughout this discussion, the return of the repressed is in fact conditioned and limited by a male desire that is itself confined by or preoccupied with an anxiety to move away from the margins. On the one hand, unlike Zhang Chengzhi's portrayal of heroism, these stories choose a marginalized male devoid of conventional heroic traits as the major character. In so doing, they carve out new (discursive) space for the formerly villainized, the neglected, the rebellious, and the insignificant. The success of these stories signifies the establishment of a new aesthetic order where the once heroic image of men is replaced by what is now often referred to as antiheroes. No one can miss the political implications in all of this when these new images of men indicate a moving away from the official Chinese ideology and into the murky realms of "human nature."

On the other hand, the antiheroes are by no means innocent. Indeed, the desire coming from these new heroes is to identify with men who have an attitude, and the attitude is that of a *da ye*. This *da ye* mentality underlies the politics of marginality in question which is aimed at restoring manly man as the object of male identity. It is in this sense, if we return to Yu Hua and Han Shaogong, that their marginal male figures, like Wang Shuo's antihero, are presented, via modernism (and satire), in hopes of being reestablished as archetypal figures with sublime and masculine qualities.

To conclude, somewhere in the creation of the new images of Chinese men, the marginal(ized) male, when conflated with a new aesthetic order that exonerates a different version of the self, is turned into another kind of hero. This hero, at the same time, though seemingly new, has turned out to be not *that* new after all. If the texts I have examined start from the margins in telling the stories of their male characters, it is not the margins where these marginal men eventually remain or to which they return. Binzai, whose marginality is employed to satirize various discursive practices (of the villagers), mysteriously returns (cleaned up and center stage in relation to the children), symbolizing the mythical father figure Xingtian. Yu Hua's protagonist, whose eventual departure leaves behind the "camera" that captures and the gazing subject that watches the departure, has always signaled the presence of a knowing self who plays with the fragmentation of himself. Finally, in the film based on Wang Shuo's story, the protagonist's return is the most telling of all because he takes the place of the father, literally becoming *da ye* again. In other words, what appears to be fragmented and decentered as the characteristics of this new hero is each time sutured (to use another psychoanalytic term) to a seemingly more triumphant male subject position.

With this, we come back to the question I set out to explore: If representations of the marginal male figure symbolize the return of the repressed, where do the repressed return to? And how do we understand the male subject position of the writers and critics who appear to identify themselves with the repressed? Through analyzing marginality politics, I have argued that in essence, the male marginality embodied by the seemingly adjunct figures or antiheroes is ultimately rejected by the male intellectuals. What returns is not so much the marginalized or repressed adjunct figures as a male desire for a strong and powerful identity.

This desire and the male preoccupation with it, as I explore further in the next two chapters, continue to be manifested in other ways so long as male writers continue to subject themselves to their own anxiety over the perceived Chinese male marginality. Because of this preoccupation, Chinese writer/critic intellectuals will also continue their search for powerful masculine identities.

Chapter 4

Zazhong gaoliang

and the Male Search

for Masculinity

In this chapter, I pick up where I ended in the previous chapter, to examine specifically the issue regarding male desire for masculinity. Contrary to some critics' contention, I argue that masculinity—of a sort closely identified with a strong-male image and certain male traits deemed manly—is an essential part of the post-Mao male search for identity. At the same time, I also argue that this particular male search is full of twists and turns conditioned by modern Chinese history, and that the dynamics within that history are what constitute the specificity of Chinese male desire for masculinity.

As *zazhong gaoliang* (hybrid/bastard sorghum) in the title indicates, the focus of my examination of the male search for masculinity will be closely related to Mo Yan's novel *Red Sorghum* (*Hong gaoliang jiazu*; literally, red sorghum family). Indeed, the two kinds of sorghum, red and hybrid/bastard, found in Mo's novel have, at least on the surface, distinct symbolic implications associated with masculinity and a lack thereof: red sorghum represents manly men, and hybrid/bastard sorghum less manly (or weakened) men. Instead of focusing on the former, however, I begin my discussion by foregrounding the latter, which is embodied by the voice of the first-person narrator, and examine why this voice is (seemingly) riddled with a strong *self-contempt* when he refers to himself as *zazhong gaoliang*. This voice holds the key to a better way of deconstructing (and eventually reaching a better understanding of) the relationship between the hybrid/bastard sorghum and the red sorghum, two related and yet (seemingly) contrasting symbols employed by Mo to represent two generations of men. Following the "sound track" of this voice, I then examine the implications of its accented notes, such as expressions of pain, shame, and a seemingly strong desire for punishment. I do so to understand further the essence of this voice, how the self-contemptuous hybrid/bastard sorghum eventually identifies itself with the (masculine) red sorghum, and what this identification indicates to us in our efforts to understand the male desire and search for a masculine identity represented by Mo's novel in particular and expressed strongly by other male writers in general in post–Cultural Revolution literature.

What/Who Is *Zazhong gaoliang*?

Generally speaking, the Chinese word *zazhong* is a swearword that means bastard. Like any swearword, when it is used against someone else, its purpose is to insult. But what does it mean when it is used against oneself? Perhaps it is not so much to insult as to *shame oneself.*

Before I go further, let me briefly summarize Mo Yan's novel. Set in the Republic era (1911–1949), the novel tells the lives of the narrator's parents and especially his grandparents living in Gaomi County of Shandong Province before and during the Resistance War against the Japanese (1937–1945). The major characters are "my grandpa" (Yu Zhanao) and the two "grannies" (Jiuer and Lianer). The story orients around the life of Yu, a self-styled commander (known as Yu Siling or Commander Yu) of a group of peasants-turned-bandits, who leads them in fighting, at first, other bandits, and later, the Japanese invaders. It also tells of the relationships between the grandfather and the two women. Although at the time of the narration the grandparents are dead and the father's generation constitutes the backbone of the country's power structure, the narrator concentrates on the grandfather in his prime, when the narrator's own father was just a child (and the grandfather's illegitimate son). As I will demonstrate later, the novel focuses on the grandparents' generation for a reason.

However, the novel is more than tales of the lives of some peasants in the past. By focusing on the untamed nature of both the natural and human worlds of that time as he imagines it, Mo manages to create a new type of hero who is in many ways different from the heroes celebrated by the CCP, whose primary heroism is their loyalty to the Party. Yu Zhanao, the grand-father, is a free-spirited man who, though highly patriotic, obeys no particu-lar ideology, whether communist or nationalist, and who fears no enemies, be they his rival bandit commanders or the Japanese invaders. Furthermore, Mo emphasizes the grandfather's true heroism not only by placing him in what seems to be a primitive and yet intensely rich natural world but also by granting him a sexual free spirit in associating with women. In short, through what many critics celebrate as a refreshing narrative style,[1] Mo en-thusiastically presents the story of Yu Zhanao, his relationships with two women, his life as a bandit leader, and his dealings with various outside forces mentioned above.

At the same time, the novel is more than the sum of these characters and their lives in the past. It also concerns the descendants of this past genera-tion, who are referred to by the narrator as *zazhong gaoliang* (hybrid/bastard sorghum). Although since its publication, Mo's novel has attracted much critical attention in China and its popularity outside of China has been espe-cially enhanced by the film *Red Sorghum,* which is based on the first two chap-ters of the novel, few critics have focused directly on the voice of the first-person narrator.[2]

In the film, the voice-over—that of the first-person narrator—functions mainly (technically) to frame the story line and is devoid of personal emo-tion. Still, his voice suggests the presence of his generation in direct reference to the representations of a past generation whose lives unfold on the screen. This subtextual reference to the narrator's own time is, however, far more prominent and significant in the novel because the first-person narrator in-vests stronger emotions, some of which (and this is what draws my attention) are forcefully expressed, when he lashes out at himself on various occasions. Indeed, the presence of the first-person voice is prominent, especially at both ends of the novel: the dedication, the last ten pages, and the epilogue, in which the "I" sets himself up as a sharp contrast to the heroes of the story. To be sure, it is the author's voice in the dedication and the epilogue and it is the first-person narrator's in the last ten pages of the novel, but in this case the two converge and one identifies directly with the other, both expressing a contempt toward the same "I."

The dedication reads, in part, as follows:

> Solemnly, I dedicate this book to those heroic and unjustly treated souls that used to be wandering among the boundless red sorghum fields. I am your unworthy descendent. I wish to pull out my darkened, soy-sauce-soaked heart, chop it up, put it in three bowls, and place them in the sorghum fields.[3]

In highly dramatic and violent language, the author is apologizing for being unworthy of his ancestors: his "darkened" and "soy-sauce-soaked heart" is the very symbol of his unworthiness, and he is ready to punish his "ugly" heart by pulling it out, cutting it up, and sacrificing it in hope of redemption.

These expressions of figurative self-mutilation may appear exaggerated and drastic. The image they evoke, however, is not excessive if we remember certain legendary tales in China, moral lessons of how sons, daughters, and daughters-in-law save their parents or show their filial piety by inflicting self-mutilation. Nor is the language drastic if we compare it to a similar kind used in the discourse of criticism and self-criticism (*piping yu ziwo piping*) and of mass criticism (*da pipan*) during the various political campaigns/movements in the first thirty years of the CCP's regime, and especially during the Cultural Revolution. What is most intriguing here, then, is not so much the degree of exaggeration as the fact that this linguistic pattern is repeated in a post-Mao novel whose thematic and stylistic dynamics are every bit as different from and implicitly in protest against those promoted by the CCP's dominant ideology. In her discussion of the novel *Red Sorghum,* Lu Tonglin offers a poignant discussion of this linguistic resemblance and its implications.[4] Here, I take a somewhat different approach by focusing on the psychic economy of the self-lashing, self-loathing, and self-contemptuous sentiment manifested through such language.

The self-lashing does not end with the dedication. Toward the end of the novel, the author/narrator returns to his hometown, where he contemplates his own time and space. It is also then, while commemorating his forefathers, that he sets up the contrast between the red sorghum and the hybrid/bastard sorghum, with the former representing the heroic ancestors and the latter their unworthy descendants. The narrator depicts himself this way:

> Ten years after I fled my hometown, I once again showed up at my Second Granny's grave with a false display of affection acquired from the upper-class society and with a stinking body from which each pore was emitting the bad smell . . . of the dirty urban life.[5]

We cannot but note the negativity of the "I," blatantly conveyed through such expressions as "false display of affection," "a stinking body," and "bad smell." When he links all of this with the "dirty urban life," incidentally, Mo falls within the literary ethos in post–Cultural Revolution China, where many writers turned to the rural for renewed inspiration.[6] What distinguishes Mo, however, is the intensity of the contrast between the urban (which for him would be synonymous with the modern) and the rural (which is related to the past, or history, where he believes the beauty of life can be found) and his strong contempt toward the former and uncompromising preference for the latter.[7]

After the lines quoted above, the negative image of the self continues. In his imagined dialogues with his ancestors, we find these words spoken by the Second Grandmother:

> You, our pitiful, weak, jealous, and stubborn child. Go to the Mo Shui River and immerse yourself in it for three days—not one day longer nor one day shorter. Wash clean your body and soul and then you may return to your own world. Between the Yang side [the male side or the side facing the sun] of the Bai Ma Mountain and the Yin side [the female side or the side away from the sun] of the Mo Shui River, there is yet one piece of pure red sorghum. You must find it at all cost and hold it high up when you temper yourself in this terrible world.[8]

Apparently, the filth of his body which needs a thorough washing is closely identified with his soul, which is characterized as "pitiful," "weak," and "poisoned." Complete with the strong wording depicting the ugliness of his body and soul and together with the dedication and epilogue, in which he is ready to sacrifice his "darkened" heart, we are presented with a negative image of a male self connected to his unworthiness.

Unworthy of what, and why does it matter? Within the literary ethos of the 1980s, such an attack carried strong political implications. On that level, one can argue that this attack on the self may not be directed at the self at all. As the Second Granny's speech demonstrates—via such phrases as "your own world" or "this terrible world"—it is aimed (albeit indirectly) at the CCP's power machine and its ideology, which, as her tone of voice suggests, are responsible for the "darkening" of the heart of the "I's" generation. The self-lashing, therefore, can be viewed as an allegorical attack on that power structure. But at the same time, also in accord with this ethos, the novel is more than just a political allegory. The repeated self-bashing is also part of the author/narrator's attempt to rethink history, to reconfigure the relationship between his own generation and that of the past, and above all (perhaps via negativity), to search for and redefine his or her generation's identity. As a result, there is a subtext running through Mo's novel that is highly self-conscious and distinctly male. It is the combination of these two elements, which characterizes the subtext, that I explore further below. Through examining this subtext, I hope to demonstrate the historicity of the self-debasing male voice and how it is in essence part of the manifestation of the male desire for masculinity. In what follows, therefore, I first take a few detours away from the novel for the purpose of mapping out the possible implications of the male self-detesting voice. I examine the notion of shame and male intellectuals' interest in it, and their strategies in addressing pain and suffering that (re)surface with the sense of shame. I am interested in seeing how a desired masculine identity is figured in male expressions of self-contempt. I then return to the novel's representation of the grandfather in light of these detours and examine how the red sorghum and the hybrid/bastard sorghum eventually converge, manifesting a strong male desire for masculinity.

(Male) Shame as Personal and Historical Expressions

The strong dissatisfaction toward the self expressed in Mo Yan's novel does not stand alone in modern Chinese literature. It has, among other things, an intertextual reminiscence in another prominent story, Yu Dafu's "Chenlun" (Sinking). Indeed, as early as the 1920s, Yu Dafu's story made the (male) ambivalence toward himself part of modern Chinese discourse, even though few critics then and now have examined it extensively from a gendered and psychic-economic point of view.

Published in 1921, "Sinking" concerns a young Chinese man's experience studying in Japan. It is written in an intensely self-absorbed way, in which the male protagonist demonstrates strong inner turmoil (stemming from his shame) both as a Chinese and as a young man. He is shy and excessively sensitive to those around him. He is filled with (sexual) desires but is extremely ashamed both at having them and at being unable to act on them. As time passes during his stay in Japan, he withdraws and eventually becomes completely isolated. Together with some detailed episodes in which the protagonist is seized with anger (toward the Japanese boys and girls he believes always laugh at him), with a seemingly unfulfillable sexual desire, and with a strong sense of shame, the story has created one of the first images of modern Chinese men suffering from the modern sentiment of alienation.

Toward the end, the story takes a sharp turn, channeling the protagonist's personal lack of self-confidence into a lament over the lack of his own country's strong and powerful standing. When the story ends, the protagonist stands by the ocean ready to commit suicide. He faces the direction where China lies and laments, "Oh, my downtrodden country, when are you going to become strong one day?!"[9] This final conflation of the personal and the national lack has been understood by most critics as part of modern Chinese intellectuals' anxiety over the national standing of modern China. The tension within this protagonist and the existence of a narrative perspective have also led Yi-tse Mei Feuerwerker to identify the self manifested in this story as a "problematic self," a modern Chinese (male) subject who is simultaneously troubled and personified by this tension.[10]

At the same time, underlying the dissatisfaction voiced toward the self is a strong sense of shame (identified by some critics as guilt) and a detestation of one's own desire for pleasure. C. T. Hsia, for example, identifies the self-loathing as guilt and comments that "the guilt and remorse of Yu Ta-fu is to be understood in the framework of a Confucian ethic, which had conditioned his upbringing. Even when engaged in casual amorous pursuits, Yu Ta-fu or his fictional alter ego always suffers from the acute awareness of his truancy as son, husband, and father."[11] Like Hsia, most critics have also seen the struggling self in this story in connection with his sense of guilt for not fulfilling his duty as son, husband, and father.[12] But due to the rapid changes taking place in the modern context in which the story was written, the presence of moral guilt cannot alone yield such a strong sentiment against the self. As part of a modern Chinese sentiment generated in China's struggle for recognition, a corresponding psychological component—shame, which is closely related to self-uncertainty—should not be overlooked.

In Chinese, shame is *chi* and is often used with *ru* (humiliation), as in *chiru* (humiliation) or *shouru* (to be humiliated). *Chi* is also often combined with *xiu,* as in *xiuchi* (shame). In this sense, we can say that "humiliation" expressed in Chinese would always involve a strong connotation of shame. It so happens that the word *chiru* (humiliation/shame) had become part of the nationalist discourse at the time China was inflicted with *guochi* (national humiliation) by foreign powers (particularly since the Opium War in 1841), a sentiment that further caused a sense of *shouru* (feeling humiliated) shared by many young intellectuals around the turn of the century. Though the protagonist in "Sinking" may feel guilty about his desires for and futile pursuit of pleasure, he is more ashamed of himself when watching what seems to him the exclusionary behavior of the boys and girls of his host country. It is this latter sentiment—not being *recognized* and therefore feeling both humiliated by and *ashamed* of the lack of recognition—that prompts the sentimentality embedded in the problematic self discussed by Feuerwerker. The self becomes problematic when caught, for instance, between a past and the present in which he, the modern self, suffers from an inferiority complex in relation to the other (in this case, Japanese and Western cultures).

With this, I would like to briefly return to Mo Yan's novel, to revisit and pause at the images evoked by the self-lashing language in the passages quoted earlier. There are two groups of contrasting images. On the one side, there is the color red, the last piece of "pure red sorghum," and the "boundless red sorghum fields," all registering the beauty and the untaintedness of the natural world of his ancestors, who are themselves pure, beautiful, and untainted. On the other side, we have the "darkened" heart, "a stinking body" with a "bad smell," and the "dirty urban life" that "poisoned" and "weakened" its inhabitants, including the author/narrator, who has learned to wear the mask of a "false display of affection." With the color red, the first group of images conjures up the concept of life in its (supposedly) most natural state, full of hope and vitality. The specific body images—the chopped-up heart, the stinking body, and the bad smell—in the second group, on the other hand, indicate the ugliness related to modern life and conjure up a sense of pain and a lack of satisfaction, among other things. Compared with the former, the latter appears ugly and unworthy and, above all, makes the "I" feel *ashamed* (of his weakened, tainted, and impure body and soul). Echoing the narrative voice in "Sinking," Mo's narrator expresses an even stronger sense of dissatisfaction with himself, although he does so with less melodramatic sentiment, marking a degree of difference (in the male psyche) effected by the changes that have taken place between one era and the other.

Characterized in this way, the implications of these images suggest, once again, that Mo's novel is not just a tongue-in-cheek tale protesting authority or, for that matter, a self-indulgent show that is carnivalistic in nature. The narrative voice is serious, with little irony, and the contrast between *hong gaoliang* and *zazhong gaoliang* is stark. Together with the manifested shame and self-contempt on which these ugly images converge, the narrator identifies himself with the negative connotation of *zazhong gaoliang,* seemingly setting himself up as the target for attack. How do we make sense of this self-bashing and self-debasing sentiment? If it in essence indicates a male desire for masculine identity, how do we go about understanding its peculiar manifestation?

Perceived from a psychological or, more specifically, psychic-economic, point of view, the strong wording of self-contempt is perhaps a powerful manifestation of what Jean Laplanche terms the "vital order" of "life and death" in his interpretation of the significance of Freud's psychoanalytic theory. It is a metaphor that can be appropriately understood as the complexity of social relations both affecting and affected by interactions between the individual and society. In this sense, we can say that what is embedded in the image of *zazhong gaoliang* signifies, at least in part, the complexity of the human—modern Chinese male, to be exact—psyche deeply entangled in relation to a particular social and political reality.

To better understand this point before moving on to the question of masculinity, we must further explore the ways we can understand this manifested self-detestation and how it is entangled with the specific sociocultural and political reality as it is perceived in modern and contemporary China.

What's Ah Q Got to Do with It?

Ah Q is the main character in Lu Xun's "A Q zhengzhuan" (The story of Ah Q).[13] But to bring him up when we discuss the self-detestation, the sense of pain and shame, and the desire for punishment expressed by the first-person narrator of *Red Sorghum* may appear somewhat peculiar. Indeed, what is the relevance of Ah Q, whose character is such that he seems to be just the opposite of Mo Yan's self-detesting narrator? Anyone familiar with the story knows that Ah Q never seems to suffer from much psychological pain or a sense of shame. He is always able to turn pain or shame into a self-deceiving narrative and see himself as the winner when he is actually being bullied. Lu Xun's creation of this character, as it is generally understood, is aimed at showing, and therefore criticizing, the absurdity of such a mentality, which Lu Xun believed to be central to the Chinese psyche (otherwise known as the Chinese national character, *guoming xing*). In this sense, once again, what's Ah Q got to do with my discussion here? Part of the answer lies in the fact that Ah Q is also evoked by the post-Mao intellectuals themselves and in the historical implications that accompany such evocations.

In a (re)reading of Lu Xun's character offered by Liu Zaifu and Lin Gang, the two critics revisit the psychology of Ah Q.[14] They argue for a need to reexamine in the 1980s Ah Q's psychology, and focus their critique on the essence of Ah Q's *jingsheng shengli fa* (a self-deceptive mentality that blindly believes in one's superiority over others). "What is its core meaning?" they ask, and

> what is Ah Q's way of thinking that supports this mentality? If we turn
> to Ah Q's behavior, we may find some revelations. Throughout his life,
> Ah Q is a complete failure. From the moment when he appeared in the
> Wei Village and was taken to Master Zhao's home where he was slapped
> to the time when he was executed after drawing a circle [a substitute for
> a signature due to his illiteracy] at the court, he suffered a lot and was
> always badly treated. . . . However, despite his actual situation in which
> he was constantly subject to bullying and unfair treatment, subjec-
> tively, he never realized his life was a big failure. What is more, after
> every mistreatment, he managed to turn it into a psychological success.
> To Ah Q, therefore, such is the real and most satisfactory success. . . . All
> he has is one treasure—his *jingsheng shengli fa*.[15]

The absurdity of Ah Q's psychology, as these two critics state, lies in his lack of self-awareness and an inability to feel pain and shame as social norms would have him feel. The subversiveness of the *jingsheng shengli fa,* if there is such, not only does not change the reality but also brings him more suffering. Ah Q represents stagnancy and a lack of desire for change. Most of all, according to Liu and Lin, he represents a lack of consciousness of one's own suffering and pain.

Obviously, Ah Q is evoked here because of his negative implications, espe-cially because of his lack of any sense of pain and suffering. As part of the post-Mao intellectual endeavor, Mo Yan's narrator's strong expression of shame and a desire to be punished can undoubtedly be understood as a direct negation of what Ah Q represents. And yet one wonders why this negation has to entail self-contempt, and because of this, one also wonders whether the former is in fact more than just a negation of the latter. With these questions, Ah Q, as I will demonstrate shortly, becomes more relevant in my discussion than otherwise might appear.

To get to that point, however, I need to bring into the picture the notion of masochism. It is a concept that specifically concerns male subjectivity that appears to be on the margins. As such, I find some existing and contested interpretations of the concept in the West potentially useful. More specifically, curious about the connection between the "I" in Mo's novel and Lu Xun's Ah Q, I wonder why, though both display what can be seen as a masochistic tendency, each registers different (and sometimes opposite) intellectual responses. So by way of a discussion of masochism, I will explore the implications of the contempt expressed by Mo's narrator in conjunction with Ah Q for a better understanding of the former's displayed self-contempt.

(Male) Masochism: Understanding the Politics of Pain and Suffering

For Freud, masochism is first and foremost a form of sexual perversion in which men want to be punished. It is characterized as neurotic, with anxiety as its primary symptom. Although similar to most of Freud's concepts, which were developed in a clinical context in his efforts to understand abnormality or perversions, it is nevertheless one of the notions frequently used by later critics to understand certain forms of interpersonal and social relations. As Deleuze argues, according to Silverman, although "the suffering position is almost necessarily male," it does not have to be pathological.[16] Expanding the notion into the social realms, Freud divided it into three forms, feminine, masculine, and moral masochisms, the last being the most important.[17] His interest lay in exploring a seeming contradiction between the pleasure principle and a desire for punishment. "For," Freud wonders aloud, "if mental processes are governed by the pleasure principle in such a way that their first aim is the avoidance of unpleasure and the obtaining of pleasure, masochism is incomprehensible."[18] Whether or not one agrees with Freud's taking the pleasure principle as a given and a seemingly self-evident concept, my interest here lies in the sociocultural implications suggested by this paradox and by Freud's characterization of moral masochism as unconscious (a concept, understood in today's theoretical context, that alludes to the sociocultural and historical components of the human psyche).

Since Freud, definitions of masochism vary depending on what the theorists emphasize.[19] Besides Deleuze, Kaja Silverman also uses this notion extensively in her discussion of masculinity at the margins. Because of the relevance of the subject matter of her book to that of mine (i.e., male subjectivity and marginality), I want to focus on her reformulation of the concept a little more. In Silverman's reading of Freud's masochism, she sees a binary relationship between pain and "end-pleasure." The binary, according to her, is specifically demonstrated in Freud's definition of moral/social masochism—a Christian masochism, for example—in which a person endures pain for the benefit of the end-pleasure, namely, the promised paradise. Understood in this sense, masochism implies a passivity that always fails to challenge the existing social order.

As such, Silverman argues, Freud's writings on moral/social masochism are problematic precisely because they are subject to binary oppositions (especially between pain and end-pleasure) that offer no alternatives for change. As a counter move, she proposes to explore the social implications of the role of perversion by focusing on its "libidinal politics." Such a move, she argues, can help shift away from, transcend, and subvert those binaries "upon which the social order rests."[20] Instead of focusing on the Freudian binary opposition between pain and end-pleasure, therefore, Silverman suggests one examine the notions of pain, suspense, and end-pleasure independently, outside of the binaries, to see how they relate to each other in other ways. She contends that masochists do not necessarily desire an end-pleasure through punishment. "The masochist," she argues, "in fact seeks out punishment"; "some individuals' pleasure might actually inhere in pain and in the psychic destabilization to which it leads" (199). This happens when a man "leaves his social identity completely behind—actually abandons his 'self'—and passes over into the 'enemy terrain' of femininity," and "does not there manifest any desire to fill his [father's] boots" (189–90, 212). (This reminds me of the Taoist alternative to social norms, which is believed by many to be embedded in the social and cultural mechanisms of various Chinese societies or, for that matter, as being embodied by Ah Q. However, there is a twist, which I will explore shortly.)

Silverman's efforts are aimed at theorizing the resistance value of the "real perverts" who defy norms by not wanting to escape pain (or by refusing to experience pain as such). If masochism represents a perversion to Freud, Silverman hopes to erase the negativity attached to the notion and argues for the resistance and agency that exist, as she sees it, in this "perversion," in which the key to the resistance is when the masochist "knows how to transform punishment into pleasure, and severity into bliss" (213).

I quote Silverman extensively for a reason. The tactic she advocates and the new paradigm she hopes to establish for discovering agency in late capitalist society hinge on a masochistic model that seeks out pain for pleasure and rejects end-pleasure, which signifies the "dominant fiction" or the status quo (of postcapitalism).[21] Interestingly, however, the essence of her argument does not seem entirely new to the Chinese, especially if we remember the main character in Lu Xun's "The True Story of Ah Q."

If we take this character out of proper context for a moment, we can see that in many ways Ah Q is a quintessential example of the (male) masochist discussed by Silverman. Anyone who is familiar with the story can recall why this character may be identified as such: he is a village idiot whose aimlessness and wondrous status constantly subject him to people's ridicule. At the same time, however, he is also an expert in transforming punishment into something else, so that he not only deflects the pain but also finds pleasure in it. Whenever he is beaten up, for example, he turns the punishment into pleasure by resorting to (an unconscious play with) the normal social order: he says that he was (only) beaten by his "son" and then he feels as if he had won the fight (morally) while completely oblivious to his suffering of just one minute earlier. In traditional China, as we know, social relations were governed by the *sangang* hierarchy, the three cardinal guides: ruler guides subject, father guides son, and husband guides wife. By seeing himself as the one that guides (for example, as the father), Ah Q always manages, in his mind, to place the tormenter in an inferior position, a mental twist that helps diminish or, to use Freud's word, defuse the pain inflicted on him and even make him feel pleased. After each punishment, therefore, Ah Q quickly forgets what has just happened to him, gets himself into the same situation, and the same scenario repeats itself.

In short, Ah Q's psychic pattern fits that which Silverman attempts to argue for and theorize. Even though Silverman emphasizes seeking out pain for pleasure as a form of resistance and one may argue that Ah Q does not actively do so, it still remains to be seen whether there is an inherent resisting value in this seeking-for-pain model of masochism. Indeed, placed in the context of Silverman's search for an alternative psychic relation to the Law of the Father, Ah Q appears to be an ideal candidate for analysis.

The irony here (and it is an important one) is that Ah Q was created by Lu Xun to symbolize the negative national character of the Chinese people. Ah Q's tactic, *jingsheng shengli fa,* was meant to be viewed by the Chinese (intellectuals) as a barrier to change rather than a possibility for personal transformation or as a subversive act. What we have, therefore, is a discrepancy between Silverman's desire to see certain examples of (male) masochism as a way to "negotiate a different psychic relation to the Laws of Language and kinship structure than that dictated by the dominant fiction" (212) and Ah Q, who was created by Lu Xun as representative of the negative characteristics of the Chinese psyche. According to Lu Xun's perspective, Ah Q's psychological indifference to pain and his inability to stop inflicting pain on himself amount to nothing more than his continuing to operate on his own fantasies. And his fantasies, perceived within the context of modern Chinese history, appear to be totally self-defeating. When viewed from Silverman's perspective, on the other hand, Ah Q would seem to be a positive model because he operates on a "different psychic relation." Accompanied by such words as "abandon," "leave," "rejects," and "passes over," Ah Q the masochist—one that resembles or fits Silverman's description—appears to be somebody who is actively seeking to pervert himself; he is, in other words, an active masochist.

The activist nature of the masochist invoked by Silverman, we must realize, is overdetermined by the theoretical move on her part to search for agency provoked by the contemporary Western theoretical context. Her overall argument must be understood within the context where the question of (male) subjectivity is also overdetermined by postcapitalist conditions. It is in this context that her stance is to be understood as one that hopes to find the values in the adjunct, in hopes of discovering new forms of agency. But at the same time, her model not only cannot escape the fact that "masochism in all of its guises is as much a product of the existing symbolic order as a reaction against it," as she herself acknowledges (212), but also, when viewed in a different context (the context in which Ah Q is portrayed and understood, for example), may not be able to demonstrate its radical nature either.

Even though Ah Q was meant to represent the mentality constructed by Chinese traditional culture, he was also created as a modern project for Chinese intellectuals. The character, in other words, was created to personify the central weakness of the Chinese psyche, viewed by Lu Xun, against the modern context, as a lack of self-recognition and self-protection. In comparison with Silverman's positive view of masochism, therefore, Chinese intellectuals such as Lu Xun would not be inclined to see Ah Q's mentality as signifying a "journey and trajectory of reaching the 'enemy terrain'" taken by the Chinese male subject. Nor would they praise it as the Chinese male self "completely abandoning the self" or as his outright refusal "to fill [the father's] boots." In the modern Chinese context, the opposite is true. As part of their desire and urge to become modern, Chinese intellectuals have continued to feel the need to call for an awakening of, as opposed to an abandoning of, the (male) self, and hence their rejection of Ah Q and his psyche.

The question now is this: If Chinese intellectuals reject Ah Q's way of negotiating a psychic relation with the laws of language and kinship structure, what is *their* preferred way of negotiation? When they call for a recognition—an awakening—of one's self, what do they do with the pain that is thereby realized? Here, we need to return to Freud's definition of moral/social masochism for further analysis. And perhaps not so coincidentally, I find that the self-loathing "I" in Mo Yan's novel, the one who appears to wallow in a painful attack on himself, signifies an inner split that is to a degree reminiscent of the Freudian moral/social masochist living in "suspense."

According to Silverman's interpretation, suspense has a "double face": "It signifies both the endless postponement of libidinal gratification, and the perpetual state of anxiety and apprehension which is the result of that renunciation and the super-ego's relentless surveillance." Furthermore, "forms of suspense are not limited to the moral masochist; they are also part of the cultural legacy of even the most conventionally structured subjects" (200–201). The usefulness of the notion of suspense lies in the fact that it illuminates what I see as a paradox central to the self-loathing sentiment in question: a desire to be free and to satisfy one's "libidinal gratification" by becoming a "real man," and an anxiety on the part of the self wanting to be able to respond to a higher order, to something sublime that ultimately transcends the self. The "I" in Mo's novel is the self who lives precisely in this suspense, punishing himself for the sake of and in hope of something else.

The next question is obvious: What is this something else? And what is its relationship with the (male) subject in question? Even though her point is to move away from Freud's focus on the Christian version of masochism, Silverman's description of the moral/social masochist is relevant (and I quote it here for clarification). Using Christian masochism as an example, Silverman interprets the moral/social masochist this way:

> The Christian . . . lives his or her life in perpetual anticipation of the second coming. The figural meaning which this anticipation implants in present sufferings makes it possible for them to be savored as future pleasures, with time folding over itself in such a way as to permit that retroactivity to be already experienced now, in a moment prior to its affectivity. Such is the fundamental perverse nature of Christian suspense and the pain it sanctifies and irritates, a suspense which works against anything approximating psychic coherence. (200)

For that end-pleasure, the Christian is willing to endure pain, and even "seeks to increase rather than decrease [the] tension" between "the endless postponement of libidinal gratification, and the perpetual state of anxiety" (200). The moral/social masochist, that is, increases the tension by undertaking the suffering for the purpose of *the greater good*. The presence of a greater good is what lies behind the rejection of Ah Q in contemporary China (and, for that matter, in Mo's narrator's voice).

(Male) Shame and Suffering as Redemption

In their reappraisal of Lu Xun's creation of Ah Q, Liu and Lin, like many critics before (and since) them, insist that Ah Q should be seen as a negative (symbolic) mirror for self-reflection and self-examination in contemporary China. They reiterate that in the case of Ah Q, the unforgivable sin is his indifference toward pain (they do not see Ah Q as seeking pain) and his tactic of alleviating it via self-deception. Any modern (Chinese) person looking into the mirror of Ah Q, they argue (also like many critics before them), must realize that Ah Q's model has gotten him (as well as China) nothing but pain, suffering, and, above all, a marginal position. They make the link between Ah Q and what they see as the traditional cultural elements (such as Buddhism and Taoism) embedded in this character. They argue, for example, that the ability (cultivated in Taoism) to retreat into one's inner world (or to nature) hinders the development of a mentality that aims to change the world.[22] (Incidentally, these critics use "traditional culture" rather broadly; in many ways, their use of the term encompasses a mishmash of the various social and religious theologies that in one way or another have played a major role throughout Chinese history.) To remedy all this, Liu and Lin make the following remarks, considering specifically the necessity for experiencing pain (i.e., becoming aware of it but not seeking it):

> Human suffering starts with learning. . . . The story of Adam and Eve embodies a deep metaphor: wisdom is defined as/by pain. The world is [made] this way, so is human life. Human beings have no alternative but to take and confront pain. It is the first step in their lives. Only from taking this step can there be future and promise. Human beings have to create their own future through experiencing endless pains and worries. Only in this way can we find a way to survive, to develop, and to create a more beautiful living environment.[23]

What is significant in this quote is the last two sentences, where the two critics finally make the link between pain and the greater good. Like Lu Xun, they want to awaken more people from the "iron house" to *feel* the pain and to *see* their own ugly image (in Ah Q). More than Lu Xun, however, they connect pain closely with an end-pleasure or a greater good, which in their words is "a more beautiful living environment," thereby foregrounding a suspense as *the* place to be (in which the Chinese must experience "endless pains and worries") before they reach that end.

There is, of course, nothing wrong in wanting and creating "a more beautiful living environment." What is at issue is the meaning of such a greater good—what it is, who defines it, and to whom it ultimately belongs—and the role of the self in relation to it, namely, in what ways he is sustained (or unable to be sustained) by such a greater good. In the modern Chinese context, the meaning of greater good cannot be separated from China's quest for modernization (and for modernity). Manifested in concrete terms, such a quest has in fact always been entangled with what Benjamin Schwartz, in his analysis of Yan Fu's thought and its historical implications, calls a Chinese "search [for] wealth and power."[24] Put more plainly, it is a modern project that desires a modernization modeled on the material success of the West. In the late twentieth century, when China's intellectuals are once again made to confront Western modernization and its glamour, the two contemporary critics' view of the "more beautiful living environment" continues to echo that search started and advocated by intellectuals such as Yan Fu more than a century ago. Ah Q, perceived in this context, would also continue to appear ill-fitted and ill-prepared to undertake such a search.

What is lacking in Ah Q's mentality, therefore, is a connection with this greater good. The quintessential example is his mental habit of affirming a decaying hierarchical system that does not sustain him, and his wish to transfer shame and humiliation onto the other (his tormenter) without having to change his way of thinking and feeling. His deep connection with the past (and therefore his inability to connect with what intellectuals believe needs to be changed for China to modernize) is the essence of Ah Q's problem.

By (re)setting Ah Q up as a negative image that symbolizes the Chinese national character and by linking the need for suspense with the purpose of achieving the (modern) greater good as an ultimate end-pleasure, the two critics urge the Chinese people to become more sensitive to the pain inflicted on them by outside forces (be it state power or the West). More specifically, they urge the Chinese to realize the shame associated with the pathetic nature of the character of Ah Q. It is, one can say, contemporary Chinese male intellectuals' maneuvering to resensitize shame by way of resensitizing pain, all, once again, for the purpose of realizing the greater good.

The pain implied in the (imagined) chopping up of one's heart in Mo Yan's *Red Sorghum* can be understood along this line. It is this pain that is directly associated with the self-loathing and self-bashing *zazhong gaoliang,* which in turn suggests an acknowledgment of one's own lacking, a realization that entails a sense of shame. Unlike Ah Q, then, the subject sensitized by pain and shame—the author/narrator—is eager to search for a "better" identity, namely, a better—masculine—self. In the end, therefore, the call for rejecting Ah Q also transcends the level of regaining the sensation of pain and the sense of shame. It is to become aware of the self. More significantly, for the intellectuals in question, it is to recognize one's own (ugly) image reflected in the mirror of Ah Q in order to search for a new and better one (so as to find the agent for achieving the greater good).

At this point, with words and phrases like "mirror," "reflection," "recognition," and the search for a "better self," we are beginning to confront a somewhat different but a more important set of issues regarding the self-contempt in question. It goes without saying that what makes the reflection appear ugly to the (male) subject should be considered one of the consequences of China's modern encounter with the West. The implications effected by such an encounter have generated and continue to generate a strong self-awareness. Such an awareness has, throughout modern Chinese history, generated various responses and efforts to strengthen both the national standing of China and the mentality of its people. In the 1980s, as we can see, the efforts continue, albeit with their own historically conditioned idiosyncracy. Part of its idiosyncratic manifestation is a strong male self-contempt, which in essence manifests a male desire for a better self. The question, then, is: Where does he turn to look for it? One seemingly paradoxical answer, which (perhaps not so ironically) is found in the manifestations themselves, is: himself. To clarify this point before I turn to Mo Yan's novel for textual evidence, I want to take a brief look at the relationship between self-loathing and self-love.

From Self-Loathing to Self-Love: Searching for a Better Self

When translated into psychoanalytic terms, self-love means narcissism. Originating in the Greek mythological figure Narcissus, who falls in love with his own image reflected in the water, narcissism means, simply, the love of self. Although what we have here, as the textual examples from *Red Sorghum* show, appears to suggest just the opposite—self-loathing—according to Freud's interpretation of narcissism, there is nothing incompatible between the two. In fact, self-love, according to Freud, is manifested precisely through the self's awareness of criticism (or rejection) from the other, which in turn generates pain and an instinct to preserve one's self, with the self turning inward. The manifestation of such a psychic activity often takes the form of shame. Shame, in turn, generates intense dissatisfaction toward the self, hence the self-loathing sentiment.

Narcissism understood in this sense (as a social in addition to a clinical phenomenon) cannot be formulated without what appears to be the opposite of self-love: shame and dislike of one's self. Indeed, today's Western pop psychology even goes so far as to suggest that shame is to narcissism what guilt is to neurosis, and that an increasing number of Westerners are suffering from a strong sense of shame, which results from the formation of collective norms in the age of modern (and highly visualized) media.[25] Even though one needs to be wary of pop psychology interpretations of various social and personal problems, the claim indicates one thing that is tangibly connected to my discussion: the sociocultural implications embedded in the notion of narcissism.

In "On Narcissism: An Introduction," Freud identifies pain as the very basis on which the fundamental problematics reside. From the role of the physical pain suffered by a sick person to its metaphorical function, Freud states, "It is possible that for every . . . change in the erotogenicity of the organs there is a parallel change in the libidinal cathexis in the ego. In such factors may lie the explanation of what is at the bottom of hypochondria and what it is that can have upon the distribution of the libido the same effect as actual organic disease."[26] In this sense, the formulation of the ego/self is shown as materially based on the complex relationship of bodily senses to the outside world in which the ego/self is said to be constantly challenged to learn to manage what is experienced as pain or painful, or, in Freud's term, as the "damming-up of libido in the ego" (42).

To the question why a "damming-up of libido in the ego" should be experienced as painful, Freud says, "There I shall content myself with the answer that 'pain' is in general the expression of increased tension, and thus a *quantity* of the material event is, here as elsewhere, transformed into the *quality* of 'pain' in mind" (42). Pain, in other words, can be experienced both physically and mentally. When experiencing pain in both ways, the person stops loving, and this, according to Freud, is psychically necessary for self-preservation; it also plays a crucial part in the formation (or damaging) of the ego. It is especially the case when, "as he develops, he is disturbed by the admonitions of others and [when] his own critical judgement is awakened" (51). Such an awakening, related to pain, is part of the psychic-economic where the relationship between the (narcissistic) self and the outside world will be formulated, and which, also according to Freud, paves the "paths leading to object-choice" as a way to recover a new form of an ego-ideal. The aim of Freud's theory, and the reason I have quoted him here, is to argue that the formation of the self is deeply entangled with the external world and that part of the formation cannot escape the role of standards and ideals of the (psychologically specific) social reality. And interacting with them (in the Lacanian sense, entering the language and Symbolic order) can be painful.

In his interpretation and critique of Freud's theoretical formulation of narcissism, Jean Laplanche points out that "the discovery of narcissism as a kind of object-choice and as a mode of identification, in fact, provides an indispensable clue" to a better way of understanding the concept.[27] In Laplanche's interpretation of narcissism, he takes us back to the question of *identification*. Any identification, according to Laplanche, involves object, process, and result, which are "reciprocally and rigorously related." And such "is the case with the genesis of the ego" (80). The concrete nature of the object-choice, the process, and the result of any identification, I might add, has to be socially, culturally, and historically conditioned. With this, we have reached the point where my evocation of Freud and Laplanche leads: how self-loathing in Mo Yan's narrator is in fact self-love manifested by the male subject's object-choice, namely, the representations of the masculine hero: the grandfather.

As I have suggested, both the loathing of the self and the desire for a better one hinge on a recognition of the author/narrator's own ugliness. With the recognition comes a desire to *identify* with a more desirable object (so as to preserve the self). In the novel, the more desirable object is a strong and masculine male figure, someone—according to two of the four narcissistic object-choices defined by Freud—the subject himself "would like to be" and someone "who was [or was believed to be] once part of himself."[28] Accordingly, it is this narcissistic object-choice that in Mo's novel manages to transform some of the grandfather's ignoble behavior—robbery, murder, drunkenness—into desirable masculine qualities, which the first-person narrator desires to recover (as "once part of himself"). It is also in this sense I now turn to examine the representations of the grandfather (and his masculine qualities) in Mo's novel, and I do so in conjunction with a popular phrase found in post–Cultural Revolution China: *xunzhao ziwo,* or "looking for the self." The masculine grandfather is part of the search in which the male self is looking for himself.

The Masculine Self and the Irony of *Zazhong gaoliang*

In *Red Sorghum,* there are two sets of immediate and biological father-son relationships: the narrator's grandfather and father, and the narrator and his father. Although narratively the story line is focused on the lives of the grandparents, especially that of the grandfather, and although the novel portrays the father-son relationship between the grandfather and the father while deliberately leaving the narrator's own relationship with his father conspicuously missing, symbolically the identification in question does not take place in either of these relationships. It takes place elsewhere.

Even though there is no grandfather-grandson relationship in the story itself, the first-person narrator deliberately presents his relationship with the former by bringing himself directly into the narrative toward the end of the novel (when he goes to visit his ancestors' tombs and engages in a mental dialogue with his Second Grandmother). There, the narrator communicates with his forefathers and listens to the reprimand, delivered to him by his grandfather's second mistress, for having lost the purity, sincerity, and the essence of being red sorghum. His grandfather, as we can judge from the whole story, represents everything that the ugly "I" is not but should be. The grandfather's masculine qualities, filtered through the ink of the writer's pen, turn him into an archetypal (male) hero, whose myth is meant to be repeated, reevoked, and, above all, (re)erected as a (modern) masculine identity. Before I expand on what I mean by modern masculine identity, we need to understand the image of the grandfather as portrayed by Mo Yan.

What kind of unsung hero is this man? In the novel, there are several thematic threads involving him, and together they weave a story of a peasant who supposedly lived an uninhibited life. The first and perhaps most significant thread pertains to his role as a self-proclaimed commander of a group of bandits. As noted in my earlier brief description, this phase of his life involves a variety of actions carried out under his command, ranging from robbery to murder to fighting against Japanese invaders. His relationship with the Japanese is a key structural element that maintains part of the novel's historical significance and weight. For the most part, he is portrayed as a free spirit rejecting control by any of those groups. He is not, in other words, a man made of doctrines represented by other groups but one who relies on his own instinct and bravery. This celebrated independence signifies a negation of the dominant ideology and constitutes a not so subtle criticism of part of recent Chinese history and of what the "I's" generation does not possess.

The second thread comes from the grandfather's relationship with two women, Jiuer and Lianer. In portraying these relationships, the narrator also emphasizes the free-spiritedness of the grandfather, a peasant who defies conventions. He saves Jiuer from a marriage to a leper by killing the man; he then maintains an illicit relationship with her without ever marrying her. By presenting the relationship in this way, the novel manages to depict the sexual relationship between the two as untamed by conventions, wild, and (supposedly) close to nature. Just as the grandfather is a hero wandering in and out of the sorghum fields, his male potency is also associated with those fields, where his first illicit relationship with Jiuer is consummated. The wild nature of his sexual relationship with Lianer, on the other hand, comes from the untamed sexual power of the woman herself. Because he is a free-spirited man, Jiuer's anger and jealousy do not stop him from going to Lianer. In this triangular relationship, Yu Zhanao is a man loyal mainly to his own needs and desire, a man supposedly closer to nature than to culture. Both women, incidentally, die at the hands of the Japanese soldiers, and their deaths, especially that of Lianer, are depicted in an extremely graphic and gruesome way, thereby once again situating the novel in the weightiness of history (i.e., the Chinese resistance against the Japanese invasion during the 1930s and 1940s and the potentially explosive nature of the memory of the atrocities committed by the invaders).

The third thread stems from Yu Zhanao's role as a father, but not in a conventional sense; he is not married to the child's mother and the child calls him *gandie* ("adoptive father"). Like his other activities, the fathering also takes place mostly in the wilderness of sorghum fields, where he hopes to make the son into a fighter. In the chapter titled "Dog's Path," for example, the story centers on the two when the grandfather takes the narrator's father to shoot packs of dogs that have run wild and are fighting over the dead bodies left after the rampage through the village by the Japanese invaders. The dogs take on the symbolic role of the invaders and thus become the peasants' enemies. The father-son relationship depicted during this fight is concentrated on how the former teaches the latter in a most inhumane environment to look for and maintain human dignity. Another telling moment of Yu's role as a father takes place when his son's sexual organ is wounded and may be permanently damaged. Yu is so determined to save his son's organ—*gen,* or "root," is his word—that he makes his daughter-in-law-to-be massage the organ back to sensitivity!

In short, the grandfather is a peasant (supposedly) without any trace of ideological construction. His unconventionality, as we can see, hinges partly on his earthiness, which the novel celebrates. This earthiness resembles the primitivity identified by Rey Chow in *Primitive Passions,* which, through what she terms "'primitivism' in politicized modernity," turns the grandfather, a common man, into a mythical character.[29] Together with his natural surroundings, whose intense beauty and pure quality are symbolized by stretches of red sorghum fields, a fiery red color that floats above the heads of the sorghum, the pitch-black silt lying at the bottom of the Moshui River, and the crystal-clear water that flows over the river bed, the grandfather is represented as a hero who is, in essence, as pure, vital, transparent, and wild as that beautiful natural world. The image of a masculine (and therefore better) self is thus established.

In his understanding of the film *Red Sorghum,* Wang Yuejin concludes that the masculine traits of the grandfather were never the ideal male traits traditionally aspired to in China and that, if anything, they were despised by the (patriarchal) elite establishment. Therefore, he argues, one should not take seriously the celebratory representations in the film of such male activities as drinking, drunkenness, killing, and fighting. These seemingly masculine traits, he effectively concludes, are not what modern Chinese men aspire to either. What is not taken into consideration in this argument, as I mentioned in the first chapter, are the historical context and the psychological condition affected by that context. These masculine traits are evoked and aestheticized for a reason. Though it may be true that those particular traits are not what modern Chinese men aspire to, it is the historical context in which these traits are represented and exonerated that is at issue here, and the modern Chinese context in which the rather crude masculinity embodied by the grandfather is glorified or beautified. In the context of the modern(ist) aesthetic order, Chinese men are not necessarily aspiring to become a *junzi* (a Confucian-style gentleman) but are definitely encouraged to be a *nanzihan* (a manly or masculine man). The *nanzihan* qualities celebrated as such are conditioned by a context within which modern Chinese male intellectuals continue to struggle for recognition.

Indeed, the modernity of this context is much emphasized by some Chinese critics, even though the point they intend to make differs from mine. According to Li Tuo, for example, writers like Mo Yan are invested in modernism as well as in going back to traditional Chinese culture. Modernism and Chinese traditional culture, Li argues, are not contradictory but complementary; together they "create a Chinese literature of both international and national characteristics."[30] For Rey Chow, alternatively, the turn to the primitive made by some contemporary Chinese filmmakers is to be understood in the complex context of a Chinese maneuver to undercut the West by assimilating a foreign—Western—media to search for one's own ethnography. Chow's argument offers a postcolonial way out for Mo's primitive passions by granting it an ethnographic value in the current global context and an implicit explanation as to why his novels are more easily translated (both into the visual and into the West) than many other Chinese writers'. More important, according to Chow's reading of Chinese contemporary primitive passions, the primitivity, understood in the postcolonial context, can be translated into an "active force in life" that offers the possibility of neither Western nor Eastern representation of a non-Western culture.[31]

There is, however, a difference between Zhang Yimou's film version of *Red Sorghum* and Mo's novel: the film does not treat the grandfather as the same kind of hero as in the novel; in fact, the grandfather in the film is not even the main character, the grandmother is. Because of this difference, which may affect Chow's conclusion in her argument about Chinese primitive passions, I want to make the following observation: in the novel, the heroic grandfather signifies a different kind of ethnography in which his glorification raises the question of the "ethnographer," namely, the narrator, and the issue of identity. Besides the political implications and the new aesthetic values embedded in the image of the grandfather, the latter also constitutes the new self the "I" is in search of.

This leads me back to the question of identification. It is clear by now that the grandfather, who appears to embody a new ethnographic possibility for modern Chinese men, is represented as an alternative father figure that the grandson hopes to identify with. It is on that level that the latter aspires to find a way out of his own ugliness. It is also on that level that we can see another allegorical implication: this alternative father figure is embraced by many male Chinese writers of the 1980s as both a negation and a way out of the CCP's dogmatic ideology and its version of history. If we recall Li Tuo's words here, what Mo's novel does, through a combination of modernism and a return to traditional culture, is to doubly negate the anti-Western and antitraditional or iconoclastic nature of the CCP's ideology, along with the Party's dogmatic notion of literature. What Li fails to point out, of course, is that the return to the traditional (in post–Cultural Revolution literature) is not a simple return; it is realized by way of borrowing Western humanism and modernism, and its evocations of the past, the remote, and the primitive constitute the desire of a modern male self who is in search of a renewed identity. That is, even though the grandfather signifies the author/narrator's search for an alternative father figure—hence a new self-image—who is not contaminated by the problems of the modern age, especially those that characterize modern China, the desire, nevertheless, is a modern one conditioned (or, for that matter, contaminated) precisely by the problems facing modern China.

The dynamics and the problematics of this identification, interestingly enough, are further echoed and exemplified by Liu Heng's story "Fuxi Fuxi" (Ju Dou). In this story, echoing Mo's novel (and perhaps not so coincidentally), is a similar pattern regarding father-son relationships. At the same time, however, the story focuses on the middle generation—the equivalent of the generation of Mo's narrator's father—who, though conspicuously missing in Mo's novel, is nevertheless the main character and is portrayed as physically strong (potent) and psychologically weaker. But my interest in bringing up Liu's story here is not because of the main character. Rather, I am interested in the third generation represented by Yang Tianbai, the (illegitimate) son of Yang Tianqing, and more specifically, by his choice of identification.

In "Fuxi Fuxi," Yang Tianqing is the nephew of Yang Jinshan, an old rich peasant who relates to the former as uncle, foster father, and master simultaneously. The relationship between the two, therefore, resembles one between father and son. Meanwhile, Tianqing also develops an illicit relationship with the old man's young wife, Huang Judou, with whom he has a son named Tianbai. On the one hand, Tianqing is portrayed as a young man with a strong body filled with male desire that bursts out in rebellion when he forms a secret relationship with the old man's young wife, a scenario that at least superficially reminds one of the Oedipus story. On the other hand (and it is also what is interesting about this story), Tianqing's triumph is not one that is represented ceremoniously. Instead, he is described as being fearful of the consequences of his illicit relationship: he refuses to run away with Judou (when she suggests it) because he is afraid of leaving the land; he rushes to look for the old man when the latter fails to return home on time; and he suspects Judou and accuses her of killing the old man when he is found dead. Even though to a large extent he has defeated the old man, he remains on the margins both out of his own fears and because he, among others, cannot claim that he is the real father of Tianbai.

In the next father-son relationship, that of Tianbai and Tianqing, the implications are more complex. As the child grows up and learns (through rumor) about the illicit relationship between his mother and Tianqing, he rejects his real father outright and is portrayed as one who is cold-hearted, violent, hateful, and above all preferring to identify Yang Jinshan as his real father. His existence as Tianqing's real son and his refusal to acknowledge him leave Tianqing in complete despair. Throughout the story, the two are publicly known as cousins of the same generation. The naming of the two with the same middle name, Tian, indicating that they belong to the same generation, not only further consolidates their relationship in the family tree of the Yangs but also effectively eliminates the possibility of one being the father of the other. Structurally, therefore, they have to respond to the old man's generation in the same way: they are his "sons." Although an important part of both their identities is not acknowledged, Tianqing certainly appears more pathetic—as a man without a family and offspring—in the eyes of the villagers and in his own mind. The strongest protest (or is it also a form of self-punishment?) that he can stage is to kill himself (although in the film *Ju Dou* he is killed by his son).

The alternative ending in the film makes one wonder further about the role of his son: What does it mean in this context when the son rejects his real father by destroying him? Does it alleviate the inner struggle of the self by externalizing the cause of his destruction? Either way—whether Tianqing is killed by himself or by his son—however, Tianbai appears to have the upper hand. His position can come only from his outright rejection of Tianqing's role as his father, and this rejection, I repeat, identifies him directly with his father in name. Additionally and importantly, by way of rejecting his own bastard status, Tianbai manages to transfer the illicit status onto Tianqing and forces him eventually to occupy the bastard status in the eyes of the "father."

Although there exists in Liu's story a degree of criticism aimed at the mindless and destructive nature of the third generation and although there is some sympathy expressed toward Yang Tianqing, the latter, nevertheless, belongs to the weak and the pitiful and is stuck with his transferred bastard status. This status, coming back to Mo's novel, is precisely what the "I" professes to reject. In rejecting his own father—by not showing him as an adult and as a significant figure in the novel and by conflating the father's adulthood with the deterioration of the existing power structure—the "I," like Tianbai, subscribes himself symbolically to an alternative father figure.

This, however, is not the end of the story. The symbolic transference (away from bastard status) manifested in both stories is enabled, narratively, by a modernist radicalism. As Rey Chow points out, this is a radicalism that stems from a modern paradigm in which Western modernism seeks a way out of its own condition by turning toward "primitive" cultures—or, in this case, a (supposedly) traditional past. It is this combination, modernism and primitivity, that in post–Cultural Revolution Chinese literature has functioned as a possible ticket for Chinese men to move away from the margins, or better yet (and in Silverman's words), from the "enemy camp."

More important (and perhaps not so ironically), this combination is itself hybrid—and bastard—in nature. This hybridity (aided by modernist radicalism in combining Western modernist sensibility and Chinese tradition) is what ultimately helps blur the distinction between red sorghum and hybrid/bastard sorghum and effectively uplifts the latter in direct identification with the former (and vice versa).

Zazhong gaoliang as a Desired Masculine Identity

In the end, *zazhong gaoliang* is *hong gaoliang,* or, better yet, this particular bastard status is meant to be shown as masculine. Together they constitute the essence of the desired masculine identity.

In the epilogue (originally a speech) of her book *Tuwei biaoyan* (Performing "Breaking out of an encirclement"), Can Xue, one of few Chinese women writers who dared to take on the male literary establishment of the 1980s, voices her critique of the male desire represented in the literature of the era. Assuming a straight face and pretending to discuss and celebrate new literary trends and criticism in contemporary Chinese literature, she satirizes it by way of parodying male writers such as Mo Yan.

She begins by explaining why the title of her speech is "*Yanggang zhiqi yu wenxue pinglun de dahao shiguang*" (Masculinity and the heyday of literary criticism). A male *zhanyou* (comrade-in-arms) of hers, she relates, titled it for her when he learned that she had been invited to give a talk at a literary conference. He complained that he should have been the one to be invited, for he knew all about the importance of today's literature. "What does a woman have to say?" he asked. "Such questions should be answered by men. And not any kind of men, but those who have deep philosophical knowledge about things and who have also maintained their masculinity."[32]

As he went on, Can Xue writes, he became increasingly angry, so much so that he kicked her tea table and stomped it into pieces before taking off. Can Xue comments, "Comrades, I must say that it was well done. In this ancient country of ours with its thousands of years of feudal control, he undoubtedly kicked awake human nature and his kicks are the prelude of the birth of a new people" (336). Then, by way of explaining where this comrade-in-arms originates, she parodies Mo's stories of his grandparents and other male writers' representations of men of the past:

> His hometown is in the country where all his ancestors were bandits. The village raises so many dogs to bite strangers that no outsiders can go in. It is a special village situated on top of a mountain which is covered by clouds and fog all year round. The village consists of eight hundred strong men and bewitching women with bound feet. . . . Every evening at sunset, the mountains would be filled with unconstrained and sexually suggestive songs. (336–37)

Her parodying represents what Can Xue sees as the essence of male representations of the past: men then were potent and masculine.

The most amusing and poignant satirical observation in Can Xue's speech comes from her retelling of a story about a legendary figure named Lao Meng (old fool), an eighty-year-old man best known for his sexual potency, who is clearly set up to parody the grandfather in Mo's novel. "What is masculinity?" she asks, tongue in cheek. "Isn't it true that all we are looking for is embodied in Lao Meng? Our number one task now, then, is to salvage our ancient culture which is on the verge of extinction and to make sure that Lao Meng's masculinity will be inherited by the younger generations" (340).

As writers, she goes on, "our task is to set up a Lao Meng–like model."

> This model must be most masculine among all masculine men . . . when he sings on a mountain, his voice must overwhelm all the voices;

his spare-time life must be both sublime and tragically glorious. It will never take place in bed but always in a barn or wheat fields; he will never be interested in women from good families and would always have a specific interest in bound-footed women . . . he will . . . be able to make every misguided person return to his own self; he will have a special aesthetic interest in the primitive lifestyle . . . finally, he must have integrity. He must achieve integrity by sitting on top of a hut to weather the elements and by chewing on hay when hungry until his superiors come in a car to take and send him abroad. Even then, he will still be reluctant to come down. The day after he returns from abroad, he will immediately climb back on the hay roof and will not come down even when others try to get him down by poking him with a bamboo post. (344–45)

The image of the masculine man here is hilarious. With a number of such amusing images apparently taken from various contemporary male writers, Can Xue manages to expose the unquestioned masculinist logic embedded in the portrayal of such a masculine man and the link between the desire of contemporary Chinese male writers and critics and their search for an alternative self-image. The poignancy of her satire lies, in part, in problematizing the male desire for masculinity and their masculinizing the past (an issue to which I will return in the next chapter).

It goes without saying that the "he" Can Xue repeatedly refers to conflates with Mo's "I." Her satire helps further reveal the implications of the self-imposed status of hybrid/bastard sorghum. In Mo's novel, employed initially as negative terms denoting the ugliness or the weakness of the male subject in question, the negative images of *zazhong gaoliang* and the narrator are gradually transferred, via an identity with *hong gaoliang,* into part of the masculine propensity. Its sexually charged implications echo the search for masculinity where *zazhong* (bastard) is only one step away from *haohan* (strong and therefore masculine man). In this sense, the grandfather becomes the quintessential embodiment of a strong bastard, untainted by either modern or traditional culture. In the end, self-contempt does not entail self-denial on the part of writers such as Mo Yan. If anything, the opposite is true. The *zazhong gaoliang,* which is used to refer to the unworthy offspring of the grandfather, comes to equate with the *chunzhong gaoliang* (the pure sorghum). Through this identification, the offspring's suffering from the knowledge of his un-worthiness also gets redeemed and transformed into a form of masculinity.

In making visible the identification between the two kinds of sorghum—hybrid/bastard sorghum *is* pure red sorghum—we realize that, combined with the male desire for potency and for being *da ye* (the master), *zazhong gaoliang* or bastard in the final analysis is transformed into a desired manly identity and as such into part of post-Mao modernist discourse. The confla-tion of the two sorghums provides legitimacy to a bastard masculine identity, which in turn legitimizes male chauvinism, misogyny, and other embedded masculinist assumptions about what it means to be men and women. In the end, *zazhong gaoliang* is not so much a self-debasing as a self-endearing male identification, one that is closely associated with a strong-male image and certain male traits deemed manly. In this way, the red sorghum–enhanced bastard comes to be foregrounded as the desired male identity, to be admired and (self-)loved.

Chapter 5

Manhood, Cultural Roots,

and National Identity

The significance of Can Xue's remarks quoted in the previous chapter goes beyond satirizing a male desire for masculine identity. Her critical tone also points toward a link between this male search for a better self and a cultural phenomenon known as *wenhua xungen* ("searching for cultural roots") that saw its heyday in China during the second half of the 1980s. Indeed, the desire for manhood or masculinity and the *xunzhao ziwo* ("searching for the [male] self") phenomenon I discussed in chapter 4 should be recognized as part and parcel of the cultural ethos of the new era (*xinshiqi*, 1978–),[1] in which (male) intellectuals once again took Chinese culture to task, advocating *wenhua fansi,* or "rethinking and reexamining the culture."[2] In this chapter, I examine the link between the male search for masculine identity and the intellectual movement in search of cultural roots.

Of particular relevance to my study is the movement's most vocal and visible component: a body of literature known as *xungen wenxue* ("roots-seeking literature"), which, perhaps not accidentally, happens to have been written almost exclusively by men.[3] Incidentally, a linguistic element can be noted here to bring this male connection into greater clarity. The word *xun* (search) is found in both *xungen* and *xunzhao ziwo;* it is a transitive verb that in each case carries an object: *gen* (roots) and *ziwo* (the [male] self), respectively. What connects the two objects thematically, however, is not the verb itself. Rather, it is the invisible subject of the verb *xun,* whose presence has eluded most critics but is made visible by Can Xue in her satire of the male search for a masculine identity in the "glorious past" (of Chinese culture). In this chapter, focusing on notions of *gen* and *zhong* (seeds), I explore the ways in which the reconfiguration of male subjectivity in *xungen* literature, while functioning as a liberating space for the male subject in question, is also part of the *xungen* writers' reevocation of the essence of Chinese culture, and how the literary representations of the "historically traumatized" male subject (to borrow Silverman's term) help recenter the self via a search for cultural roots. In my examination of the roots-seeking literature, I have in mind the *desiring (male) subject* whose search for the self is ultimately conflated with a search for cultural roots.

I begin with a discussion of the existing definitions of roots-seeking both as a cultural and as a literary phenomenon. I first contextualize the search and explore the features of *xungen* literature as characterized by critics and by writers themselves. Focusing on the notion of identification, I then examine how and why certain characteristics are celebrated as representative of the essence of China's traditional past (hence cultural roots) and are in turn reestablished as the symbolic identity for Chinese culture and for the Chinese male subject simultaneously. On that symbolic level, I examine how concerns about cultural roots are in fact deeply ingrained in Chinese modernity, part of which has been a constant struggle in which intellectuals try to come to terms with China's past, present, and future. It is a legacy and an ongoing negotiation that continues to walk a fine line between asserting a cultural (and national) identity and becoming either culturally nihilistic or (male) chauvinistic, all of which can be understood as manifestations of the tension among Chinese men, issues of masculinity, and intellectuals' quest for modernity.

Xungen as a Cultural Movement: A Necessary Clarification

Even though critical attention to the *xungen* movement and literature has long since subsided in China (largely due to the fact that rapid economic changes have shifted writers' and critics' attention to modern urban settings), views from the existing discussions concerning the phenomenon remain rather enigmatic. Its political implications (i.e., its allegorical significance) notwithstanding, critics have offered different interpretations regarding the meaning of this movement. Some understand it as a post–Cultural Revolution return to the past for a renewed cultural identity, some see it as another intellectual critique of traditional Chinese culture, and still others treat it as yet another manifestation of Chinese intellectuals' pursuit of a modern utopia (Western-style).[4]

Part of the difference in definition may be effected by the word *xun* itself. When used to characterize the cultural movement, *xungen* or roots-seeking implies that there is something to be sought (from an entity called Chinese culture and its past). Because of this, it also suggests that the relationship between contemporary Chinese intellectuals and (traditional) Chinese culture is not simply antagonistic (as is assumed by some critics), with the intellectuals critiquing and attacking the culture.[5] In fact, one can argue that, almost by design, it is a term that obscures the nature of this relationship and complicates the historical significance of this cultural movement, which, given its specific context, is different from the May Fourth cultural movement (in spite of a constant identification between the two). Here, a brief historical comparison is in order.

In modern China, the role of intellectuals (as it is understood in the West today) did not truly evolve until the turn of the century, especially before and during the May Fourth movement. When it finally did evolve, intellectuals constituted a formidable force instrumental in challenging (and eventually helping to smash) the existing cultural structure based on traditional culture or *chuantong wenhua,* better known as *lijiao* (Confucian ethics). For the leading May Fourth intellectuals (such as Chen Duxiu, Li Dazhao, Hu Shi, and above all Lu Xun), traditional Chinese culture represented by Confucian codes of belief and behavior stood for everything that was inhumane in the existing Chinese social order, caused China to fall behind the Western powers and Japan, and constituted China's biggest obstacle to change, to progress, and above all, to becoming a strong modern nation. They supported a devastatingly critical (or iconoclastic) view of traditional Chinese culture with little ambivalence toward what it represented. (Indeed, the idea of *xungen* would have been alien to these May Fourth intellectuals.)

When it comes to (especially) writer/critic intellectuals in post–Cultural Revolution China, however, if there is an oppositional stance on their part, it is surely not against traditional Chinese culture. For obvious political reasons, it is the Party-state—its power structure and its ideology—that came to stand in the place where traditional culture once stood for the May Fourth intellectuals. In the 1980s, that is, after decades of wars and revolutions, after *lijiao* as the dominant social theology and organizational principle had long been smashed, and after thirty years of the People's Republic, Chinese intellectuals faced a different context in which to tackle the notion of culture. Although their impulse to take on the (big) question of culture still remained, they found themselves in an oppositional position against a dominant discourse that had itself long co-opted or assimilated the May Fourth legacy in denouncing traditional culture. The complexity of the contemporary cultural movement thus lies in the fact that these intellectuals were in for a hard time understanding for themselves what kind of cultural issues they needed to think through, examine, and reexamine, and why those issues were important. *Xun* or search in this sense is a particularly appropriate word; it conveys a sense of uncertainty embedded in the origin of this cultural movement with regard to Chinese culture.

To most PRC Chinese and to many contemporary Chinese intellectuals, traditional Chinese culture tends typically to mean mainly one thing: the negative remnants of Confucianism. Indeed, part of the contemporary Chinese cultural movement consists of intellectuals criticizing the influence of such negative remnants in the existing power structure and ideology. Because of this critical stance, they identify themselves and are identified with the May Fourth intellectuals and their legacy. There is, however, a second aspect of the issue concerning traditional culture that makes contemporary intellectuals different from their May Fourth predecessors. Although criticizing the negative remnants of traditional culture, they also looked beyond the May Fourth definitions of traditional culture and began to flirt with it by advocating the necessity and the importance of searching for cultural roots. It is in this sense, I think, that the search (*xun*) motif comes into the picture in the contemporary era, signifying a renewed intellectual interest in traditional Chinese culture.

What Is *Xungen* Literature?

As mentioned, *xungen* literature emerged in the 1980s when a group of young male writers, responding to the new cultural movement, turned to rural China and to the past for another look at Chinese culture. Like many contemporary Chinese oppositional critics who insist on identifying the CCP with the oppressive and conservative aspects of Confucianism, and thus lump the two together as *zhuliu wenhua* ("mainstream culture"),[6] *xungen* writers search for alternative cultural roots by turning to other versions of Chinese culture they believe to have been marginalized, repressed, and twisted by the official or mainstream culture (be it Confucianism or the CCP). Instead of totally negating traditional Chinese culture, therefore, these writers set out to search for alternative, authentic roots they believe to have been covered by layers of historical scars. Some insist that Confucianism in its most authentic form may still be a viable cultural force, for it is, after all, deeply entrenched in Chinese culture; others look to (their versions of) Taoist influences for revitalizing what is believed to be the unique strength of Chinese culture; still others turn to various regional cultures for new identities. Almost all of them turn to rural China.[7] Indeed, both in Mo Yan's novel and in the satirical remarks made by Can Xue, we have already seen this pattern of turning to the rural and to the past.

In 1985, a series of male writers made public announcements to declare the connection between their writings and their cultural roots and to argue the importance of recognizing that connection. Han Shaogong, for example, wrote "Wenxue de gen" (Roots of literature), which is characterized by critics as the manifesto of *xungen* literature.[8] Following Han were Zheng Wanlong's "Wo de gen" (My roots), Li Hangyu's "Li yi li wo de gen" (Put my Roots in order), and Ah Cheng's "Wenhua zhiyue zhe renlei" (Culture conditions humankind).[9] In his "manifesto," Han claims that writers should "look into the deeper level of the national spirit and cultural characteristics to *search for 'roots' of the self*" (emphasis mine).[10] Even though the self here is not specified as male, the conflation of the search for roots and for the male self is implicit in this statement and the connection between the two is from the very beginning central and categorically essential to this literary movement.

In an interview with the Taiwanese writer Shi Shuqing, Han Shaogong made it clear that he is interested in Chu culture (Chu being the area covering parts of today's Hunan and Hubei Provinces), which, according to him, had long been assimilated by the all-powerful Confucian culture. The roots he seeks, he insists, are not in the traditional Confucian dominant culture. Chu culture, rather, is a "nonorthodox and nonstandardized culture, assimilated and marginalized by Confucianism." For one thing, "Chu people used to worship birds, and that makes them 'descendants of birds' rather than 'of the dragon of the Yellow River.' "[11] "Chu culture," Han continues, "is partly primitive and holds the belief in the union of humans and gods, and . . . of time and space" (16). Moreover, Chu culture is not only "mysterious," but "it also has an intuitive way of thinking. Unlike Confucianism, which is based on rational thinking . . . , Chu culture resembles Taoist theology, which expresses its ideas aesthetically through fairy tales" (18). In short, Chu culture is almost everything that Confucianism is not. Like many of his fellow Chinese, Han's notion of Confucianism is totalizing, to be sure, but his contention can be understood in part as a strategic positioning, signaling an opposition to any officially sanctioned ideology. Contrasting Chu culture with Confucian culture in this sense, Han sets up a series of dichotomies: official/unofficial, civilized/primitive, rational/intuitive, culture/nature, and Confucianism/Taoism. Chu culture represents everything on the right side of the dichotomies and challenges those on the left. In searching for the origin of Chu culture, Han hopes to set up the primitive, the natural, and the unofficial to counterbalance the other side of the dichotomies, namely, Confucianism. Additionally, in stories such as "Bababa," the primitive, the natural, and the unofficial are often personified and represented by an estranged outsider, who can be seen as either remaining on the margins (as a form of resistance) or having failed to assimilate. At this point, therefore, we can begin to wonder whether it is Chu culture or something else that is actually at issue. I will return to this question later, but it is necessary to indicate that Han's seemingly enthusiastic remarks concerning Chu culture have other implications.

Ji Hongzhen, a Chinese critic, has offered some extensive thoughts on how to understand *xungen* literature. According to her, the history of twentieth-century China, with its mixture of "ignorance that exists in the rural society" and the "hypocrisy found in urban civilization," has produced a deep depression in writers like Mo Yan.[12] The expression of such depression is "an anxiety over the 'deterioration of the [Chinese] race' [*zhong de tuihua*], and a desire to look back through the dust of history for memories of his ancestors and for that piece of 'red sorghum' which belongs to him" (23). In fact, Ji continues, this anxiety is expressed in different ways by a number of writers, such as

Zhang Chengzhi, Han Shaogong, Li Hangyu, Jia Pingwa, and Ah Cheng. Through "the dust of history," these writers attempt to "remember," and they focus their "memories" on representing the marginalized or the forgotten. The roots they search for, according to Ji, vary on the surface: sometimes they are to be found in the inassimilable or unassimilated parts of various sub- or regional cultures (be it Chu, Xiangxi, or Lu culture), sometimes in the colorful and almost sensual landscape that Mo describes, sometimes in the unconstrained desires many of their characters have displayed, and sometimes in the close ties that Ah Cheng's characters have with nature. Together, however, Ji suggests, the *xungen* writers intend to celebrate and often deliberately beautify the "irrational," the "primitive," and the mysterious that have been marginalized by mainstream culture. At the same time, Ji's remarks seem to imply, the *xungen* writers are not simply celebrating these alternative Chinese cultures. There is, as her characterization of their anxiety indicates, a historically informed "heaviness" behind all of their writings, which, given the declarations made by the writers themselves, also suggests an embedded sense of mission: to rechart, as it were, the maps of Chinese culture. And it is both the historical weightiness and the sense of mission that ultimately elevate *xungen* literature to the level of, for lack of a better word, the sublime (a point to which I will return later).

Another Chinese critic, Li Qingxi, characterizes *xungen* literature this way:

> Two years ago, in my discussion of Han Shaogong's "Bababa," I mentioned the issue of writers moving away from the individual consciousness of their characters to the national collective [un]consciousness, and argued that the roots-seeking fiction emerging at that time marked the turning point of that move. In another article on Han Shaogong, I also analyzed, from an artistic perspective, his move toward representing the atypical, switching from portrayals of individuals to depicting the collective psychology. Now . . . I think this is truly a promising way to go.[13]

To Li, what marks the difference between *xungen* writers and others is the former's moving away from writing about themselves to writing about other people. That is, in representing their (male) characters, the writers are not interested in them as individuals per se but as part of a cultural landscape within which the characters interact. *Xungen* literature, in this sense, means a move toward intellectual inquiry into something more general and significant, such as the collective psyche of the Chinese.

From Li's comments, we get a sense that he is praising *xungen* writers for moving beyond lamenting their own fate (and failure) as individuals and for having become much less sentimental in their telling of stories: they no longer indulge in the pains of their "petty" selves but confront cultural issues instead. Li assumes a subject-object relationship between the writers and their characters and identifies the characters as the writers' *shenmei duixiang* (literally, objects of [their] aesthetic activity). He also assumes that, when the writers move to represent the collective (un)conscious, they are no longer stuck with their self-lamenting mentality, and thus the self is not the issue anymore. To be sure, in *xungen* literature, writers did move beyond writing about personal wounds and were less interested in lamenting pains from an individual character's point of view; their personal pains, in other words, were no longer the subject matter of their stories. And because of this, such transcendence (from an individual consciousness to a collective unconscious) is aesthetically more acceptable to and appreciated by many critics. But for Li, it also means that in this new way of writing the writers are somehow positioned outside the (imagined) world they created, and hence the self is no longer an issue. As a result, in his marveling at the aesthetic values and changes that *xungen* literature represents, Li also manages to obscure the presence of a desiring subject that is itself part of those changes.

In fact, as is shown in Han Shaogong's statement quoted above, the presence of the desiring subject is made quite clear by writers themselves, who have stated that, in proposing to search for roots, what they are really interested in is exploring their own *ganjue* (personal or subjective feelings). In his essay "My Roots," for example, Zheng Wanlong connects his search for roots with the notion of *ganjue:* "Personal [or subjective] feelings are important. They leave deeper traces in one's mind than rational understanding based on reason."[14] Based on such subjective feelings, he wants to "establish [his own] ideals, values, ethics, and culture, and, by way of describing human behavior and human history, to represent a universal human essence in [his] novels" (45). In addition to Han's manifesto, Zheng's words indicate an interesting point regarding *xungen* literature: on the one hand, there is a direct identification between the writers' own subjective feelings and the aesthetic qualities of their works, and on the other, a desire to turn the combination of the two, to echo Žižek, into the sublime object of their search.

The Sublime of *Xungen* Literature

It is almost inevitable that when we discuss the qualities (as defined by the critics quoted above) of *xungen* literature, writings such as Mo Yan's, with saturated imagery and symbolism of the natural world, come to mind.[15] In the novel *Red Sorghum,* for example, Mo combines color, taste, smell, and sound to describe landscape, killing, death, sexual desires, rituals, and many other activities to such an extent that his reader often finishes his stories deeply affected. Throughout the novel, various sensory images are employed in association with his depictions of red sorghum fields. There, for instance, one smells "an unusual, fishy and sweet smell mixed in yellow and red."[16] There, "the sorghum leaves were sizzling amidst the fog through which one could hear the bright commotion of Moshui River . . . sometimes loud, sometimes weak, sometimes nearby, and sometimes far away" (3). There, as a child, the narrator's father witnesses a scene in which Commander Yu (the narrator's grandfather) tries to stop a man, Wang Wenyi, from coughing by smothering him, after which "father saw two purple-colored fingerprints like two ripe grapes, and Wang Wenyi's ghostly blue and frightened eyes" (4). There, on the "pitch-black soil" once lay his grandmother's "jade-like smooth body" and also many of her life dramas. There, hundreds of "black, green, and red dogs" once ran wild, and many had to be killed by his grandfather. And there, battles against the Japanese were fought, and his grandmother and many others shed their blood, which further enriched the color of the red sorghum.

The same richness is also found in many other *xungen* writers' works. In describing his birthplace, for example, Zheng Wanlong writes of a river with "pitch-black water," "white fish, swimming among purple-colored undergrowth in water."[17] From the forests, "warm blood gushes out, together with unrestrained laughter, iron-like faces, and songs that worship Nature's primitivity" (45). "Heilong River," he declares, "is the root of my life and my fiction. I seek to represent the strong rich colors of mountains and forests, the bold and unconstrained melody, and the cold and chilly sensations" (45).

This is also reminiscent of Zhang Chengzhi's representations of all the rivers in his "Rivers of the North." By now, we can see a pattern emerging from these and other representations of the richness of the landscape, a pattern that is epitomized in *Red Sorghum*. There, we find that the sorghum fields are of pure red color, the soil is pitch-black and rich, dogs are truly untamed, people live to the fullest of their desires, and above all, men are exceptionally energetic, brave, and free-spirited, and women are "free" and yet devoted to their men. It is a world where natural desires, rather than cultural reasons, dominate.

From the examples given above, we can say that the natural world encompasses the rural, the past, and the non- or precultural (represented by such characters as Binzai in "Bababa" and the grandfather in *Red Sorghum*), whereas culture includes the urban, the present, and the learned (books, reading, writing, and propaganda). Depicted as pure, rich, untamed (and therefore strong), the natural world is shown as an ideally clean place—in this case, free of ideological contamination. The urban or the present, on the other hand, is shown as hellish, dirty, and above all, deteriorated. Here, other examples also come to mind. In Han's "Bababa," for example, we recall a twisted relationship between culture and nature and how culture is made to appear ridiculous by natural forces whose mystery is forever beyond human comprehension.

In Rey Chow's reading of the film *King of Children,* she offers a brilliant discussion of how the film manages to turn nature into a symbol of progressive force.[18] We find a similar message in other stories by Ah Cheng. In another of his king novellas, *King of Trees,* for example, Ah Cheng, in his usual detached manner, tells the story of a man whose life is destroyed when his beloved tree is felled as the result of others' (the "educated youth," who are sent to the countryside for "reeducation") zealous but blind following of "ideas."[19] In both of these stories, learning (and therefore culture) is questioned because of its destructiveness, and the writers invest more feelings in nature, which is represented with a sense of mystery and awe. Together, these stories indicate a familiar dichotomy, one between nature and culture, with the latter represented as the villain and the former elevated as the sublime.

To be sure, this villainization of culture in favor of nature is not a new invention by the *xungen* writers. It is a literary motif commonly found in classical Chinese and other literatures (e.g., the nineteenth-century English

Romantic poets and the modernist turn to the "primitive" natural world in protest against the perceived decay of the modern world). *Xungen* writers' dichotomization of nature and culture is in effect yet another literary moment in which writers turn to nature for inspiration and for a way out of a cultural maze. But, as we know, in each of these cases there is nothing purely natural about nature, and the nature/culture dichotomy is employed for political, cultural, and socioeconomic reasons specific to the times. As such, the important questions to ask here are in what ways nature signifies for and is signified by the *xungen* writers and why.

At this point, I am reminded of the observation by Ji Hongzhen in her characterization of the searching-for-roots writers I quoted earlier: that what preoccupies the *xungen* writers is primarily their "anxiety over the *'deterioration of the [Chinese] race'*" (*zhong de tuihua*). What kind of anxiety is this? What does *zhong* or "race" mean? Does it mean the Chinese people, or does it mean Chinese culture? Or is it both? What exactly does *tuihua* or "deterioration" mean? If it means that, once upon a time, the Chinese *zhong* was the opposite of *tuihua,* what does this predeterioration past have to do with the present?

Zhong is an interesting word here. It can mean a number of things: species, race, seeds, and guts, all indicating something biologically (hence naturally) masculine, crucial, or essential to life. In the sociocultural context, the word *zhong* also carries a strong patriarchal implication. It is, for example, a key word in the tenacious traditional belief in the importance of having sons; only sons are considered *chuanzong jiezu de zhong,* or the "seed" to pass on the family line. In this phrase, *zong* (ancestry) and *zhong* are patrilineally connected as a natural passage for the family (and metaphorically for the "race") to continue. Without *zhong,* namely sons, the lineage is doomed. Furthermore, not only might having no sons threaten the lineage, having sons who are weak may also constitute a threat to continuity. This latter implication is precisely what the phrase *zhong de tuihua* suggests: the "deterioration of the (Chinese) race." Used in the context of *xungen* literature, in this sense, *zhong* first and foremost evokes something natural: the quality of the (Chinese) race and, literally, of men (of the race). On a symbolic level (for this is what it actually means), *zhong* becomes a male-gendered symbol denoting the essence of the Chinese "race" (and by extension, its culture and China as a nation), its survival, identity, and power (or lack thereof). What makes *xungen* literature particularly relevant to my overall discussion is precisely this embedded concern centered on *zhong* with a strong patrilineal and masculinist implication. This, incidentally, is also the point where the word *gen* becomes relevant.

Gen, as should be clear by now, means "roots." As such, it also has a biological base for meaning that, by extension, carries the connotation of being the source, the origin, or the base of life, without which life cannot exist. Culturally and especially patrilineally in China, it is also often used to refer to the only son of a family (the only source for continuing the family line). In this sense, it is a synonym for the word *zhong.* Both have a natural basis for their original meanings; both, by extension, have strong patriarchal and patrilineal connotations; and both, when used metaphorically, suggest something that is essential and independent of cultural contamination and that can therefore be recovered in its original form.

There are proverbs using the word *gen* that convey these implications. *Shuda genshen,* for example, is a *gen*-phrase that means a big tree with deep roots, hence the vitality of the tree and its longevity. *Genshen digu* suggests something so deeply rooted that it is hard to remove or eradicate. *Luoye guigen* ("fallen leaves return to their roots") is a favored phrase used by many "uprooted" Chinese who would like to go back to rediscover their roots. *Xungen,* similar to the last phrase, also implies (in a reverse way) an uprootedness. In the context of *xungen* literature, it suggests an uprootedness that, without relocating its roots, will lead to deterioration or *tuihua* of the Chinese race or, as we recall from the discussion in the previous chapter, will lead to an emergence of *zazhong* (bastard) offspring who are deemed not as pure or as strong as their ancestors.

It should also be clear by now that words such as *zhong* and *gen* both signify something naturally essential and, as key words in *xungen* literature, carry strong patriarchal implications. Together, they focus on men/masculinity as the (naturally) essential source for a renewal of the Chinese race. This male-centeredness harks back to the point made at the beginning of the chapter: the *subject* matter of *xungen* literature and the relationship between the (male) *subject* who seeks and the *roots* that he searches for.

In his book *The Sublime Object of Ideology,* where he discusses how ideology manages to "hold us," Slavoj Žižek makes a distinction between "imaginary identification" and "symbolic identification." In the former, he argues, "we imitate the other at the level of resemblance—we identify ourselves with the image of the other in as much as we are like him." In the latter, "we identify ourselves with the other precisely at the point at which he is inimitable, at the point which eludes resemblance."[20] The difference between imaginary identification and symbolic identification, concepts that were significantly developed and expanded by Lacan in the twentieth century, can be traced back to Hegel. In defining what identity is, to echo a point made in chapter 1, Hegel argues that the so-called law of identity is wrong when we say "The sea is the sea, The air is the air, The moon is the moon . . ." because these objects themselves do not have "bearing on one another," and "what we have before us therefore is not Identity, but Difference."[21] Identity, on the other hand, is to be found in things that "are not the same, not identical with each other" (141). This, I think, is how Žižek's definition of symbolic identification is to be comprehended. It is an identification that takes place when "we identify ourselves with the other precisely at the point at which he is inimitable, at the point which eludes resemblance." Because of a lack of direct resemblance between the subject and the symbolic, Žižek continues, a sense of autonomy is realized at the symbolic level, because "the interplay of imaginary and symbolic under the domination of symbolic identification constitutes the mechanism by means of which the subject is integrated into a given sociosymbolic field—the way he/she assumes certain 'mandates.' "[22] Put plainly, symbolic identification takes place precisely at the moment when the subject assumes his or her own autonomy following the social norms that differentiate the self from the other. The subject's sense of autonomy, at the same time, can only be achieved when the subject subscribes to "certain 'mandates' " that sustain his or her sense of uniqueness.

This point is illuminating for my discussion here: the male search for a masculine identity in *xungen* literature also exceeds the male subject's identifying with the image of manly men (as discussed in the previous chapter). The search for the (better) self, that is, does not remain merely as an imaginary identification in which the better self is a masculine man. It also takes place symbolically in the search for authentic Chinese cultural roots. In *xungen* literature, more specifically, it resides in *zhong* (a race with guts) and *gen* (roots), symbolized by the rich, sensual, and untamed natural world and to be recovered to represent Chinese cultural essence (roots) and, ultimately, a new Chinese cultural identity.

An interesting twist takes place when a symbolic identification is realized: in identifying with nature, which is marginalized by mainstream culture, Chinese male intellectuals in essence gravitate toward it precisely at the point where Chinese intellectuals and nature do not resemble each other. And yet, when the natural world is celebrated through pure red sorghum, pitch-black silt at the bottom of a river, the untamed wilderness of the sorghum fields, and the free-spirited men and women inhabiting that world, what is sublime about all of this is not the sorghum, the river, or the fields themselves, but what they symbolize: the (masculine) power that the Chinese *zhong* and *gen* once had and that should be rediscovered and recovered. In their representations of geographical landscapes, of people found in those landscapes, and of regional ritualistic practices, beliefs, and ways of living, *xungen* writers hope to resurrect aspects of Chinese culture in which they believe vital forces still exist and with which they wish to identify.

The celebration of nature, in the final analysis, is a celebration of a (masculine) power that is believed to have been trapped or constrained (or even weakened) by mainstream culture. Allegorically speaking, the beautified primitive natural world is meant to symbolize the sublime of Chinese culture, and the beautification is aimed at challenging and decentering the existing mainstream culture. Nature as the sublime is thus equated with cultural roots (*wenhua de gen*) as an alternative cultural identity. By way of nature (which, again, includes the past, the natural, and the prelinguistic), "a return of culture" (*wenhua de huigui;* its Chinese equivalent is an important phrase to keep in mind) is subsequently realized. Additionally, because *zhong* and *gen* are employed to signify the innate or natural strength of Chinese culture, *wenhua de huigui* in this sense also entails *zhong de huigui,* or the return of the (Chinese) men/race.

This point echoes my earlier questioning of Li's point about the "disappearance" of the (writer's) self in *xungen* literature. The self has in fact never disappeared; rather, he is veiled by cultural roots on a symbolic level where, once again in Žižek's words, the resemblance is least likely. Here, male identification, or masculine identity, takes place at the beautification of the past, the rural, the prelinguistic, and above all, the natural world, all of which, on a symbolic level, constitute the sublime of Chinese culture, which is located in the essence of *zhong*. *Zhong de huigui,* in turn, is *wenhua de huigui.*

Zhong de huigui: Masculine Chinese Cultural Identity

With nature represented as an alternative cultural identity and established as the sublime of Chinese culture, cultural roots—as a new cultural identity— become conveniently conflated with *zhong* (race) and *gen* (roots). Thus, the return of culture (*wenhua de huigui*) simultaneously means the return of the (Chinese) race (*zhong de huigui*), and by extension, as I have argued so far, the return of a Chinese masculine identity.

Huigui in Chinese means "to return." To return, at the same time, does not entail only "coming back"; it also suggests an elsewhere from which to return and, more important, a past that returns together with the returning. *Huigui,* in other words, evokes the notion of history and the past.

In his discussion of a dialectical concept of history, Walter Benjamin reexamines the notion of the past. He identifies it in two ways: history/past as "the epic element/dimension of history," and history/past as "the specific/particular epoch, the specific/particular life, and the specific/particular work."[23] He argues that when history is understood in an epic fashion, historians tend to ignore the particulars of history. History perceived in the former sense has a totalistic tendency toward seeing historical continuity. "The historical materialist," he contends, "must sacrifice the epic element/dimension of history" for the "particulars" (227). Benjamin's distinction is a very important one because it undermines the monopoly of a historicism based on seeing the world and the evolution of time only in a linear and continuous fashion.

In his discussion of contemporary Chinese writers' representations of China, Ching-kiu Stephen Chan echoes Benjamin's point, although with a strong poststructuralist touch.[24] Chan perceives a built-in tension in these writers' relationship with China (either Chinese culture or China's past), which is manifested in what he terms the split between the historical and the imaginary. Chan's historical resonates with Benjamin's particulars, denoting the specific moments in an entity called Chinese history. His imaginary pairs with Benjamin's "epic dimension of history," although Chan's has a stronger poststructuralist touch in that questioning the "epic dimension of history" is only part of the issue. Chan's focus on the contemporary Chinese writers' split between the historical and imaginary, echoing Benjamin's point, can help us understand how the past is represented and why it is represented in that manner in *xungen* literature.

On the one hand, in many of their stories, *xungen* writers go back to a history that can be identified as its particular moments. In Mo Yan, for example, those moments include the Sino-Japanese War, the early twentieth century when certain Chinese provinces witnessed a Western missionary presence, the Great Leap Forward, the Cultural Revolution, and so forth, all of which have their specific and related contextual implications. What is more, in addition to the temporal specificities, there are also distinct traces of what Benjamin terms "the particulars of life," including spatial characteristics, human activities and human relations, and detailed depictions of the human condition of the time. The combination of those particulars indicates contemporary writers' specific interest in and fascination with modern Chinese history.

On the other hand, as my previous discussion has strongly indicated, the notion of *xungen* does not end with those historical particulars because there is also at issue the imaginary or the "epic dimension" of their representations of the past. It is this imaginary, named cultural roots (which would be called China in Chan's discussion), that diminishes or ultimately renders almost irrelevant the particulars of those historically specific times. The past takes on epic features, and its particulars become blurred by the depictions of a rich landscape, a primitive environment and way of living, and untamed, free-spirited, and brave people. The past is rendered into a mythical moment that is present and yet beyond tangible reach. In this way, the mythicized and mystified past is conveniently conflated with the notions of *zhong* and *gen,* which themselves help mythicize the original masculine power and strength of the Chinese race—Chinese men, to be exact—and together the combination of such a mythical past and *zhong* and *gen* conjures up a historical myth of Chineseness (a notion to which I will return shortly). In *xungen* literature, it is this mythical (in the epic sense) past that plays a major role in the writers' imagination and in their telling of the stories that are set in various particular historical moments. The imagined past becomes Chan's China, which I take one step further by naming it as a "Chineseness," which is not only an abstract concept that Chinese intellectuals are fond of toying with but also one that carries with it a strong male (chauvinistic) component.

To be sure, the past represented in this fashion should be understood as a desire for renewal or rejuvenation of the present. Given the historical context of modern Chinese history, such a desire manifests a protest against the various forces that rendered China as a nation-state weaker, especially in relation to the West. And it is expressed by writers themselves when they discuss the relationship between the past and the present. Zheng Wanlong, for instance, has made clear where his real concerns lie when he reaches into the past: "I not only live in the present, but also in the present of the past; the past exists in the present. The past is not dead, it is still alive in our presence."[25] Its historically dialectic observation with regard to the entanglement of the past versus the present notwithstanding, Zheng's repeated mixing of the two suggests that his interests in the past exist mainly for the present.

Other critics, of course, have also considered the Chinese intellectuals' relationship with the notion of the past. Rey Chow, for example, has identified some Chinese fifth-generation filmmakers' interest in and their celebration (or aestheticizing, or even exoticizing) of the past as a representation of an "illusory new beginning."[26] Their films about the past, in other words, are in essence less about the past than about a "new beginning" when a strong and masculine Chinese cultural identity will be realized. Stephen Chan, additionally, has discussed contemporary Chinese writers' interest in the past and in a "future/past" formula, seeing it as yet another manifestation of Chinese intellectuals' struggle to come to terms with Chinese modernity.[27]

As noted by these critics, this temporal concern about the past in *xungen* literature actually pertains more to the future, indicating a desire to begin again. Indeed, within the context of modern Chinese history, the desire to begin again has been embedded in various political struggles and cultural movements ranging from "self-strengthening," nation building, the New Culture Movement, and the New Life Movement (all pre-1949), to post-1949 socialist reconstruction and various efforts to modernize, to other forms of Mao Zedong's efforts to turn China into a strong nation (including the Great Leap Forward and the Cultural Revolution), to the post-1978 cultural movement, and to the marketization of China's economy and the explosive happenings of popular culture all conducted in the name of (finally) beginning to modernize and to build a strong China.

One has just to note the frequency of the word "new" (*xin*) in the naming of these moments. The post–Cultural Revolution period has been known in China as the New Era (*xin shi qi*). Each moment of renewal, understood in Benjamin's historical dialectics, is yet another cycle of becoming that is grounded in particulars and should be comprehended as such. Benjamin evokes the notion of becoming via defining origin in this way: "Origin . . . , although a thoroughly historical category, nonetheless has nothing to do with beginnings. . . . The term origin does not mean the process of becoming of that which has emerged, but much more, that which emerges out of the process of becoming and disappearing. The origin stands in the flow of becoming as a whirlpool . . . ; its rhythm is apparent only to a double insight."[28]

Contextually speaking, the New Era (hence the "new beginning") after the Cultural Revolution signified another historical moment in which the Chinese people were to confront a different reality and many new problems. The *xungen* movement and literature were part of the intellectuals' response to this different historical moment in which they participated in "the process of becoming and disappearing." What is at issue, however, is that for the *xungen* writers themselves, the process was soon to be turned from "becoming and disappearing" into "returning" (to the origin of Chinese culture), which, as I have shown repeatedly in this discussion, assumes an essential past in Chinese culture that can be rediscovered in its essential way.

This is where a shift in emphasis takes place in (our understanding of) the *xungen* cultural movement: a shift from a concern with cultural issues to an obsession with the notion of Chineseness that in many cases drifts away from the historical particulars. That is, with emphasis on the notion of *huigui, xungen* as a cultural and literary movement shifts away from questioning and challenging the existing sociocultural structures (as a politically oppositional move) and hence toward an obsession with the essence—roots—of Chinese culture and toward a self-referential indulgence in the search for a masculine self. Also, with the focus placed on an entity identified as *gen,* this literature's tendency to mystify the past and cultural roots eventually becomes less of a showcase for the diversity in Chinese culture (as the writers advocated at the beginning) than one single cultural identity with further emphasis placed on its "potency." That is how the return of culture becomes conveniently conflated with the return of the (Chinese) race and more specifically with the return of strong and potent Chinese men. The relocated Chineseness is thus buttressed by its imagined potency.

With the emphasis shifted to Chineseness, the *xungen* movement is in essence responding, albeit indirectly, to an issue that has haunted Chinese intellectuals for more than a century: China's position in relation to the West, or the China/West dichotomy. Even though in *xungen* literature itself, the concern with the dichotomy is direct, it is nevertheless manifested in the literature's search motif and in its emphasis on Chineseness. In essence, therefore, *xungen* literature echoes one of the fundamental struggles of modern China in coming to terms with its relationship with the West.

This is what differentiates contemporary Chinese writer/critic intellectuals from their May Fourth predecessors. If the concern over the survival of China as a culture and a nation constitutes a major component of Chinese modernity, when it comes to the *xungen* movement and literature, Chinese culture and China as a nation take on a concern more with their potency than with an immediate national crisis. In addition to the political and cultural implications, therefore, when the cultural movement in the 1980s entered a searching (for roots) mode, it was not so much about exposing the weakness of Chinese culture as about veiling it, by suggesting that the weakness exists elsewhere, either in the history of traditional mainstream culture or in the history of the CCP's regime. *Zhong* and *gen* function, to echo my earlier discussion of the notion of phallus, as the veil set up to signify both the original and the missing male organ. The past is glorified to symbolize the grit—hence the potency—of Chinese men that they desire to recover.

When searching for roots is conflated with searching for male potency, the question of the subject matter and the verb *xun* becomes relevant once again. As mentioned previously, in post-Mao Chinese literature, the word *xun* (*zhao*, "to search or look for") has occupied a unique discursive position, found in such frequently used terms as *xunzhao nanzihan* (looking for real men),[29] *xunzhao ziwo* (looking for the self), and *xungen* (roots-seeking). The search motif manifests, in part, the specificity of male subjectivity in contemporary China that I examine in this study. What underscores the paradox of men lamenting and despising being weak is a male anxiety whose manifestations go further and deeper than mere protests against political persecution and oppression. In resisting the dominant ideology, post-Mao male writers challenge its utopian myths and versions of history by creating seemingly decentered male subject positions and by giving voice to them through manifestations of their desires. The decentered male subject positions, however, do not necessarily equate to subject positions without center. Rather, the center is shifted or relocated. The relocated center lies in the conflation of such no-tions as Chinese cultural roots, the return of the (Chinese) race, and the search for real or masculine men. The *Chineseness* symbolized by roots and guts, in this sense, becomes the new center. When *zhong* signifies the sym-bolic of Chineseness, I must add, its patrilineal implication is exclusionary of women, who are not identified with the notion of *zhong,* and its male-centeredness implies positioning women further toward the margins because the concern of the male subject is his relationship (as *zhong*) with his ances-tors (*zong*).

Because *zhong* suggests the potency of Chinese culture as a whole, Chinese culture in the end becomes a totality (again) that can find itself only when rec-ognized as a powerful (as implied by "potency") culture and nation, especially in relation to the West. It is the combination of this masculinist stance and male anxiety and ambivalence over modern China's seeming lack of cultural potency that has constituted many modern Chinese intellectuals' relation-ships with the China/West dichotomy and has affected their views of Chinese culture. As a result, these views often tread the fine line between being cultur-ally nationalistic (and chauvinistic) and being culturally nihilistic.

In the final analysis, however, this nationalism and nihilism are two sides of the same coin. What connects them is a desire for *zhong de huigui,* that is, a desire to "masculinize" Chinese culture. In his discussion of Liang Qichao, a pre–May Fourth modern Chinese thinker, Joseph Levenson makes the fol-lowing useful observation with regard to modern Chinese intellectuals and their quest for strengthening Chinese culture and for modernity:

> How can a Chinese be reconciled to the observable dissipation of his cultural inheritance—or how can a China in full process of Western-ization feel itself equivalent to the West? This question is the inner link between Liang and the Communists, that link which is contemporaneity. . . .
>
>   If a need for conviction of China's equivalence to the West is buried in Liang's ideas, it is somewhere buried in every modern Chinese the-ory of Chinese culture, from the most traditional to the most radically iconoclastic.[30]

Levenson may downplay the Western imperialist factor in modern Chinese history when he states that "the fact that European thinkers are involved is a

Chinese fact" (5), for within the context of modern Chinese intellectual history, this "Chinese fact" is not just a one-sided obsession coming from Chinese intellectuals. It was undeniably imposed by the outside (Western and Japanese) forces. Nevertheless, Levenson's observation is important because he points out the link between different modern theories of Chinese culture, a link, he argues, that is underwritten by "a need for conviction."

Given its emphasis on *zhong de huigui* and a desire for cultural potency, *xungen* literature indicates that the male search for cultural roots is yet another moment when the (Chinese intellectuals') "need for conviction" (re)surfaced. In that search, the pendulum swings to a culturalism that often functions as the hotbed for an essentialized belief in the masculinist aspect of *zhong,* a notion that is employed to symbolize the superiority and potency of Chinese culture. In this sense, if *xungen* literature is in essence a call for *zhong de huigui,* what is ultimately called for is a desired return of three entities embodied in the one word *zhong:* manhood, cultural roots, and national identity. The conflation of the three signifies a strong masculine imprint both in the *xungen* cultural movement in particular and in China's quest for a modern identity in general.

Afterword

This book was written at a time when Chinese intellectuals had gone through a century-long quest for, and struggle to come to terms with, modernity. As the twentieth century ends, we have only begun to examine expressions of male desire in literature and culture in conjunction with that quest and struggle. My study is an exploration of that conjunction.

This is also a time when China is experiencing rapid changes in economic reforms and marketization. Although these changes and their impact have yet to completely unfold and be fully understood, economic growth has undoubtedly already changed the landscape of China and the lives of many Chinese (for better or for worse). Modernization appears to have finally arrived in China; its glamour is no longer on the other side of the ocean.

In the face of these contexts, I want to leave with the following questions: Where and how do the male writer/critic intellectuals figure in all of these changes? How are these changes impacting them as individuals, men, and intellectuals? If their quest for modernity and desire for recognition have always been entangled with the image and the geopolitical standing of China in the international arena, now that China is believed to be well on its way to modernization and a position with increasing international power, where do these intellectuals stand in relation to all of this? And finally, does *xiandaihua* ("modernization") mean that Chinese masculinity has finally reached the point where it can be liberated from its besieged status?

These are, of course, open-ended questions, but many signs indicate that contemporary Chinese male writer/critic intellectuals are standing at yet another crossroad. Although many of them appear to be overwhelmed by the rapid changes taking place in China, most have, whether enthusiastically or reluctantly, joined the process. Some actively participate in the production of popular culture, turning themselves into the darlings of the mass media. Some enthusiastically import new Western theories, including postmodernism, poststructuralism, and other "post"-isms. Some seriously ponder the need to reintroduce *renwen jingsheng* ("humanist spirit"); others find it necessary to renew a nationalist fervor. And still others begin to identify themselves, by way of a "return to the future," as *wenren* ("men of letters," as opposed to "intellectuals," *zhishi fenzi*). These reinvented men of letters evoke the image of literati in traditional China, and such an association causes one to wonder about the implications of this "newfound" male intellectual identity. At the same time, facing serious structural and social problems that have emerged with the modernization, these intellectuals are yet to find a critical edge from which to position themselves and to confront these emerging problems.

A friend of mine once asked me whether I should and would consider Chinese male intellectuals' interest in themselves as a sign of sheer boredom. My immediate answer was no (and the reason is obvious from my book!). Nevertheless, in this post–New Era (*hou xin shi qi*) there is an increasingly discernible tendency toward decadence, accompanied especially by the reinvented *wenren* image, and this cannot but make one wonder about the role and fate of the writer/critic intellectuals as China modernizes itself. One must ask: Is the post–New Era the beginning of a postintellectual era as well?

Having raised this question, however, I believe there are more important ones to pose concerning the role of Chinese male intellectuals in the context both of economic reforms and of their quest for modernity. We need to ask, for example, in what ways "decadence" is another manifestation of the male desire associated with the search for masculinity. What is more, we need to ask questions about Chinese women: Where do Chinese male intellectuals stand in relation to the new challenges women face? In what way is their stand on women's issues a manifestation of their own desires and concerns? Finally, with *wenren* or *wenhuaren* identified as (yet another version of) the authentic Chinese male, we need to continue to probe the link between representations of China and the central concerns of Chinese male intellectuals that I analyze in this book.

Notes

Introduction

1 Benjamin I. Schwartz, "The Limits of 'Tradition Versus Modernity' as Categories of Explanation: The Case of the Chinese Intellectuals," *Dedalus* (spring 1972): 76.

2 In recent years, scholars have expanded their discussion of issues of Chinese modernity beyond the triad traditional and modernity in relation to Chinese intellectuals that Schwartz outlined in the early 1970s. Recent publications, such as *Woman and Chinese Modernity* by Rey Chow, *The Sublime Figure of History* by Wang Ban, *Women and Sexuality in China* by Harriet Evans, *Sex, Culture, and Modernity in China* by Frank Dikötter have all helped open up new ways of considering Chinese modernity. I quote Schwartz's earlier observation with such recent publications in mind.

3 I understand "body" as a biological entity with physiological features that mark its sex, and as an entity with constructed gendered orientations. I am aware of the tension in this dualistic view and of Judith Butler's rethinking of the notions of sex and gender and the ongoing controversies and debate about it. As my discussions in this book indicate, in light of the ongoing debate, I continue to recognize the importance and usefulness of the concept of gender. At the same time, I also recognize the necessity of understanding the cultural implications in the concept of sex and of doing so by being fully aware that the human body is at the same time a physiological and biological entity. Judith Butler, *Gender Trouble* (New York: Routledge, 1995).

4 See, for example, Yue Ming-Bao, "Gendering the Origins of Modern Chinese Fiction," in *Gender and Sexuality in Twentieth-Century Chinese Literature and Society,* ed. Tonglin Lu (Albany: State University of New York Press, 1993), 47–66; Ching-kiu Stephen Chan, "The Language of Despair: Ideological Representations of the 'New Woman' by May Fourth Writers," in *Gender Politics in Modern China,* ed. Tani E. Barlow (Durham, NC: Duke University Press, 1993), 13–32; Carolyn T. Brown, "Woman as Trope: Gender and Power in Lu Xun's 'Soap,'" in *Gender Politics in Modern China,* 74–89.

5 There has been some critical inquiry into the literary and cultural implications of male desire for "masculinity" and the historical, cultural, political, ideological, and gendered implications related to this aspect of the culture, by Rey Chow, Lu Tonglin, and Wang Yuejin, for example. The study I intend here will take the discussion further. See Rey Chow, "Male Narcissism and National Culture: Subjectivity in Chen Kaige's *King of Children,*" in *From May Fourth to June Fourth,* ed. Ellen Widmer and David Der-wei Wang (Cambridge, MA: Harvard University Press,

1993), 327–59; Lu Tonglin, *"Red Sorghum:* Limits of Transgression," in *Politics, Ideology, and Literary Discourse in Modern China,* ed. Liu Kang and Xiaobing Tang (Durham, NC: Duke University Press, 1993), 188–210; Wang Yuejin, *"Red Sorghum:* Mixing Memory and Desire," in *Perspectives on Chinese Cinema,* ed. Chris Berry (London: BFI Publishing, 1991), 80–103.

6 By "Chinese women," I do not mean to suggest that all Chinese women are the same. However, in the context of this argument, I use the term to suggest the "other sex" or the "gendered other" in relation to Chinese male intellectuals.

7 Zhang Jie, "Fang zhou" (The ark), *Shouhuo* (Harvest) 2 (1982): 4–59.

8 See, for example, Wu Daiying, "Xinshiqi 'nuxing wenxue' mantan" (An informal discussion of "women's literature" in the new era), *Dangdai wenyi sichao* (Ideas in contemporary literature and arts) 4 (1983): 35–41; Xia Zhongyi, "Cong xianglin sao, shafei nushi dao 'fangzhou' " (From Xianglin's wife and Miss Sophia to "The ark"), *Dangdai wenyi sichao* 5 (1983): 58–63; Wang Fuxiang, " 'Nuxing wenxue' zhiyi" (Questioning "women's literature"), *Dangdai wenyi sichao* 2 (1984): 16–22; Yu Qing, "Kunan de shenghua" (Sublimate suffering), *Dangdai wenyi sichao* 6 (1987): 50–55; Xu Wenyu, *Zhang Jie de xiaoshuo shijie* (The fictional world of Zhang Jie) (Beijing: People's Literature Press, 1991).

9 Zhang Xinxin, "Zai tongyi dipingxian shang" (On the same horizon), *Shouhuo* (Harvest) 6 (1981): 172–233; "Wo zai naer cuoguo le ni?" (How did I miss you?), *Shouhuo* 5 (1980): 91–105.

10 I am not suggesting a resemblance with the Japanese "I-novel" here. The inward turning in the Chinese situation is less a projecting of the "self" than a representation of what is believed to be the true self.

11 This has continued to be the focal point of discussion among scholars of modern China. Many (Western) feminist scholars of Chinese history and society have questioned the CCP's relationship with and policies on women. See, for example, Judith Stacey, *Patriarchy and Socialist Revolution in China* (Berkeley: University of California Press, 1983); Phyllis Andors, *The Unfinished Liberation of Chinese Women 1949–1980* (Bloomington: Indiana University Press; Sussex: Wheatsheaf Books, 1983); Margery Wolf, *Revolution Postponed* (Stanford: Stanford University Press, 1985).

Responses to these studies vary. Some Chinese women scholars from the PRC currently residing in the West have taken a somewhat different stance in their assessment of the relationship among the CCP revolution, its gender policies, and Chinese women. Their discussions have been heard at various conferences and are being written into dissertations and books.

12 I discuss this phenomenon more fully in chapter 1.

13 The name of this phenomenon comes from a play by Sha Yexin entitled *Xunzhao nanzihan* (Looking for a real man), *Shiyue* (October) 3 (1986): 115–76. Starting in the early 1980s, the concern over a lack of "real men" began to be voiced in literature, in the media (limited mostly to youth magazines at the time), and on college cam-

puses. It is a phenomenon that has been examined by critics in China. See Guo Xiaodong, "Nuren zai qinxie de shijie li" (Women in a tilted world), *Pi ping jia* (Critics) 6 (1988): 15–19; Chen Huifen, "Zhaohui shiluo de naban: 'renshi ni ziji'" (In search of that lost half: "Recognize yourself"), *Dangdai wenyi sichao* (Ideas in contemporary literature and arts) 2 (1987): 8–15; and Yi Qing, "Yige chongman huoli de zhidian—ye tan 'xunzhao nanren' de nuxing wenxue" (An energizing supporting point—also about the "looking for manly men" literature by women writers), *Dangdai wenyi sichao* 2 (1987): 16–18. In most of these analyses, critics have tended to question women's desire for finding real men. Men's desire for being a real man or their lament at not being able to be one, however, has not received adequate analysis.

14 Stallone's image came from the film *First Blood,* and Takakura Ken's originated from a number of Japanese films in which he played a hero who is strong, tough, and a man of few words.

15 This image anticipated a series of similar ones found in the films of the fifth-generation directors.

16 With modern intelligentsia's function added to the role of intellectuals, modern Chinese intellectuals have certainly been anything but homogeneous. What I have in mind by "intellectuals" are mostly the writer/critic intellectuals who have, at least in modern Chinese history, stood out as most akin to the intelligentsia, being critical and oppositional to the existing power structure. In the modern Chinese context, they can range from the May Fourth intellectuals to contemporary ones. In today's context, they are mostly writers and critics who have been most vocal in critiquing the power system. I explain this point more extensively in chapter 1.

17 There have been criticisms concerning the question of men, and I refer to them when necessary in my discussion throughout the book. My study both echoes and negotiates some of these earlier discussions.

18 Martin Jay, *Adorno* (Cambridge, MA: Harvard University Press, 1984), 23.

19 Jean Laplanche, *Life and Death in Psychoanalysis,* trans. Jeffrey Mehlman (Baltimore: Johns Hopkins University Press, 1976), 50.

20 For this last point, see Rey Chow, "Postmodern Automatons," in *Writing Diaspora* (Bloomington: Indiana University Press, 1993), 55–72.

21 Fredric Jameson's well-known characterization of "Third World" literature.

22 In her paper "Gender Equality in China: Between the State and Market" presented at the conference on Chinese Women and Feminist Thoughts 21–24 June 1995 in Beijing, Lin Chun points out that because of the lack of the basics of a democracy, as individual citizens Chinese men may not necessarily always enjoy a more powerful political and economic position than do women. Others have also suggested that during the first thirty years of the CCP's regime, Chinese men as individuals did not enjoy more power than women mainly because the regime suppressed any individual rights regardless of gender.

23 See, for example, Lu Tonglin, *Misogyny, Cultural Nihilism, and Oppositional Politics* (Stanford: Stanford University Press, 1995).

24 For more on this issue, see Lu Tonglin's discussion of misogyny in ibid.

25 Kaja Silverman, *Male Subjectivity at the Margins* (New York: Routledge, 1992).

26 Arthur Brittan, *Masculinity and Power* (New York: Basil Blackwell, 1989), 4.

27 Rey Chow, "Against the Lures of Diaspora," in *Gender and Sexuality in Twentieth-Century Chinese Literature and Society,* ed. Tonglin Lu (Albany: State University of New York Press, 1993), 28.

28 Brittan, *Masculinity and Power,* 4.

1 Masculinity Besieged? Toward an Understanding of Chinese Modernity and Male Subjectivity

1 Kaja Silverman, *Male Subjectivity at the Margins* (New York: Routledge, 1990), 55.

2 Ibid.

3 Judith Butler, *Bodies That Matter* (New York: Routledge, 1993), 9.

4 For more discussion on the role of modern Chinese intellectuals, see Vera Schwarcz, *The Chinese Enlightenment* (Berkeley: University of California Press, 1986); Jerome B. Grieder, *Intellectuals and the State in Modern China* (New York: The Free Press, 1981); Lin Yu-sheng, *The Crisis of Chinese Consciousness* (Madison: University of Wisconsin Press, 1979); Hao Chang, *Chinese Intellectuals in Crisis* (Berkeley: University of California Press, 1987); Jonathan D. Spence, *The Gate of Heavenly Peace* (New York: Penguin, 1981); Xiong Yuezhi, *Xixue dongjian yu wanqing shehui* (The dissemination of Western learning and the late Qing Society) (Shanghai: Shanghai People's Press, 1994).

5 Tu Wei-ming, *Way, Learning, and Politics* (Albany: State University of New York Press, 1993), 25.

6 The recent economic crisis in Asia has further raised questions about the premise of Tu's neo-Confucianist alternative.

7 For more criticism of the revival of Confucianism based on the "successful models" of other Asian communities, see Arif Dirlik, "Reversals, Ironies, Hegemonies," *Modern China* 22, no. 3 (July 1996): 243–84.

8 For more information, see Chang, "Kang Yu-wei (1858–1927)," in *Chinese Intellectuals in Crisis,* 21–65; Kung-Chuan Hsiao, *A Modern China and a New World* (Seattle: University of Washington Press, 1975).

9 For example, Lydia H. Liu, "Narratives of Modern Selfhood: First-Person Fiction in May Fourth Literature," in *Politics, Ideology, and Literary Discourse in Modern China,* ed. Liu Kang and Xiaobing Tang (Durham, NC: Duke University Press, 1993), 102–23; Yue Ming-Bao, "Gendering the Origins of Modern Chinese Fiction," in *Gender and Sexuality in Twentieth-Century Chinese Literature and Society,* ed. Tonglin Lu (Albany: State University of New York Press, 1993), 47–66.

10 Yi-tsi Mei Feuerwerker, "Text, Intertext, and the Representation of the Writing Self in Lu Xun, Yu Dafu, and Wang Meng," in *From May Fourth to June Fourth,* ed. Ellen Widmer and David Der-Wei Wang (Cambridge, MA: Harvard University Press, 1993), 167.

11 Ibid., 179–80.

12 Lydia H. Liu, "Narratives of Modern Selfhood: First-Person Fiction in May Fourth Literature," in *Politics, Ideology, and Literary Discourse in Modern China,* ed. Liu Kang and Xiaobing Tang (Durham, NC: Duke University Press, 1993), 102–23.

13 Even though Chinese intellectuals are said to have been burdened with *youhuan yishi* throughout history, one can make a good case that their modern "anxiety complex" resulted from the changes in modern times and is therefore not to be considered a simple cultural extension characteristic of Chinese intellectuals.

14 Qian Zhongshu's *Weicheng* (The besieged city) was first published by Shanghai Chenguang Publishing House in 1947. The edition used here was published by People's Literature Publishing House (Renmin wenxue chuban she) in 1981 in Beijing.

15 In the novel, Qian Zhongshu points out the irony of the last choice of Fang's subject of study by saying that, "just as Chinese officials and merchants have to change the money obtained from exploiting their own countrymen into foreign currency in order to keep the value of the money" (ibid., 9), getting a degree in Chinese literature from a foreign university would also give more value to that degree. Qian, needless to say, was sarcastic about the Chinese enthusiasm for things Western.

16 Many Chinese commentaries of the 1980s interpreted the title of the novel as a metaphor of marriage. Although C. T. Hsia, in *A History of Modern Chinese Fiction* (New Haven: Yale University Press, 1971), gives a more psychologically oriented reading of the character Fang Hongjian, he understands the besiegedness, via Fang's marriage, as symptomatic of a "man forever seeking attachment and forever finding that each new attachment is but the same bondage" (146). For further discussion, see Lu Wenhu, ed., *Qian Zhongshu yanjiu caiji* (Collection of Qian Zhongshu study) vol. 1 (Beijing: Sanlian Publishing House, 1992); Kong Qingmao, *Qian Zhongshu zhuan* (Biography of Qian Zhongshu) (Nanjing: Jiangsu Literature and Arts Press, 1992); Zhang Wenjiang, *Yinzao babita de zhizhe: Qian Zhongshu zhuan* (The wise man and his Babel tower: A biography of Qian Zhongshu) (Shanghai: Shanghai Wenyi Press, 1993); and Theodor Huters, *Qian Zhongshu* (Boston: Twayne Publishers, 1982).

17 Qian Zhongshu, Xu (preface) to *Weicheng* (The besieged city) (Beijing: People's Literature Press, 1981), 3. This translation and others in this book are mine unless otherwise noted.

18 Ibid., 359.

19 For an extensive discussion on the origin of the concept of the individual in mod-

ern China, see Wang Hui, "Geren guannian de qiyuan yu zhongguo de xiandai rentong" (Issues of modern Chinese identity and the origin of the concept of the individual), *Chinese Social Sciences Quarterly* (autumn 1994): 51–84.

20 For more information and discussion about the debate, see Liu Kang, "Subjectivity, Marxism, and Cultural Theory in China," in *Politics, Ideology, and Literary Discourse in Modern China,* ed. Liu Kang and Xiaobing Tang (Durham, NC: Duke University Press, 1993), 23–55; Mu Ling, "Literary Criticism in the 1980s," *Modern China* 4 (October 1995): 420–27.

21 See, for example, G. W. F. Hegel, "Self-Consciousness," and "Free Concrete Mind," in *The Phenomenology of Mind,* trans. J. B. Baillie (New York: Harper Torchbooks, 1967), 215–67, 269–308; and "Identity," and "Difference," in *Hegel Selection,* ed. J. Loewenberg (New York: Scribner's, 1957), 135–48.

22 Juliet Flower MacCannell, "Desire," in *Feminism and Psychoanalysis,* ed. Elizabeth Wright (Oxford: Blackwell, 1992), 63.

23 Ibid.

24 Tom Rockmore, *Before and after Hegel* (Berkeley: University of California Press, 1992), 5.

25 When such study did take place, it usually was done for the purpose of comparison with their Western counterparts.

26 Sun Longji, " 'Mutaihua' zhi jingsheng xianxiang xue" (The psychological phenomenon of "wombnization": Male Characters in Modern Chinese Fiction), *Nuxingren* (W.M. semiannual) 5 (1991): 112.

27 Ibid., 113.

28 Anthony Giddens has argued in *The Consequences of Modernity* (Stanford: Stanford University Press, 1990), that modernity is a Western project defined historically by "two distinct organizational complexes" that "are of particular significance in the development of modernity: the *nation-state* and *systematic capitalist production.* Both have their roots in specific characteristics of European history and have few parallels in prior periods or in other cultural settings" (174). Though I agree with the need to offer a historicized view of modernity, I also believe that such a view should not be turned into this equation: modernity = West = superior model for the rest of the world. This equation is precisely what is assumed in Sun's argument.

29 When used conventionally, both femininity and masculinity refer to sets of configurations or traits that are identified as being "naturally" feminine or masculine, with the former belonging to women and the latter to men. In Wang's argument, I believe, the notion of masculinity is itself not questioned and is used conventionally.

30 Wang Yuejin, "*Red Sorghum:* Mixing Memory and Desire," in *Perspectives on Chinese Cinema,* ed. Chis Berry (London: BFI Publishing, 1991), 85, 86.

31 A psychoanalytic notion denoting part of male subjection.

32 Elisabeth Bronfen, "Castration Complex," in *Feminism and Psychoanalysis,* ed. Elizabeth Wright (Oxford: Blackwell, 1992), 41.

33 Jacques Lacan, *The Four Fundamental Concepts of Psycho-Analysis,* ed. Jacques-Alain Miller, trans. Alan Sheridan (New York: Norton, 1981), 281.

34 Silverman, *Male Subjectivity at the Margins,* 3.

35 Judith Butler, "Melancholy Gender/Refused Identification," in *Constructing Masculinity,* ed. Maurice Berger, Brian Wallis, and Simon Watson (New York: Routledge, 1995), 33.

36 Silverman, *Male Subjectivity at the Margins,* 388.

37 Butler, "Melancholy Gender," 23.

38 Please see note 13 of the introduction.

39 By "post-1949" I do not mean to suggest that the CCP's own quest for modernity began after it took over China. I focus on post-1949 mainly because some of the major concerns of the new regime would have a unique relationship with the post-Mao writer/critic intellectuals, most of whom grew up in the Mao era.

40 Zheng Shiping, *Party vs. State* (Oxford: Oxford University Press, 1998); Wang Ban, *The Sublime Figure of History* (Stanford: Stanford University Press, 1997).

41 Huang Ping, "You mudi zhi xingdong yu wei yuqi zhi houguo" (Purposeful behavior and unintended consequences), *Chinese Social Sciences Quarterly* (autumn 1994): 37–38.

42 One can argue for the necessity of such a move by pointing toward the latest "Mao craze" and nostalgia for the Laosanjie or the Red Guards generation over their own upbringing. Because memory of the past is always about the present, the question is, What about that past is particularly relevant to the present?

43 For studies regarding the CCP-led revolution and Chinese peasantry, see William Hinton, *Fan Shen* (New York: Monthly Review Press, 1966); Phillip Huang, *The Peasant Economy and Social Change in North China* (Stanford: Stanford University Press, 1985); Helen F. Siu, *Furrows, Peasants, Intellectuals, and the State: Stories and Histories from Modern China* (Stanford: Stanford University Press, 1990); and Shumin Huang, *The Spiral Road* (Boulder, CO: Westview Press, 1989).

44 Benjamin I. Schwartz, *In Pursuit of Wealth and Power* (Cambridge, MA: Harvard University Press, 1964).

45 Mao's words: "It is possible to catch up with Britain in fifteen years. We must summon up our strength and swim vigorously upstream." "Speech at the Supreme State Conference" (28 January 1958), in *Chairman Mao Talks to the People,* ed. Stuart Schram (New York: Pantheon, 1974), 94.

46 Nikolai Ostrovsky, *Kak zakalialas' stal'* (How the steel was tempered) (Moscow: Molodaia gvardiia, 1935).

47 Many Soviet films were being dubbed into Chinese and widely shown in China in the 1950s. *How the Steel Was Tempered* was one of them. See Wu Lun, "Sulian dianying zai zhongguo" (Soviet film in China), *Shijie ribao* (World journal) 6 April 1997, 18.

48 I discuss this point more fully in chapter 3.

49 See note 6 of the introduction.

50   "The Ark" is a story of three divorced and to-be-divorced middle-aged women and their relationships among themselves and with men, husbands, ex-husbands, coworkers, and superiors. Most of the male characters are portrayed negatively, which made the story a controversial one. Most of the controversies centered around whether the author's portrayal of men was fair or not. The assumption behind the criticism is that Chinese men were weakened by the power structure and should not be held responsible for the way they are.

51   For such criticism, see *Gender and Sexuality in Twentieth-Century Chinese Literature and Society,* ed. Tonglin Lu (Albany: State University of New York Press, 1993).

52   This is one of the most commonly quoted lines by Mao on gender equality. In Chinese, it goes like this: "Shidai bu tong le. Nan tongzhi neng zuodao de, nu tongzhi ye neng zuodao." The line first appeared in "To Fully Bring out Women's Initiative in the Revolutionary Construction," *Hongqi* (Red flag) 10 (1971): 63.

53   For an analysis of the CCP's policies on women, see Su Hongjun's discussion of the Party's organ, *Hongqi* magazine: "A Feminist Study on Mao Zedong's Theory of Women and the Policy of the Chinese Communist Party toward Women through a Study of the Party Organ *Hongqi* (1958–1988)," *Chinese Historians* 2 (July 1990): 21–35. Additional analyses can be found in the books listed in note 8 of the introduction.

54   Elisabeth Croll, *Feminism and Socialism in China* (London: Routledge & Kegan Paul, 1978), 185.

55   See ibid., chap. 7, " 'Woman Work': Communist China."

56   Phyllis Andors, *The Unfinished Liberation of Chinese Women 1949–1980* (Bloomington: Indiana University Press; Sussex: Wheatsheaf Books, 1983); Margery Wolf, *Revolution Postponed* (Stanford: Stanford University Press, 1985).

57   Mary Ann Doane, *The Desire to Desire* (Bloomington: Indiana University Press, 1987), 36.

2   Sexuality and Male Desire for "Potency"

1   Zhang Jie, "Ai, shi buneng wangji de" (Love must not be forgotten), *Beijing wenyi* (Beijing literature and arts) 11 (1979): 19–27; Zhang Xianliang, *Nanren de yiban shi nuren* (Half of man is woman), *Shouhuo* (Harvest) 5 (1985): 4–102.

2   In the early 1980s, a woman named Yu Luojin wrote a few nonfiction pieces about her life during the Cultural Revolution. Her stories attracted a wide range of public attention partly because she was the sister of Yu Luoke, a young man who had been executed during the Cultural Revolution for his political views, and partly because she candidly told stories of her first marriage and her love affair with other men afterwards. The public was fascinated by who she was and what she wrote, but the critics generally dismissed her for airing her own "dirty laundry" (*geren yinsi*). Because her stories were mostly about herself, they were not considered "real" literature. Issues of sexuality in her writings were thus ignored.

3 See, for example, Zhang Xinxin, "Wo kan 'nanren de yiban shi nuren' de xing xinli miaoxie" (My view on the depiction of sexuality in "Half of man is woman"), *Wenyi Bao* (Newspaper on arts and literature) 28 December 1985, 2; Wei Junyi, "Yiben changxiaoshu yingqi de sikao" (Thoughts triggered by a best-seller), *Wenyi Bao* 28 December 1985: 2; *Ping "Nanren de yiban shi nuren"* (Reviews of "Half of man is woman") (Yinchuan: Ninxia People's Press, 1987).

4 By this comparison, I do not mean to suggest a lack of interest by women writers in addressing issues of sexuality. Many have, especially since the mid-1980s, but they often do so differently from their male counterparts. It exceeds the scope of this study to discuss the difference except to point this out.

5 In the second half of the 1980s, Wang Anyi, a woman writer, wrote a series of stories loosely known as *san lian* (three love stories) exploring the theme of sexuality: "Huangshan zhilian" (Love on a barren mountain), "Xiaocheng zhilian" (Love in a small town), and "Jinxiugu zhilian" (Love in a brocade valley). She caused some sensation as a woman writer writing on the subject, but her exploration of the subject came after the ice had been broken. The way she addresses the theme requires a separate study that exceeds the scope of this one.

6 There is, of course, also a difference between women writers' representations of sexuality and that of male writers, but due to the scope of this study, I am not able to elaborate on the difference here except to point it out.

7 Esther Yau, "*Yellow Earth:* Western Analysis and a Non-Western Text," in *Perspectives on Chinese Cinema,* ed. Chris Berry (London: BFI Publishing, 1991), 62– 79.

8 Tani Barlow has argued that, though both are modern terms and both refer to women, the word *nuxing* (female) is a modern Chinese category formulated under the influence of Western ideas at the turn of the century, whereas the word *funu* is more commonly used by the CCP with its own historically conditioned implications. Her distinction between *funu* and *nuxing* is pointed (even though questions can be raised regarding her claim of the premodern linguistic references used to refer to women). In correspondence to modern and premodern Chinese contexts, the suffix *xing* in *nuxing* helps indicate that, in modern Chinese, the connotation of the word *xing* in the classical sense—"the nature of things"—finds an echo in modern Chinese and becomes a "natural" choice for a modern humanistic discourse. Tani E. Barlow, "Theorizing Woman: Funü, Guojia, Jiating," in *Body, Subject and Power in China,* ed. Angela Zito and Tani E. Barlow (Chicago: University of Chicago Press, 1994), 253–89.

9 Nancy Hartsock, *Money, Sex, and Power* (Boston: Northeastern University Press, 1985), 156.

10 Quoted in Stephen A. Mitchell, *Relational Concepts in Psychoanalysis* (Cambridge, MA: Harvard University Press, 1988), 101.

11 Hartsock, *Money, Sex, and Power,* 156.

12 Judith Butler, *Bodies That Matter* (New York: Routledge, 1993), 1.

13 Michel Foucault, *The History of Sexuality,* trans. Robert Herly (New York: Vintage Books, 1980), 1:3.

14 Judith Butler, *Gender Trouble* (New York: Routledge, 1990), 76.

15 Privately, it could be a different matter, even though the public silence on sex and sexuality would have undoubtedly affected the private space in which sexuality was concerned. For a sense of what it might have been like, see Gail Hershatter and Emily Honig, *Personal Voices* (Stanford: Stanford University Press, 1988).

16 Harriet Evans, *Women and Sexuality in China: Female Sexuality and Gender Since 1949* (New York: Continuum, 1997).

17 In Chinese, *po xie* ("old shoe") is a term used against women with supposedly illicit relationships. During the Cultural Revolution women were subject to public humiliation being labeled as such. There is not a term in Chinese for men that has the same negative and humiliating connotation as *po xie* does for women. The effect of such humiliation of women was more than warning people against illicit sexual relationships; it also continued to reenforce some of the conventions of the patriarchal ideology.

18 Butler, *Bodies That Matter,* 3.

19 Zhong Xueping, "Male Desire and Male Suffering: The Politics of Reading *Half of Man Is Woman,*" in *Engendering China,* ed. Christina Gilmartin et al. (Cambridge, MA: Harvard University Press, 1994), 175–94.

20 David Macey, "Phallus: Definitions," in *Feminism and Psychoanalysis,* ed. Elizabeth Wright (Cambridge, MA: Blackwell, 1992), 318.

21 Jane Gallop, *The Daughter's Seduction: Feminism and Psychoanalysis* (Ithaca: Cornell University Press, 1982); Jane Gallop, *Reading Lacan* (Ithaca: Cornell University Press, 1985).

22 Jean-Joseph Goux, "The Phallus: Masculine Identity and 'Exchange of Women,'" *Differences* 4 (spring 1992): 40–75.

23 Kaja Silverman, *Male Subjectivity at the Margins* (New York: Routledge, 1990), 3.

24 Rey Chow, *Writing Diaspora* (Bloomington: Indiana University Press, 1993), 107.

25 Whereas the publication of "Mimosa" won him tremendous notoriety, the publication of *Half of Man Is Woman* did not seem to meet with the same critical acclaim. Many critics, both men and women, were critical of the story especially with regard to the protagonist's relationship with the woman character Huang Xiangjiu.

26 Zhang Xianliang, *Xiguan siwang* (Accustomed to death) (Taipei: Yuansheng Press, 1989), 2.

27 Silverman, *Male Subjectivity at the Margins,* 3.

28 Zhang, *Xiguan siwang,* 12.

29 Liu Heng, *Dong zhi men* (Winter's gate), in *Xiao shuo jia* (Novelists) 3 (1992), 5.

30 Marie-Claire Huot, "Liu Heng's *Fuxi Fuxi:* What about Nuwa?" in *Gender and Sexuality in Twentieth-Century Chinese Literature and Society,* ed. Tonglin Lu (Albany: State University of New York Press, 1993), 98–99.

31 Ibid., 85.

32 Silverman, *Male Subjectivity at the Margins*, 58–59.

33 Ibid., 58.

3 From Heroes to Adjuncts, Nobodies, and Antiheroes: The Politics of (Male) Marginality

1 Zhang Chengzhi, "Beifang de he" (Rivers of the north), *Shiyue* (October) 1 (1984): 4–49; "Hei junma" (Black stallion), *Shiyue* 6 (1982): 66–95; "Huangni xiaowu" (A yellow-earthen hut), *Shouhuo* (Harvest) 6 (1985): 4–41.

2 Zhang, "Beifang de he," 69.

3 "Revolutionary realism and romanticism" was the motto for literary creation during the first thirty years of the CCP's regime. Literature was used as a form of propaganda; literary creation, therefore, was based on already fixed doctrines, ideals, and truth. The extreme versions of such literature, mostly produced during the Cultural Revolution, are filled with larger-than-life heroes.

4 Wang Ruoshui, "Guanyu 'yihua' de gainian" (About the concept of "alienation"), in *Waiguo zhexue shi yanjiu jikan* (Collection of research essays on the history of foreign philosophies) (Shanghai: Shanghai People's Press, 1978), 1–34.

5 Following the alienation debate was the debate on the notion of subjectivity (*zhutixing*), argued mainly by Li Zehou and Liu Zaifu. For more information on these two, see chapter 1, n. 20.

6 Art Berman, *Preface to Modernism* (Urbana: University of Illinois Press, 1994), 24.

7 Modernist literature existed in China by the 1930s. However, by and large it did not emerge the same way as did post–Cultural Revolution modernism. For one thing, the earlier modernism was not as closely associated with politics as its latter version for specific historical reasons.

8 *Geren* (individual) is too close to *geren zhuyi* (individualism), a term given a strong negative connotation (selfishness, or self-centeredness) by the CCP's dominant discourse.

9 Berman, *Preface to Modernism*, 22.

10 Nan Fan, "Wenxue: fu yu zi" (Literature: Father and son), *Shanghai wenxue* (Shanghai literature) 10 (1991): 73.

11 Li Tuo, Zhang Ling, and Wang Bing, " 'Yuyan' de fanpan" (The revolt of "language"), *Wenyi yanjiu* (Literature and arts studies) 2 (1989): 75–80.

12 Howard Goldblatt, ed., *Chairman Mao Would Not Be Amused* (New York: Grove Press, 1995).

13 Lu Tonglin, "Can Xue: What Is So Paranoid in Her Writings?" in *Gender and Sexuality in Twentieth-Century Chinese Literature and Society,* ed. Tonglin Lu (Albany: State University of New York Press, 1993), 177.

14 Yu Hua, "Siyue sanri shijian" (The April third incident), in *Zhongguo xinchao xiaoshuo xuan* (Selections of new wave stories in China), ed. Cheng Youxin (Shanghai: Shanghai Academy of Social Sciences Press, 1989), 225.

15 Cheng Yongxin, "Bianhou yu" (Editor's notes), in *Zhongguo xinchao xiaoshuo xuan,* 266.

16 Han Shaogong, "Wenxue de gen" (Roots of literature), *Zuojia* (Writers) 4 (1985): 2–5.

17 Wu Liang and Cheng Peide, eds., *Xinxiaoshuo zai 1985 nian* (New fiction in 1985) (Shanghai: Shanghai Academy of Social Sciences Press, 1986), 1.

18 Many contemporary Chinese avant-garde (male) writers are said to be very interested in Gabriel García Márquez's magic realism, an interest seen in many of their writings.

19 Han Shaogong, "Bababa" (Dad Dad Dad), in *Xinxiaoshuo zai 1985 nian* (New fiction in 1985), ed. Wu Liang and Cheng Peide (Shanghai: Shanghai Academy of Social Sciences Press, 1986), 1–2.

20 Walter Benjamin, *The Origin of German Tragic Drama,* trans. John Osborne (London: NLB, 1977), 178.

21 Han, "Bababa," 6.

22 Both interpretations can be seen as absurd because Xingtian is a legendary figure in traditional Chinese tales. The legend goes that he struggles for power with Tiandi (the God of Heaven) and is beheaded when defeated. But he is so determined to fight on that he turns his nipples into eyes and his belly button into a mouth and his arms continue to carry weapons.

23 Han, "Bababa," 38.

24 Rey Chow, *Primitive Passions* (New York: Columbia University Press, 1995), 111–12.

25 See Geremie Barmé, "Wang Shuo and *Liumang* ('Hooligan') Culture," *Australian Journal of Chinese Affairs* 28 (July 1992): 23–64, for his definitions of the notion of hooligan and its historical connotations.

26 Unless, of course, it is translated visually. The film *In the Heat of the Sun* (which is based on Wang's *Dongwu xiongmeng* and directed by Jiang Wen), for example, is able to use the visual to produce the comical effects of Wang's language. As a result, it has received acclaimed international recognition.

27 Barmé, "Wang Shuo," 23, quoting Wang Shuo, "Wode xiaoshuo" (My fiction), *Renmin wenxue* (People's literature) 3 (1989): 108.

28 Barmé, "Wang Shuo," 31.

29 Wang Meng, "Duobi chonggao" (Stay away from the sublime), *Dushu* (Reading) 1 (1993): 14.

30 There are books of criticism published in China critiquing Wang Shuo. Among them, Xiao Yuan, *Wang Shuo zai pipan* (Recriticizing Wang Shuo) (Changsha: Hunan Publishing House, 1993).

31 *In the Heat of the Sun* is the name of the film based on this story. Its national and international success (its leading actor won the leading actor award at the Cannes Film Festival in 1995) has yet to attract the attention of critics to examine the film's implications. In China, the success of the film is partly a spin-off of the success of the Wang Shuo phenomenon.

32 Wang Shuo, *Dongwu xiongmeng* (Animal vicious), *Shouhuo* (Harvest) 6 (1991): 130–207. Even though this novella was published in 1991, I see it as part of the Wang Shuo phenomenon, which essentially belongs to the ethos of the 1980s.

33 It is possible that Jiang is poking fun at the seemingly triumphant "sons" in the last scene of the film. Such a reading, however, is not convincing. Although the scene is a playful one, in accordance with the satirical nature of the entire film, the playfulness is not aimed at undermining the power of these newcomers. Given the director's own interest in portraying Chinese manliness via a carnivalistic spirit, it is necessary to realize that, though on the one hand there might be a degree of self-deprecation on the part of the director's poking fun at the young men themselves, on the other, there is too strong a masculinist self-love displayed in the film for the director to poke serious fun at these "sons" at the end of the film.

4 *Zazhong gaoliang* and the Male Search for Masculinity

1 Li Tuo, Xu (preface) to *Touming de hong luobo* (The transparent red radish) (Beijing: Writers Press, 1986), 1–10.

2 See, for example, Lu Tonglin, *"Red Sorghum:* Limits of Transgression," in *Politics, Ideology, and Literary Discourse in Modern China,* ed. Liukang and Xiaobing Tang (Durham, NC: Duke University Press, 1993), 188–210; Zhu Ling, "A Brave New World? On the Construction of 'Masculinity' and 'Femininity' in *The Red Sorghum Family,"* in *Gender and Sexuality in Twentieth-Century Chinese Literature and Society,* ed. Tonglin Lu (Albany: State University of New York Press, 1993), 121–34; Wang Yuejin, *"Red Sorghum:* Mixing Memory and Desire," in *Perspectives on Chinese Cinema,* ed. Chris Berry (London, BFI Publishing, 1991), 80–103. There are also papers presented at such conferences as the AAS annual meetings discussing either the film or the novel.

3 Mo Yan, *Hong gaoliang jiazu* (The red sorghum family) (Beijing: PLA Arts and Literature Press, 1987), 1.

4 Lu, *"Red Sorghum:* Limits of Transgression," 188–210.

5 Mo, *Hong gaoliang jiazu,* 450.

6 For further discussion on the ruralness of contemporary writers, see Nan Fan, "Wenxue: chengshi yu xiangcun" (Literature: City and country), *Shanghai wenxue* (Shanghai literature) 4 (1990): 29–33, 80; Xueping Zhong, "Shanghai *Shimin* Literature and the Ambivalence of (Urban) Home," *Modern Chinese Literature* 1 (1995): 79–100.

7 This reminds me of Rey Chow's discussion of contemporary Chinese film in *Primitive Passions* (New York: Columbia University Press, 1995), in which she explores the relationship between the rise of modernist art and its aesthetic objects, the so-called primitive peoples, societies, and cultures.

8 Mo, *Hong gaoliang jiazu,* 453.

9 Yu Dafu, "Chenlun" (Sinking), *Yu Dafu zaoqi zuoping xuan* (Selection of Yu Dafu's early works) (Guangzhou: Huacheng Publishing House, 1982), 57.

10 See chapter 1, n. 9.

11 C. T. Hsia, *A History of Modern Chinese Fiction* (New Haven: Yale University Press, 1971), 109.

12 See, for example, Leo Ou-fan Lee, *The Romantic Generation of Modern Chinese Writers* (Cambridge, MA: Harvard University Press, 1973).

13 Lu Xun, "A Q zhengzhuan" (The story of Ah Q). It first appeared in installments in *Chenbao fukan* (Morning newspaper) from December 1921 to February 1922. In 1923, the story was collected and published in *Nahan* (Call to arms) (Beijing: Xinchao Publishing House, 1923).

14 Liu Zaifu and Lin Gang, "Zhongguo chuantong wenhua he 'A Q moshi'" (Traditional Chinese culture and the "Ah Q model"), *Zhongguo shehui kexue* (Chinese social sciences) 3 (1988): 133–52. The reason I focus on these two critics' discussion of Ah Q is because they were part of the intellectual endeavor of the 1980s. As such, their reexamination of Ah Q was carried out within the intellectual climate that manifested itself, in part, in the male search for masculine identity.

15 Ibid., 134.

16 Silverman, *Male Subjectivity at the Margins,* 189.

17 Sigmund Freud, "Economic Problem of Masochism," in *The Standard Edition of the Complete Psychological Works of Sigmund Freud,* trans. James Strachey (London: Hogarth Press, 1961), 161.

18 Ibid., 159. For further discussion of this paradox, see the opening remarks of this essay.

19 See, for example, R. Stoller, *Observing the Erotic Imagination* (New Haven: Yale University Press, 1985); Stephen A. Mitchell, *Relational Concepts in Psychoanalysis* (Cambridge, MA: Harvard University Press, 1988).

20 Kaja Silverman, *Male Subjectivity at the Margins* (New York: Routledge, 1990), 187.

21 For a discussion of the notion of dominant fiction, see ibid., 15–51.

22 This reminds me of many arguments made by Chinese intellectuals over the years about why China has fallen behind in the modern world and why the West became the leading force into modernity. They argue that Christianity is an aggressive religion that functions to push a Christian culture to move forward, whereas Chinese culture does not have a religion that functions this way. Instead, their argument assumes, Chinese culture has been deeply hindered by the oppressive hierarchical structure of neo-Confucianism and the Taoist way of counterbalancing the oppressiveness. To a large extent, the TV series *He shang* (River elegy, 1988) represents such an argument. For more debate on these issues, see Chen Xiaomei, "Occidentalism as Counterdiscourse: 'He Shang' in Post-Mao China," *Critical Inquiry* 18 (summer 1992): 686–712.

23 Liu and Lin, "Zhongguo de chuantong wenhua yu 'A Q moshi,'" 152.

24 Benjamin I. Schwartz, *In Search of Wealth and Power* (Cambridge, MA: Harvard University Press, 1964).

25 I heard this distinction made on a radio program in Boston ("The Connection" on WBUR, 1 July 1996). The discussion on this program focused on how shame has

become part of the psychological pattern in the United States, where traditionally, according to the guest on the program, it used to be defined as being preoccupied by guilt. Even though this kind of claim leaves much to be desired, it can at least trigger responses that may lead to interesting discussions.

26 Sigmund Freud, "On Narcissism: An Introduction," trans. Cecil M. Baines, in *Collected Papers* (New York: Basic Books, 1959), 4:40–41.

27 Jean Laplanche, *Life and Death in Psychoanalysis,* trans. Jeffrey Mehlman (Baltimore: Johns Hopkins University Press, 1976), 79.

28 Freud, "On Narcissism," *Collected Papers,* 47.

29 Chow, *Primitive Passions,* 37.

30 Li, Xu, 10.

31 Chow, *Primitive Passions,* 198.

32 Can Xue, " 'Yanggang zhiqi' yu wenxue pinglun de haoshiguang" ("Masculinity" and the heyday of literary criticism), in *Tuwei biaoyan* (Performing "Breaking out of an encirclement") (Shanghai: Shanghai Literature and Arts Press, 1990), 336.

5   Manhood, Cultural Roots, and National Identity

1 *Xinshiqi* is a term coined to name the post–Cultural Revolution era. Lately, there is another term floating among critics in China, post–New Era (*hou xinshiqi*), which is used mainly to refer to the 1990s.

2 See, for example, Ji Hongzhen, "Lishi de mingti yu shidai jueze zhong de yishu chanbian—lun 'xungen wenxue' de fasheng yu yiyi" (On the origin and significance of the "searching-for-roots literature"), *Dangdai zuojia pinglun* (Review of contemporary writers) 1 and 2 (1989): 13–22, 69–75.

3 The exception may be Wang Anyi's (a woman writer) novella *Xiao Bao zhuang* (Bao town), *Zhongguo zuojia* (Chinese writers) 2 (1985): 43–84, which many critics categorize as a piece of *xungen* writing. This, however, is the only piece by Wang that has been recognized as such. None of her other writings published in the 1980s fit this category.

4 For further discussion in addition to Lu Tonglin's and Rey Chow's works, see Jing Wang, *High Culture Fever* (Berkeley: University of California Press, 1996).

5 I put "traditional" in parentheses for a reason. There are a few terms often used interchangeably when people refer to Chinese culture: "traditional Chinese culture" (*chuantong zhongguo wenhua*), "traditional culture" (*chuantong wenhua*), "Chinese culture" (*zhongguo wenhua*), "cultural tradition" (*wenhua chuantong*), and others. Little effort has been made to clarify these terms, which do not always mean the same thing. In some cases, "Chinese culture" is used to refer to "traditional Chinese culture," a term that bears a negative connotation. Therefore, I find it necessary to put "traditional" in parentheses for clarification.

6 Unlike many May Fourth writers whose relationship to Chinese traditional culture was a critical one and who did not set out to attack it because they desired to find their "real" self in it, the *xungen* writers find themselves in a different historical

moment. They are faced with a paradox: by the time they emerged in contemporary China, the May Fourth writers' object of attack, the Confucian value system, was destroyed as a system but inherited at a deeper structural level in the CCP's power structure. The question became: What do they mean by *xungen*, or "searching for roots"?

7 For historical reasons, most of the *xungen* writers belong to the Red Guard generation and many of them went to the countryside (if they were not originally from there) during the Cultural Revolution to receive "reeducation." Their encounter with rural China made them come closer to parts of China where modern influence remained at a minimum level and where the traditional cultural practices still dominated in a more obvious way than in urban areas. Years later, after they had left those places and began to ponder the question of Chinese culture, many of them "naturally" returned to rural China, where they believe "traditional Chinese culture," both its problems and its glory, exist.

8 Han Shaogong, "Wenxue de gen" (Roots of literature), *Zuojia* (Writers) 4 (1985): 2–5; 6:62.

9 Zheng Wanlong, "Wo de gen" (My roots), *Shanghai wenxue* (Shanghai literature) 5 (1985): 44–46; Li Hangyu, "Li yi li wo de gen" (Examining my roots), *Zuojia* (Writers) 9 (1985): 75–77; Ah Cheng, "Wenhua zhiyue zhe renlei" (Culture conditions humankind), *Wenyi bao* (Newspaper on arts and literature) 6 (1985).

10 Han, "Wenxue de gen," 2.

11 Han Shaogong, *Mousha* (Murder) (Taibei: Yuanjin Publishing House, 1989), 16. *Long de chuanren* ("descendants of the dragon") is a phrase often used to refer to the Chinese.

12 Ji Hongzhen, "Youyu de tudi, buqu de jinghun" (The melancholic land and the unyielding spirit), *Wenxue pinglun* (Literary review) 6 (1987): 23.

13 Li Qingxi, "Gulao dadi de chengmu" (Silence of the ancient land), *Wenxue pinglun* (Literary review) 6 (1987): 54.

14 Zheng, "Wo de gen," 44.

15 This section, indeed my entire book, was written before Wang Ban's book *The Sublime Figure of History* was published. I find his discussion of the notion of the sublime brilliant and thought-provoking. I hope my discussion here can offer an additional dimension to his argument.

16 Mo Yan, *Hong gaoliang jiazu* (The red sorghum family) (Beijing: PLA Arts and Literature Press, 1987), 3.

17 Zheng, "Wo de gen," 44.

18 Rey Chow, "Male Narcissism and National Culture," in *Primitive Passions* (New York: Columbia University Press, 1995), 108–41.

19 Ah Cheng, "Shuwang" (King of trees), in *Qiwang Shuwang Haiziwang* (Kings of chess, trees, and children), ed. Leo Lee et al. (Taibei: Xindi Literary Publishing House, 1988), 61–118.

20 Slavoj Žižek, *The Sublime Object of Ideology* (London: Verso, 1989), 109.

21 G.W.F. Hegel, "The Doctrine of Essence," in *Hegel Selections,* ed. J. Loewenberg (New York: Scribner's, 1957), 140.

22 Žižek, *The Sublime Object of Ideology,* 110.

23 Walter Benjamin, "Eduard Fuchs, Collector and Historian," in *The Essential Frankfurt School Reader,* ed. Andrew Arato and Eike Gebhardt (New York: Urizen Books, 1978), 227. In this translation, the translator uses "element" and "specific." In another translation, "element" is "dimension" and "specific" is "particular" (D. R. Howland, "Constructing Perry's 'Chinaman' in the Context of Adorno and Benjamin," *Positions* 2 [fall 1995]: 329).

24 Ching-kiu Stephen Chan, "Split China, or, The Historical/Imaginary: Toward a Theory of the Displacement of Subjectivity at the Margins of Modernity," in *Politics, Ideology, and Literary Discourse in Modern China,* ed. Liu Kang and Xiaobing Tang (Durham, NC: Duke University Press, 1993), 70–101.

25 Zheng, "Wo de gen," 46.

26 Rey Chow, *Primitive Passions* (New York: Columbia University Press, 1995), 37.

27 Chan, "Split China," 83.

28 Susan Buck-Morss, *The Dialectics of Seeing* (Cambridge, MA: MIT Press, 1989), 8. Buck-Morss cites from *Ursprung des deutschen Trauerspiel,* 1:226.

29 See introduction, n. 11.

30 Joseph R. Levenson, *Liang Chi-chao and the Mind of Modern China* (Cambridge, MA: Harvard University Press, 1953), 5.

Bibliography

Ah Cheng. "Shuwang" (King of trees). In *Qiwang shuwang Haiziwang* (Kings of chess, trees, and children), ed. Leo Lee et al. Taibe: Xindi Literary Publishing House, 1988, 61–118.

——. "Wenhua zhiyue zhe renlei" (Culture conditions humankind). *Wenyi bao* (Newspaper on arts and literature) 6 (1985).

Anderson, Benedict. *Imagined Communities.* London: Verso, 1983.

Anderson, Marston. *The Limits of Realism.* Berkeley: University of California, 1990.

Andors, Phyllis. *The Unfinished Liberation of Chinese Women 1949–1980.* Bloomington: Indiana University Press; Sussex: Wheatsheaf Books, 1983.

Barlow, Tani E. "Theorizing Woman: Funu, Guojia, Jiating (Chinese Woman, Chinese State, Chinese Family)." In *Body, Subject and Power in China,* ed. Angela Zito and Tani E. Barlow. Chicago: University of Chicago Press, 1994, 253–89.

——, ed. *Gender Politics in Modern China.* Durham, NC: Duke University Press, 1993.

Barmé, Geremie. "Wang Shuo and *Liumang* ('Hooligan') Culture." *Australian Journal of Chinese Affairs* 28 (July 1992): 23–64.

Benjamin, Walter. *The Origin of German Tragic Drama,* trans. John Osborne. London: NLB, 1977.

——. "Eduard Fuchs: Collector and Historian." In *The Essential Frankfurt School Reader,* ed. Andrew Arato and Eike Gebhardt. New York: Urizen Books, 1978, 225–53.

Berman, Art. *Preface to Modernism.* Urbana: University of Illinois Press, 1994.

Berry, Chris, ed. *Perspectives on Chinese Cinema.* London: BFI Publishing, 1991.

Boone, Joseph A., and Michael Cadden, eds. *Engendering Men.* New York: Routledge, 1990.

Brittan, Arthur. *Masculinity and Power.* New York: Basil Blackwell, 1989.

Bronfen, Elisabeth. "Castration Complex." In *Feminism and Psychoanalysis,* ed. Elizabeth Wright. Oxford: Blackwell, 1992, 41–45.

Brown, Carolyn T. "Woman as Trope: Gender and Power in Lu Xun's 'Soap.' " In *Gender Politics in Modern China,* ed. Tani E. Barlow. Durham, NC: Duke University Press, 1993, 74–89.

Buck-Morss, Susan. *The Dialectics of Seeing.* Cambridge, MA: MIT Press, 1989.

Butler, Judith. *Gender Trouble.* New York: Routledge, 1990.

——. *Bodies That Matter.* New York: Routledge, 1993.

——. "Melancholy Gender/Refused Identification." In *Constructing Masculinity,* ed. Maurice Berger, Brian Wallis, and Simon Watson. New York: Routledge, 1995, 21–36.

Can Xue. " 'Yanggang zhiqi' yu wenxue pinglun de haoshiguang" ("Masculinity" and the heyday of literary criticism). In *Tuwei biaoyan* (Performing "Breaking out of an encirclement"). Shanghai: Shanghai Literature and Arts Press, 1990, 332–51.

Chan, Ching-kiu Stephen. "The Language of Despair: Ideological Representations of the 'New Woman' by May Fourth Writers." In *Gender Politics in Modern China,* ed. Tani E. Barlow. Durham, NC: Duke University Press, 1993, 13–32.

———. "Split China, or, The Historical/Imaginary: Toward a Theory of the Displacement of Subjectivity at the Margins of Modernity." In *Politics, Ideology, and Literary Discourse in Modern China,* ed. Liu Kang and Xiaobing Tang. Durham, NC: Duke University Press, 1993, 70–101.

Chang, Hao. *Chinese Intellectuals in Crisis.* Berkeley: University of California Press, 1987.

Chen Huifen. "Zhaohui shiluo de naban: 'renshi ni ziji' " (In search of that lost half: "Recognize yourself"). *Dangdai wenyi sichao* (Ideas in contemporary literature and arts) 2 (1987): 8–15.

Chen Xiaomei. "Occidentalism as Counterdiscourse: 'He Shang' in Post-Mao China." *Critical Inquiry* 18 (summer 1992): 686–712.

Chow, Rey. *Woman and Chinese Modernity.* Minneapolis: University of Minnesota Press, 1991.

———. "Against the Lures of Diaspora." In *Gender and Sexuality in Twentieth-Century Chinese Literature and Society,* ed. Tonglin Lu. Albany: State University of New York Press, 1993, 23–46.

———. "Male Narcissism and National Culture: Subjectivity in Chen Kaige's *King of Children.*" In *From May Fourth to June Fourth,* ed. Ellen Widmer and David Der-wei Wang. Cambridge, MA: Harvard University Press, 1993, 327–59.

———. *Writing Diaspora.* Bloomington: Indiana University Press, 1993.

———. *Primitive Passions.* New York: Columbia University Press, 1995.

Cixous, Hélène, and Catherine Clement. "Glossary." In *The Newly Born Woman.* Trans. Betsy Wing. Minneapolis: University of Minnesota Press, 1975, 163–69.

Clark, Paul. *Chinese Cinema.* Cambridge: Cambridge University Press, 1987.

Croll, Elisabeth. *Feminism and Socialism in China.* London: Routledge & Kegan Paul, 1978.

De Lauretis, Teresa. *Technologies of Gender.* Bloomington: Indiana University Press, 1987.

Dikötter, Frank. *Sex, Culture, and Modernity in China.* Honolulu: University of Hawaii Press, 1995.

Dirlik, Arif. "The Postcolonial Aura: Third World Criticism in the Age of Global Capitalism." *Critical Inquiry* 20 (winter 1994): 328–56.

———. "Reversals, Ironies, Hegemonies." *Modern China* 22, no. 3 (July 1996): 243–84.

Dittmer, Lowell, and Samuel S. Kim, eds. *China's Quest for National Identity.* Ithaca, NY: Cornell University Press, 1993.

Doane, Mary Ann. *The Desire to Desire.* Bloomington: Indiana University Press, 1987.

Evans, Harriet. *Women and Sexuality in China: Female Sexuality and Gender Since 1949.* New York: Continuum, 1997.

Feuerwerker, Yi-tsi Mei. "Text, Intertext, and the Representation of the Writing Self in Lu Xun, Yu Dafu, and Wang Meng." In *From May Fourth to June Fourth,* ed. Ellen Widmer and David Der-wei Wang. Cambridge, MA: Harvard University Press, 1993, 167–93.

Foucault, Michel. *The History of Sexuality,* vol. 1. Trans. Robert Herly. New York: Vintage Books, 1980.

Freud, Sigmund. "On Narcissism: An Introduction." Trans. Cecil M. Baines. In *Collected Papers*, vol. 4. New York: Basic Books, 1959, 30–59.

——. "Economic Problem of Masochism." In *The Standard Edition of the Complete Psychological Works of Sigmund Freud*. Vol. 19. Trans. and ed. James Strachey. London: Hogarth Press, 1961, 155–72.

Gallop, Jane. *The Daughter's Seduction*. Ithaca: Cornell University Press, 1982.

——. *Reading Lacan*. Ithaca: Cornell University Press, 1985.

Giddens, Anthony. *The Consequences of Modernity*. Stanford: Stanford University Press, 1990.

Gilmartin, Christina K., Gail Hershatter, Lisa Rofel, and Tyrene White, eds. *Engendering China*. Cambridge, MA: Harvard University Press, 1994.

Gilmore, David D. *Manhood in the Making*. New Haven: Yale University Press, 1990.

Goldblatt, Howard, ed. *Chairman Mao Would Not Be Amused*. New York: Grove Press, 1995.

Goldman, Merle, Timothy Cheek, and Carol Lee Hamrin, eds. *China's Intellectuals and the State*. Cambridge, MA: Council on East Asian Studies/Harvard University, 1987.

Grieder, Jerome B. *Intellectuals and the State in Modern China*. New York: The Free Press, 1981.

Goux, Jean-Joseph. "The Phallus: Masculine Identity and the 'Exchange of Women.'" *Differences* 4 (spring 1992): 40–75.

Guo Xiaodong. "Nuren zai qinxie de shijie li" (Women in a tilted world). *Pi ping jia* (Critics) 6 (1988): 15–19.

Han Shaogong. "Wenxue de gen" (Roots of literature). *Zuojia* (Writers) 4 (1985): 2–5; 6:62.

——. "Bababa" (Dad Dad Dad). In *Xinxiaoshuo zai 1985 nian* (New fiction in 1985), ed. Wu Liang and Cheng Peide. Shanghai: Shanghai Academy of Social Sciences Press, 1986, 1–38.

——. *Mousha* (Murder). Taibei: Yuanjin Publishing House, 1989.

Hartsock, Nancy. *Money, Sex, and Power*. Boston: Northeastern University Press, 1985.

Hegel, G.W.F. *Hegel Selections*. Ed. J. Loewenberg. New York: Scribner's, 1957.

——. *The Phenomenology of Mind*. Trans. J. B. Baillie. New York: Harper Torchbooks, 1967.

Hershatter, Gail, and Emily Honig. *Personal Voices*. Stanford: Stanford University Press, 1988.

Hinton, William. *Fan Shen*. New York: Monthly Review Press, 1966.

Howland, D. R. "Constructing Perry's 'Chinaman' in the Context of Adorno and Benjamin." *Positions* (fall 1995): 329–66.

Hsia, C. T. *A History of Modern Chinese Fiction*. New Haven: Yale University Press, 1971.

Huang, Phillip. *The Peasant Economy and Social Change in North China*. Stanford: Stanford University Press, 1985.

Huang Ping. "You mudi zhi xingdong yu wei yuqi zhi houguo" (Purposeful behavior and unintended consequences). *Chinese Social Sciences Quarterly* (autumn 1994): 37–50.

Huang, Shumin. *The Spiral Road*. Boulder, CO: Westview Press, 1989.

Huot, Marie-Claire. "Liu Heng's *Fuxi Fuxi*: What about Nuwa?" In *Gender and Sexuality in Twentieth-Century Chinese Literature and Society*, ed. Tonglin Lu. Albany: State University of New York Press, 1993, 85–106.

Huters, Theodore. *Qian Zhongshu.* Boston: Twayne Publishers, 1982.

Hsiao Kung-Chuan. *A Modern China and a New World.* Seattle: University of Washington Press, 1975.

Jameson, Fredric. "Third-World Literature in the Era of Multinational Capitalism." *Social Text* (fall 1986): 65–88.

Jay, Martin. *Adorno.* Cambridge, MA: Harvard University Press, 1984.

Ji Hongzhen. "Youyu de tudi, buqu de jinghun" (The melancholic land and the unyielding spirit). *Wenxue pinglun* (Literary review) 6 (1987): 20–29.

——. "Lishi de mingti yu shidai jueze zhong de yishu chanbian—lun 'xungen wenxue' de fasheng yu yiyi" (On the origin and significance of the "searching-for-roots literature"). *Dangdai zuojia pinglun* (Review of contemporary writers) 1 and 2 (1989): 13–22, 69–75.

——. "Wenhua xungen yu dangdai wenxue" (Cultural roots-seeking and contemporary literature). *Wenyi yanjiu* (Literature and arts studies) 2 (1989): 69–74.

Kong Qingmao. *Qian Zhongshu Zhuan* (Biography of Qian Zhongshu). Nanjing: Jiangsu Literature and Arts Press, 1992.

Lacan, Jacques. *The Four Fundamental Concepts of Psycho-Analysis.* Ed. Jacques-Alain Miller, trans. Alan Sheridan. New York: Norton, 1973.

——. *Ecrits: A Selection.* New York: Norton, 1977.

Laplanche, Jean. *Life and Death in Psychoanalysis.* Trans. Jeffrey Mehlman. Baltimore: Johns Hopkins University Press, 1976.

Laplanche, Jean, and J.-B. Pontalis, eds. *The Language of Psycho-Analysis.* Trans. Donald Nicholson-Smith. New York: Norton, 1973.

Lee, Leo Ou-fan. *The Romantic Generation of Modern Chinese Writers.* Cambridge, MA: Harvard University Press, 1973.

——. *Voices from the Iron House.* Bloomington: Indiana University Press, 1987.

Levenson, Joseph R. *Liang Chi-chao and the Mind of Modern China.* Cambridge, MA: Harvard University Press, 1953.

Li Hangyu. "Li yi li wo de gen" (Examining my roots). *Zuojia* (Writers) 9 (1985): 75–77.

Li Qingxi. "Gulao dadi de chengmu" (Silence of the ancient land). *Wenxue pinglun* (Literary review) 6 (1987): 49–54.

Li Tuo. Xu (preface) to *Touming de honggaoliang* (The transparent red radish). Beijing: Writers' Press, 1986.

Li Tuo, Zhang Ling, and Wang Bin. " 'Yuyan' de fanpan" (The revolt of "language"). *Wenyi yanjiu* (Literature and arts studies) 2 (1989): 75–80.

Lin Chun. "Gender Equality in China: Between the State and Market." Paper presented at Chinese Women and Feminist Thoughts Conference, Beijing, 21–24 June 1995.

Lin Yu-sheng. *The Crisis of Chinese Consciousness.* Madison: University of Wisconsin Press, 1979.

Liu Heng. *Dong zhi men* (Winter's gate). In *Xiao shuo jia* (Novelists) 3 (1992): 5–21.

Liu Kang. "Subjectivity, Marxism, and Cultural Theory in China." In *Politics, Ideology, and Literary Discourse in Modern China,* ed. Liu Kang and Xiaobing Tang. Durham, NC: Duke University Press, 1993, 23–55.

Liu Kang and Xiaobing Tang, eds. *Politics, Ideology, and Literary Discourse in Modern China.* Durham, NC: Duke University Press, 1993.

Liu, Lydia H. "Narratives of Modern Selfhood: First-Person Fiction in May Fourth Literature." In *Politics, Ideology, and Literary Discourse in Modern China,* ed. Liu Kang and Xiaobing Tang. Durham, NC: Duke University Press, 1993, 102–23.

Liu Zaifu and Lin Gang. "Zhongguo de chuantong wenhua yu 'A Q moshi' " (Traditional Chinese Culture and the "Ah Q Model"). *Zhongguo shehui kexue* (Chinese social sciences) 3 (1988): 133–52.

Lu, Tonglin. "Can Xue: What Is So Paranoid in Her Writings?" In *Gender and Sexuality in Twentieth-Century Chinese Literature and Society,* ed. Tonglin Lu. Albany: State University Press of New York, 1993, 157–74.

——. *"Red Sorghum:* Limits of Transgression." In *Politics, Ideology, and Literary Discourse in Modern China,* ed. Liu Kang and Xiaobing Tang. Durham, NC: Duke University Press, 1993, 188–210.

——. *Misogyny, Cultural Nihilism, and Oppositional Politics.* Stanford: Stanford University Press, 1995.

Lu Wenhu, ed. *Qian Zhongshu yanjiu caiji* (Collection of Qian Zhongshu study), vol. 1. Beijing: Sanlian Publishing House, 1992.

Lu Xun. "A Q zhengzhuan" (The story of Ah Q). In *Nahan* (Call to arms). Beijing: Xinchao Publishing House, 1923.

MacCannell, Juliet Flower. "Desire." In *Feminism and Psychoanalysis,* ed. Elizabeth Wright. Oxford: Blackwell, 1992, 63–68.

Macey, David. "Phallus: Definitions." In *Feminism and Psychoanalysis,* ed. Elizabeth Wright. Cambridge, MA: Blackwell, 1992, 318–20.

Macherey, Pierre. *A Theory of Literary Production.* London: Routledge & Kegan Paul, 1978.

Mao Zedong. "To Fully Bring out Women's Initiative in the Revolutionary Construction." *Hongqi* (Red flag) 10 (1971): 60–64.

——. "Speech at the Supreme State Conference." In *Chairman Mao Talks to the People,* ed. Stuart Schram. New York: Pantheon, 1974, 91–94.

Mitchell, Stephen A. *Relational Concepts in Psychoanalysis.* Cambridge, MA: Harvard University Press, 1988.

Mo Yan. *Hong gaoliang jiazu* (The red sorghum family). Beijing: PLA Arts and Literature Press, 1987.

Mu Ling. "Literary Criticism in the 1980s." *Modern China* 4 (October 1995): 420–27.

Nan Fan. "Wenxue: chengshi yu xiangcun" (Literature: Urban and rural). *Shanghai wenlun* (Shanghai review) 4 (1990): 29–33, 80.

——. "Wenxue: fu yu zi" (Literature: Father and son). *Shanghai wenxue* (Shanghai literature) 10 (1991): 70–75.

Ostrovsky, Nikolai. *Kak zakalialas' stal'* (How the steel was tempered). Moscow: Molodaia gvardiia, 1935.

Parkers, Andrew, Mary Russo, Doris Sommer, and Patricia Yaeger, eds. *Nationalisms and Sexualities.* New York: Routledge, 1992.

Ping "Nanren de yiban shi nuren" (Reviews of "Half of man is woman"). Yinchuan: Ninxia People's Press, 1987.

Qian Zhongshu. *Weicheng* (The besieged city). Beijing: People's Literature Press, 1981.

Rockmore, Tom. *Before and after Hegel.* Berkeley: University of California Press, 1992.

Schwarcz, Vera. *The Chinese Enlightenment.* Berkeley: University of California Press, 1986.

Schwartz, Benjamin I. *In Search of Wealth and Power.* Cambridge, MA: Harvard University Press, 1964.

——. "The Limits of 'Tradition versus Modernity' as Categories of Explanation: The Case of the Chinese Intellectuals." *Daedalus* (spring 1972): 71–88.

Sedgwick, Eve Kosofsky. *Between Men.* New York: Columbia University Press, 1985.

Semanov, V. I. *Lu Hsun and His Predecessors.* New York: M. E. Sharpe Inc., 1980.

Sha Yexin. *Xunzhao nanzihan* (Looking for a real man). *Shiyue* (October) 3 (1986): 115–76.

Silverman, Kaja. *The Subject of Semiotics.* New York: Oxford University Press, 1983.

——. *Male Subjectivity at the Margins.* New York: Routledge, 1992.

Siu, Helen F. *Furrows, Peasants, Intellectuals, and the State: Stories and Histories from Modern China.* Stanford: Stanford University Press, 1990.

Spence, Jonathan D. *The Gate of Heavenly Peace.* New York: Penguin, 1981.

——. *The Search for Modern China.* New York: Norton, 1990.

Spivak, Gayatri Chakravorty. *The Post-Colonial Critic.* New York: Routledge, 1990.

Stacey, Judith. *Patriarchy and Socialist Revolution in China.* Berkeley: University of California Press, 1983.

Stoller, R. *Observing the Erotic Imagination.* New Haven: Yale University Press, 1985.

Su, Hongjun. "A Feminist Study on Mao Zedong's Theory of Women and the Policy of the Chinese Communist Party toward Women through a Study of the Party Organ *Hongqi.*" *Chinese Historians* 2 (July 1990): 21–35.

Sun Longji. "'Mutaihua' zhi jingsheng xianxiangxue" (The psychological phenomenon of 'wombnization'). *Nuxingren* (W.M. semiannual) 5 (1991): 112–32.

Tu Wei-ming. *Way, Learning, and Politics.* Albany: State University of New York Press, 1993.

Wang Anyi. *Xiao Bao zhuang* (Bao town). *Zhongguo zuojia* (Chinese writers) 2 (1985): 43–84.

Wang Ban. *The Sublime Figure of History.* Stanford: Stanford University Press, 1997.

Wang Fuxiang. "'Nuxing wenxue' zhiyi" (Questioning "women's literature"). *Dangdai wenyi sichao* (Ideas in contemporary literature and the arts) 2 (1984): 16–22.

Wang Hui. "Geren guannian de qiyuan yu zhongguo de xiandai rentong" (Issues of modern Chinese identity and the origin of the concept of the individual). *Chinese Social Sciences Quarterly* (autumn 1994): 51–84.

Wang, Jing. *High Culture Fever.* Berkeley: University of California Press, 1996.

Wang Meng. "Duobi chonggao" (Stay away from the sublime). *Dushu* (Reading) 1 (1993): 10–16.

Wang Ruoshui. "Guanyu 'yihua' de gainian" (About the concept of "alienation"). In *Waiguo zhexue shi yanjiu jikan* (Research papers on the history of foreign philosophies), vol. 1. Shanghai: Shanghai People's Press, 1978, 1–34.

Wang Shuo. *Dongwu xiongmeng* (Animal vicious). *Shouhuo* (Harvest) 6 (1991): 130–207.

Wang Yuejin. "Red Sorghum: Mixing Memory and Desire." In *Perspectives on Chinese Cinema,* ed. Chris Berry. London: BFI Publishing, 1991, 80–103.

Widmer, Ellen, and David Der-wei Wang, eds. *From May Fourth to June Fourth.* Cambridge, MA: Harvard University Press, 1993.

Williams, Raymond. *Culture and Society: 1780–1950.* New York: Columbia University Press, 1983.

Wolf, Margery. *Revolution Postponed.* Stanford: Stanford University Press, 1985.

Wright, Elizabeth, ed. *Feminism and Psychoanalysis.* Cambridge, MA: Blackwell, 1992.

Wu Daiying. "Xinshiqi 'nuxing wenxue' mantan" (An informal discussion of "women's literature" in the new era). *Dangdai wenyi sichao* (Ideas in contemporary literature and the arts) 4 (1983): 35–41.

Wu Liang and Cheng Depei, eds. *Xinxiaoshuo zai 1985 nian* (New fiction in 1985). Shanghai: Shanghai Academy of Social Sciences Press, 1986.

Wu Lun. "Sulian dianying zai zhongguo" (Soviet film in China). *Shijie ribao* (World journal) 6 April 1997, 18.

Xia Zhongyi. "Cong xianglin sao, shafei nushi dao 'fangzhou'" (From Xianglin's wife and Miss Sophia to "The ark") *Dangdai wenyi sichao* (Ideas in contemporary literature and the arts) 5 (1983): 58–63.

Xiao Yuan. *Wang Shuo zai pipan* (Recriticizing Wang Shuo). Changsha: Hunan Publishing House, 1993.

Xiong Yuezhi. *Xixue dongjian yu wanqing shehui* (The dissemination of Western learning and the late Qing Society). Shanghai: Shanghai People's Press, 1994.

Xu Wenyu. *Zhang Jie de xiaoshuo shijie* (The fictional world of Zhang Jie). Beijing: People's Literature Press, 1991.

Yau, Esther. "*Yellow Earth:* Western Analysis and a Non-Western Text." *Perspectives on Chinese Cinema,* ed. Chris Berry. London: BFI Publishing, 1991, 62–79.

Yi Qing. "Yige chongman huoli de zhidian—ye tan 'xunzhao nanren' de nuxing wenxue" (An energizing supporting point—also about the "looking for manly men" literature by women writers). *Dangdai wenyi sichao* (Ideas in contemporary literature and arts) 2 (1987): 16–18.

Yue Ming-Bao. "Gendering the Origins of Modern Chinese Fiction." In *Gender and Sexuality in Twentieth-Century Chinese Literature and Society,* ed. Tonglin Lu. Albany: State University of New York Press, 1993, 47–66.

Yu Hua. "Siyue sanri shijian" (The April third incident). In *Zhongguo xinchao xiaoshuo xuan* (Selections of new wave stories in China), ed. Cheng Youxin. Shanghai: Shanghai Academy of Social Sciences Press, 1989, 224–66.

Yu Qing. "Kunan de shenghua" (Sublimate suffering). *Dangdai wenyi sichao* (Ideas in contemporary literature and the arts) 6 (1987): 50–55.

Yu Dafu. "Chenlun" (Sinking), *Yu Dafu zaoqi zuoping xuan* (Selection of Yu Dafu's early works). Guangzhou: Huacheng Publishing House, 1982, 17–57.

Zhang Chengzhi. "Hei junma" (Black stallion). *Shiyue* (October) 6 (1982): 66–95.

———. "Beifang de he" (Rivers of the north). *Shiyue* (October) 1 (1984): 4–49.

———. "Huangni xiaowu" (A yellow-earthen hut). *Shouhuo* (Harvest) 6 (1985): 4–41.

Zhang Jie. "Ai, shi buneng wangji de" (Love must not be forgotten). *Beijing wenyi* (Beijing literature and arts) 11 (1979): 19–27.

———. "Fang zhou" (The ark). *Shouhuo* (Harvest) 2 (1982): 4–59.

Zhang Wenjiang. *Yinzao babita de zhizhe: Qian Zhongshu zhuan* (The wise man and his Babel tower: A Biography of Qian Zhongshu). Shanghai: Shanghai Wenyi Press, 1993.

Zhang Xianliang. *Nanren de yiban shi nuren* (Half of man is woman). *Shouhuo* (Harvest) 5 (1985): 4–102.

———. *Xiguan siwang* (Accustomed to death). Taipei: Yuansheng Press, 1989.

Zhang Xinxin. "Wo zai naer cuoguo le ni?" (How did I miss you?). *Shouhuo* (Harvest) 5 (1980): 91–105.

——. "Zai tongyi dipingxian shang" (On the same horizon). *Shouhuo* (Harvest) 6 (1981): 172–233.

Zheng Shiping. *Party vs. State.* Oxford: Oxford University Press, 1998.

Zheng Wanlong. "Wo de gen" (My roots). *Shanghai wenxue* (Shanghai literature) 5 (1985): 44–46.

Zhong, Xueping. "Male Desire and Male Suffering: The Politics of Reading *Half of Man Is Woman.*" In *Engendering China,* ed. Christina Gilmartin, Gail Hershatter, Lisa Rofel, and Tyrene White. Cambridge, MA: Harvard University Press, 1994, 175–94.

——. "Shanghai *Shimin* Literature and the Ambivalence of (Urban) Home." *Modern Chinese Literature* 1 (spring 1995): 79–100.

Zhou, Jin. *Weicheng yanjiu* (A study of *The Besieged City*). Taibei: Yuanshen Press, 1980.

Zhu, Ling. "A Brave New World? On the Construction of 'Masculinity' and 'Femininity' in *The Red Sorghum Family.*" In *Gender and Sexuality in Twentieth-Century Chinese Literature and Society,* ed. Tonglin Lu. Albany: State University of New York Press, 1993, 121–34.

Žižek, Slavoj. *The Sublime Object of Ideology.* London: Verso, 1989.

Index

Xueping Zhong is Assistant Professor in the Department

of German, Russian, and Asian Languages and Literatures

at Tufts University.

Library of Congress Cataloging-in-Publication Data

Zhong, Xueping.

Masculinity besieged? : issues of modernity and male

subjectivity in Chinese literature of late twentieth century /

Xueping Zhong.

   p. cm.

Includes bibliographical references and index.

ISBN 0-8223-2406-7 (alk. paper)

ISBN 0-8223-2442-3 (paper : alk. paper)

1. Chinese literature—20th century—History and criticism.

2. Masculinity in literature.   3. Literature and society—China.

I. Title: Issues of modernity and male subjectivity in Chinese

literature of late twentieth century.   II. Title.

PL2303.Z48   2000

895.1'09352041—dc21   99-050298